DATE DUE

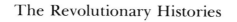

The Revolutionary Histories

The Revolutionary Histories

CONTEMPORARY NARRATIVES OF
THE AMERICAN REVOLUTION

LESTER H. COHEN

Cornell University Press

ITHACA AND LONDON

First published 1980 by Cornell University Press.
Published in the United Kingdom by Cornell University Press Ltd.,
2–4 Brook Street, London W1Y 1AA.

International Standard Book Number 0-8014-1277-3
Library of Congress Catalog Card Number 80-11243
Printed in the United States of America
Librarians: Library of Congress cataloging information
appears on the last page of the book.

FOR MARSHA

CONTENTS

ACKNOWLEDGMENTS

One has too few opportunities to express gratitude to the many scholars who, unbeknown to themselves, have helped another's work bear fruit. I wish to seize the present one and mention a few whose writings have been of special significance to me. Always important and sometimes formative on literary and philosophical issues have been the works of Hayden White, Northrop Frye, Leo Braudy, Jonathan Culler, W. B. Gallie, and Maurice Natanson (whose scholarship, happily, is matched by his superior teaching). Those of Bernard Bailyn, Ernst Cassirer, Peter Gay, Perry Miller, Edmund S. Morgan, J. G. A. Pocock, and Gordon S. Wood have been as indispensable to this study as they must be to any work that treats the intellectual history of Enlightenment and Revolutionary America.

In a sense, one writes one's first book for and even with one's teachers. I happily acknowledge my enormous debt to Page Smith, with whom I first developed my interests in the Revolutionary era and the interpretation of narrative, and whose friendship has been a limitless source of pleasure and sustenance. Parts of this study are the offspring of my doctoral dissertation; to the extent that the book bears the traces of their guiding hands, it reflects its good fortune in having been shaped under the careful direction of David Brion Davis, Edmund S. Morgan, and Sydney E. Ahlstrom, whose own works remain a reservoir of inspiration.

Thanks are due the Purdue Research Foundation and the National Endowment for the Humanities for helping to support this project with summer grants in 1975 and 1976. Portions of Chapters 5 and 7 appeared as "The American Revolution and Natural Law Theory," *Journal of the History of Ideas,* 39 (July–September 1978), and "Explaining the Revolution: Ideology and Ethics in Mercy Otis Warren's Historical Theory," *William and Mary Quarterly,* 37 (April 1980). Michael McGiffert, editor of *WMQ,* unwittingly made revision of the whole manuscript easier and more satisfying by taking such pains with a part. Some of Chapter 6 was published as "Narrating the Revolution: Ideology, Language, and Form," in *Studies in Eighteenth-Century Culture,* 9 (1979), © 1979 by the Regents of the University of Wisconsin.

I owe a great deal to the graduate students in Purdue's American Studies Program, who keep intellectual history thriving here and who have tried to make me a better thinker and teacher. I am especially obliged to the assistant professors in Purdue's History Department. Since the fall of 1976 we have met monthly to read and comment on one another's work and have generated a community of friends in what is too frequently a wilderness of lonely individuals. I am beholden to them not only for their careful attention to several chapters, but for their zealous encouragement and support during the writing: Darlene Clark Hine, Charles W. Ingrao, Lois Magner, Linda Levy Peck, Jon C. Teaford, Philip R. VanderMeer, Regina Wolkoff, and Carl Zangerl. Donald J. Berthrong, head of our department, deserves the ambivalent thanks perhaps typical of a younger colleague. His judicious (one might say persistent) application of pressure helped me to realize the volume sooner rather than later.

Marsha R. Cohen made the book possible. Besides taking care of all the little things—pursuing a career as systems engineer, rearing Joshua and David, making us a home and a family, coaxing order out of chaos—she prompted me to live up to my best intentions (sometimes in spite of my worst ones). To her the book is dedicated with love, respect, and gratitude.

LESTER H. COHEN

West Lafayette, Indiana

The Revolutionary Histories

INTRODUCTION

Accompanying the American Revolution was a historical revolution, a radical transformation of assumptions and ideas about the nature and meaning of history and about man's location in the historical process both as participant in events and as interpreter and shaper of them. This historical revolution was practical as well as conceptual, for as theory changed so did the modes in which history was written. In the revolutionary histories we see a dramatic change not only in the categories of historical explanation, the theory of causation, and the understanding of chance, human character, and will, but in the literary conventions that govern historical narrative, in the language, style, and form of historical presentation. With this group of narratives, in short, emerged a new American historical consciousness, one that decisively left behind the traditional providential interpretation of history and that projected on its horizon the mode of writing we commonly call "Romantic."

The revolutionary histories are "patriot histories," narratives written by people who actively supported resistance and revolution and later articulated their perceptions of experiential reality in historical discourse. Despite their relative homogeneity as a group—all were white, all Protestant, all male (with one very conspicuous exception), all Federalist (with the same exception), most New Englanders—the historians were talented and interesting individuals, and their works reveal the richness of their personal experiences. Among those most frequently cited in this study, David Ramsay was a South Carolina physician who had studied medicine with Benjamin Rush at the College of Philadelphia and later served as a surgeon in the Continental Army, a member of the Continental Congress, a representative to the South Carolina Assembly, and a delegate to his state's Constitution Ratifying Convention. Mercy Otis Warren of Plymouth, Massachusetts, found herself in the thick of radical politics from the early 1760s to the mid-eighties, her home a veritable salon for Boston-area dissenters, and her poems, plays, and Antifederalist essays salvos in the revolutionary contest. The Virginian John Marshall, then as now the most widely known of the historians, wrote *The Life of George Washington* during the early years of his tenure as Chief Justice of the Supreme Court. Timothy Pitkin, son of a prominent Connecticut minister and son-in-law of Yale College president Thomas Clap, served as a Federalist congressman. Jeremy Belknap, William Gordon, Abiel Holmes, and Jedidiah Morse were New England ministers who, in addition to writing history, were known for preaching sermons that advanced "the sacred cause of liberty." Belknap and Holmes, moreover, were cofounders of the Massachusetts Historical Society.[1]

This book, however, concerns not the historians themselves but the historical narratives they wrote. I am primarily interested in what unites the historians *in* their histories, in what constitutes a shared historical consciousness as evidenced by a shared vocabulary of enlightened republicanism, by a common conceptual approach to a common group of themes, and by their participation in a set of literary conventions that they all believed properly governed historical writing. As a result, despite their individual differences, which in other contexts might be important, I refer to them throughout under the collective title "the revolutionary historians."

I try here to accomplish three aims—one historiographical,

two substantive—that arise from the notion that there was a historical revolution in late-eighteenth-century America. My overriding historiographical concern is to illuminate the complex interrelationships among the philosophical assumptions, ideological values, and aesthetic qualities that the histories reveal, for the interplay of philosophy, ideology, and literary structures constitutes the significance of the histories as narratives. As a result, my approach is essentially textual, for only a textual (or formalist) approach can treat a historical narrative as what it most obviously purports to be: "a verbal structure in the form of a narrative prose discourse," as Hayden White has suggested.[2] I am (sometimes painfully) aware that textual methods contain certain hazards. To center in the interior structures and forms of literary sources frequently prompts one to ignore the personal dimension of a writer's expression, to depreciate the sense of social context in which an author writes, and to suggest that there is a paradigmatic historical imagination from which no individual historian deviated in any significant way.

Nevertheless, historical narratives, like all significant documents, not only reflect biography and society but generate their own imaginative space, worlds of interpretive possibilities that transcend their immediate sphere of influence. Historians too often fail to enter that space. In an effort to make sense of the social context within which literary documents are produced, we frequently impose on them an external order before appreciating fully the kinds of order that they create from within. In short, the revolutionary histories tell us as much about historical consciousness through their forms, structures, and language as through their contents. To approach them as texts that reveal certain assumptions, language, strategies, conventions, and ideas is to open frequently ignored domains of expression, and—in granting them a degree of autonomy by dislodging them from the protective coloration of their social background—to avoid reducing them to the *merely* idiosyncratic or the passively social. I have preferred to risk one set of evils rather than another in the hope that the result is provocative and suggestive.

I have confined myself to "patriot histories" (with an emphasis on both words) because of the nature of my historiographical concerns. Since my project is to demonstrate the integrity of philosophical, ideological, and formal literary themes, *narrative performance*—the active and creative way in which historians give voice and shape to their theories as well as to the events themselves—is a crucial dimension of the study. I have limited myself to *formal* narratives, therefore, in order to make general claims about the writing of narrative history, and particular claims about how the revolutionary histories were written. As a consequence, I have omitted full discussions of two important groups: enlightened nonhistorians, and Loyalist commentators.

The revolutionary historians were directly engaged in giving shape and focus to what they perceived to be historical reality. Unlike others of their generation, who from time to time reflected on history's lessons and the significance of events, the historians were faced with the task of molding events into patterns of meaning, shaping them into coherent lines of development. They were compelled by the very nature of writing narrative to come to grips with the range of explanatory and aesthetic problems that I discuss in this study. Unlike their contemporaries, whose historical ideas, while important, never had to be formally shaped or articulated, the historians had to achieve, with their ideas and strategies of presentation, the coherence that narrative performance not only demands but intrinsically accomplishes. To include the historical theories of nonhistorians would subvert my larger purpose. For there is no way to validate the relationship between historical ideas and historical form in nonhistorical writing, since there is precisely no historical form to "casual" historical observations. This is, then, a study neither of the historical mind of the Revolutionary generation, nor of American historical theories in the eighteenth century, although I hope that it helps to illuminate both of these important and neglected topics.

A more unfortunate omission is that of the Loyalist or Tory "histories"—unfortunate, because Loyalist writings have yet to receive the attention they deserve. In the context of my larger aims here, however, properly speaking there are no Tory histories of the American Revolution, as John Adams perceptively pointed out to Thomas Jefferson as late as 1813. No Loyalist wrote a sustained narrative history of the Revolutionary era, which by contemporary standards included the years between 1763 and 1787. Even if one were to accept as "histories" works that more accurately would be called "memoirs," the writings of Tories fall into two main groups, neither of which can bear an intense philosophical, ideological, and literary investigation as narrative history of the American Revolution: those written before the Revolution was over—indeed, even before the peace of 1783 which ended only the military conflict; and those written after the Revolution, but which cover a period ending (in almost every case) even before 1763, the eve of the Revolutionary era.[3] In addition, almost all the Loyalist histories are colony histories (indeed, self-consciously and purposefully so), which fail to express the range and scope of vision that are revealed even in David Ramsay's *History of the Revolution of South-Carolina.* I try here to suggest ways of dealing with Tory histories, for if I am correct in arguing that philosophical, ideological, and aesthetic themes operate together to constitute the narrative historical work, then Loyalist writings ought to reveal (as I believe they do) different formal elements precisely as they reflect a different ideological stance.

In short, the writings of nonhistorians and Tories are important in themselves, and I discuss both in limited and, I hope, fruitful ways. But neither group of writings qualifies as narrative history of the American Revolution and, therefore, neither can be treated in the same formal terms that I believe illuminate the revolutionary histories.

The book is divided into two parts, the first emphasizing "philosophical" issues, the second "ideological." I use quotation marks around both terms because I am not completely convinced that one can, except for heuristic purposes, separate philosophy from ideology, or that, as the construction of the book implies, philosophy ought to precede ideology. In addition, since few moderns would confuse the revolutionary historians with philosophers in almost any post-Kantian sense, it is doubly difficult to distinguish the philosophical from the ideological.

Nevertheless, the distinction is useful because it helps one to isolate certain kinds of problems. It is intended to suggest my belief, moreover, that social, political, and, broadly speaking, cultural attitudes often seem to depend on a prior commitment, independent of a thinker's particular situation, to certain fundamental principles concerning man *qua* man, society *qua* society, politics *qua* politics, and so forth. Thus, for example, I think it is fair to suppose that the historians' understanding of republicanism as an ideology that supports political freedom and requires ethical responsibility rests on a prior philosophical conviction that man *is* free and capable of ethically responsible activity. Similarly, when the historians wrote of the future as a contingent and undefined "out-there" which would be shaped by people's present actions, it is proper to conclude that they did not conceive man to be powerless to act because the future was the preconcerted and completed product of an immutable divine decree. Finally, since the historians told the story of the Revolution in fundamentally romantic rather than mythical terms, we can reasonably believe that they meant to relate the story of people and not of God (or gods). There is, then, a dialectic between the "philosophical" themes of Part I and the "ideological" themes of Part II. Articulation forms the substratum of both philosophy and ideology, as well as the medium through which both become (or refuse to become) accessible to me. Hence, language is also an essential concern throughout, since the literary aesthetics of narrative are empowered by words and their organization.

Each of the two parts of the book reflects one of my major substantive purposes. In Part I, I argue that with the revolutionary histories the providential theory of history, which had dominated American historiography for more than a century, was repudiated because, as the historians saw it, providence could no longer provide categories adequate for explaining the Revolution. Providential history was God's history; revolutionary history was man's. Thus the very concept of what history was and how it operated was dramatically changed. Before the middle of the eighteenth century, historians tended to locate historical causation and meaning in God's transcendent providence and sought to erase human efficacy and contingency from the lexicon of historical discourse. The revolutionary historians saw history as an immanent (rather than transcendent) process of self-generating moments, and founded their immanent theory on the idea that the human will and chance were central categories of historical explanation.

I am arguing, of course, for the secularization of historical thought, an argument that some historians will find obvious, while others will no doubt find it wrong-headed (if not downright obtuse). Far too many important studies have been written since the brilliant pioneering works of Perry Miller for an intellectual historian to take lightly the roles of religion and theology in American thought. But historians in recent years have come close to associating with *religious* thought virtually any thought that reveals passion, commitment, and vision. This tendency not only depreciates the richness and significance of thought that is distinctively areligious, but also runs the risk of trivializing and flattening truly significant theological formulations.

In this and other cases language is central: the revolutionary historians do indeed use the language of providence in their histories. This easily (and I believe falsely) leads us to conclude that they saw their histories arising within the traditional framework of an overarching historical providence. An examination of their language and strategies of presentation, however, indicates that providence in the histories no longer means what it once did; it indicates that providence was no longer an explanatory concept at all, though it remained a rich and highly charged cultural and ideological metaphor.

In Part II, I argue that historical writing was for the historians an ideological and ethical art. Writing history was for them not only a "scholarly" enterprise concerned with instruction in history's lessons, but was, more importantly, a present- and future-oriented instrument of political and moral values and national vision. Associated with this was the historians' profound awareness of their own social and political roles as participants in the events they sought to narrate—their sense that they were responsible to their contemporaries and to future generations for perpetuating the spirit of the Revolution and the constellation of republican principles that suffused it. The histories they wrote are, as a result, manuals of revolutionary republicanism, exhortations, propaganda tracts, collections of the lives of exemplary people, and romances, all of which are modes of supporting their principal commitment: that to write the history of the American Revolution was itself a revolutionary act.

1

Providential History and
the Problem of Contingency

In one of the most famous passages in American literature,
William Bradford re-created metaphorically the termination of
the Hebrews' search for sacred space, the end of an exodus and
the beginning of a new life as related in the Book of Joshua.
Shifting his narrative voice to the present tense in order to convey with immediacy the overpowering sense of loneliness and
dread, Bradford "cannot but stay and make a pause, and stand
half amazed at this poor people's present condition." By "condition" Bradford meant everything: the people's state of mind, the
state of their provisions, their very location in space and time at
the edge of two wildernesses: to the rear, the east and past, an
ocean crossed—"a sea of troubles"—evoking the feeling of what
was lost and irrecoverable; to the front, the west and future,
"what could they see but a hideous and desolate wilderness, full
of wild beasts and wild men—and what multitudes there might
be of them they knew not." It was nearly winter and "all things
stand upon them with a weather-beaten face, and the whole
country, full of woods and thickets, represented a wild and sav-
age hue." The possibility of disaster was imminent and it was
unrelieved for, unlike Moses, Bradford could not "as it were, go
up to the top of Pisgah to view from this wilderness a more

goodly country to feed their hopes." Bradford, like Joshua, was consigned to life, not death, and to live was to risk the future's hazards in order to win the promised land. In such a precarious situation, standing before the Jordan and the unknown dangers that lay beyond, "which way soever they turned their eyes (save upward to the heavens) they could have little solace or content in respect of any outward objects. . . . What could now sustain them but the Spirit of God and His grace?"[1]

Bradford wrote his narrative for succeeding generations of Separatists. Realizing, as Joshua did, that one of the great dangers of a new enterprise was that it quickly becomes old and conventional and that future generations would forget, he addressed his narrative to the children in an effort to remind them of their parents' mission. Thus he enjoined them to say: "Our fathers were Englishmen which came over this great ocean, and were ready to perish in this wilderness; but they cried unto the Lord, and He heard their voice and looked on their adversity. . . . Yea, let them which have been redeemed of the Lord, shew how He hath delivered them from the hand of the oppressor. . . . Let them confess before the Lord His lovingkindness and His wonderful works before the sons of men." Historical writing was a testimony and a celebration, a means of bearing witness to God's directing hand in concrete historical situations. Thus, precisely as Joshua in his last speech to the Hebrews before entering the promised land recounted the history of his people from Abraham to the present moment—warning the people that "Ye are witnesses against yourselves that ye have chosen you the Lord, to serve him," and beseeching them to "put away . . . the strange gods which are among you, and incline your heart unto the Lord God of Israel"—so Bradford offered his testimony to the children as a reminder of God's deliverances and as a challenge to reaffirm the sacred mission.[2]

At the heart of Bradford's project—indeed, at the heart of all Puritan historical narrative and theory—is a profound sense of the contingency of existence, for only by emphasizing the percariousness of life could he insist upon the ultimate authority of divine providence as the locus of historical causation and meaning and as a refuge from chance. Bradford played masterfully on that sense of contingency by constructing his narrative according to theo- instead of chrono-logic. Had he been more concerned with chronology he would, for example, have described the Pilgrims' subscription to the Mayflower Compact before he narrated their disembarkation in the wilderness.[3] To have done so, however, would have blunted the exquisite edge of dread and trepidation by allowing the reader at least a modicum of comfort in believing that the people were not completely alone, unprotected, vulnerable. By narrating events in theological (one might almost say existential) sequence, Bradford denied such feelings of security or comfort, making emphatic the notion that with God's overruling providence *nothing*—surely no human political convention—stood between man and his anxious predicament. In short, as he actually wrote the narrative Bradford placed man before God without mediation and was able to stress the reciprocally related ideas that the world appears to be contingent, precarious, even chaotic and that man's only recourse for order is God.

Bradford's American wilderness, filled with wild beasts and wild men, bears a striking resemblance to Thomas Hobbes's contemporary description of the state of nature, a state in which life is a war of all against all, and in which there is "no Knowledge of the face of the Earth; no account of Time; no Arts; no Letters; no Society; and which is worst of all, continuall feare, and danger of violent death; And the life of man, solitary, poore, nasty, brutish, and short."[4] Long before John Locke proclaimed that "in the beginning all the World was America,"[5] and spoke of the state of nature in terms benign compared with Hobbes's, the Puritans perceived the world as dangerous. So had John Calvin who, Michael Walzer argues, saw human life as "an anxious business at best." Calvin, like Hobbes, was preoccupied with "the uncertainties of existence," and beneath his concerns for order, discipline, and subjection lay "an extraordinary fearfulness." Puritan political theory involved an effort to banish contingency from man's world and to replace it with order. Recognizing the precariousness of the human situation, the Puritans constructed a political architecture of enormous stability and integrity and founded it upon a theology that propounded coherence as God's will.[6] "For Order is as the soul of the Universe, the life and health of things natural, the beauty and strength of things Artificial," wrote William Hubbard in 1676, in a sermon echoing John Winthrop's "Model of Christian Charitie." God displayed His desire for the harmony of all things by disposing the numerous elements of His varied creation into their appropriate places, "which is Order." And, Hubbard contended, this was true not only in nature, but was observable as well in "the rational and political World."[7]

Precisely as they hewed a political order out of apparent chaos and validated that order in the name of God, the Puritans used historical narrative not only to tell a story but to write order through the experiential historical process and they validated that order in the name of divine providence. Whether one judges the providential interpretation of history to be a willful denial of human freedom and responsibility—an "escape from freedom" in modern terms—or as a mode of historical explanation that liberates man from his naive devotion to the ultimacy of his own activities, historical writing, as much as political theory, science, and cosmology, represents a means of generating order through man's perceptions of contingency. No Puritan would equal William Bradford's extraordinary capacity to subdue contingency with providence without destroying the tension between them. But, heavy-handed as most Puritan histories are, they reveal the same two purposes—one theological, the other didactic—that motivated Bradford's project: to explain history according to the theology of providence, and to exhort future generations to keep alive the sense of mission that had impelled their ancestors to face a precarious world armed with little more than their faith.

Causation and Explanation: The Doctrine
of Divine Providence

From the middle of the seventeenth century to the middle
of the eighteenth—longer, some have argued—Puritan historians repeatedly sounded the same themes in essentially the
same terms. Borne on a wave of millennial hopes and expectations, they created the image of a New Israel, integrated the
apparently grim jeremiad into an optimistic historical vision, developed a historical typology that drew precise analogies between biblical history and New England life, and tied the saints'
experiences to the history of redemption.[8] While crucial dimensions of Puritan social and intellectual life have thus been well
explicated, too little attention has been directed recently to the
historical theory itself and to its philosophical assumptions.

During the century in which it dominated American historical
thinking, Puritan providential history persistently focused on
contingency, the notion that the existence and continuity of historical experience and nature were precarious. This concept
provides a key to understanding providence as an explanatory
structure and insight into the ways in which that structure broke
down in the latter decades of the eighteenth century.

In *The Doctrine of Divine Providence Opened and Applyed* (1684),
a veritable manual of Puritan historical theory, Increase Mather
dwelled on the contingency of things to remind those readers
who would feel comfortable and secure that living in the world
was hazardous. Even "great Revolutions in the world, have . . .
been occasioned by meer contingencies," Mather warned. Some
of the most momentous events in history had been entirely unpredictable, appearing to people to be accidental or fortuitous.
When, for example, Nebuchadnezzar captured Jerusalem it was
indeed "a great Revolution," yet "a meer Contingency" had
prompted him to go to that city when he initially had planned to
go elsewhere. Despite their best plans and schemes and despite
the reasonable probability of their success, people's expectations
were frequently dashed, for "*things many times come to pass contrary*

to humane probabilities and the rational Conjectures and expectations of men." Aiming to chasten people's willfulness and their exuberance over their own works, Mather pointed out that they "often times make up Purposes and resolutions and all comes to nothing in the conclusion," for the world does not operate according to their will and expectations. Instead, "time and chance happens to all." The swift runner does not always win the race; sometimes "some unexpected Accident or other Chaunceth to fall in the way" and the slow runner succeeds. In reality people could not even rely on the natural order to remain consistent, for things sometimes acted *"otherwise than according to their natures and proper inclinations."*[9]

Despite appearances to the contrary, Mather wrote of contingency not to affirm, but to deny it. He focused on chance, accident, and the precariousness of things to make an epistemological point about appearances and reality (as well as to exhort his readers to reaffirm their faith in God's providence). Rather than an ontological feature of objective reality, contingency was merely an appearance. Precisely because finite man was incomplete, he did not have access to all God's intentions for His world. Since, the revered William Ames pointed out, "the will of God is partly hidden and partly revealed," man simply could not know what God had planned for human history. According to Deuteronomy 29:29, the basis of Ames's statement, "The secret things belong unto the Lord our God: but those things which are revealed belong unto us and to our children for ever, that we may do all the words of this law." Contingency was thus an appearance to man, a conclusion man sometimes drew in the absence of knowledge of God's concealed will. But simply because man perceived contingency in the world he could not necessarily conclude that the world was in fact contingent. Mather chided people for their arrogant assumption that God should act according to human reason: "There is no such track of providence, as that men shall thereby be able fully to understand by what Rules the Holy and Wise God ordereth all events

Prosperous and adverse which come to pass in the world. His ways of Providence are unsearchable." And if the judgments of God are inscrutable, rest assured that the world conforms to those judgments, however obscure they may appear to man, and that "they are (and shall at last appear to be) Just, and Equal, and Good."[10]

Mather thus used the appearance of contingency as a touchstone for reformulating the providential historical theory that would banish contingency from the historical universe. Contingency could have, in truth, only one meaning: that all events were "contingent" upon God's will. Where fallen and finite man perceives accident or chance in the world, there in fact is God's providence. For "as to all events which come to pass in the world," Mather insisted, "he that [sitteth] upon the Throne hath an hand therein." Nothing occurs without a providence. Even those events that to man appear to be "the most Contingent and fortuitous" reveal the hand of God. "What more Fortuitous or that has a greater and more uncertain chance in it, than a *lot* has [?]" Mather asked rhetorically, and he answered: "*yet the whole disposing thereof is of the Lord.*" Thus all events— including the "Contingent," the "fortuitous," the "chance," and the "lot"—*are* events only because they are providential, empowered by God's will. God's providence extends even to the "most inconsiderable things that happen in the world." Indeed, "He would not be God if the least thing in the world should happen without him." As for the "meer Contingency" that set Nebuchadnezzar's course for Jerusalem, "Why! He that sits in Heaven ordered those casual Circumstances which put the King upon this fatal Resolve."[11]

This providential theology of history provided an explanation of historical events that guaranteed meaning and purpose not only to specific incidents but to the historical process as a whole. It was, of course, a thoroughly deterministic historical theory; as Mather wrote, "*There is an holy Decree and Praedetermination in Heaven concerning all things which come to pass in the world.*" At the same time, the providential theory was perfectly consistent with Puritan attitudes toward human nature and willfulness. For if historical events depended finally upon God's will—if, indeed, "He would not be God if the least thing in the world should happen without him"—then the will of corrupt man could be nothing more than an instrument in effecting God's design. Mather, in fact; framed his providential theory in terms of an opposition between God's will and man's will, arguing that "to make things depend chiefly upon the decrees and wills of man is to place Man in the Throne and to dethrone him that sitteth in Heaven. We must therefore know, that all Events of Providence are the issues and executions of an Ancient, Eternal, Unchangeable decree of Heaven."[12] Since all events had the same status *as* events, Mather's formulation creates an either/or: either God caused all things to happen or man did. His providential theory leaves no room to doubt that God did.

As a theoretical construct—that is, excluding consideration of the question whether the Puritans (or anyone else, for that matter) could have *lived* in terms of its implications—Mather's statements implicitly proclaimed that for man to accept responsibility for his history was to sin. For, as Thomas Hooker explained in 1659, the essence of sin was human willfulness. Sin's intention was to dethrone God—indeed, to annihilate God—and to usurp God's sovereignty for man. Sin, Hooker wrote, "would dispossess God of that absolute Supremacy which is indeed his Prerogative Royal," and therein lay its "unconceavable hainousness"—"it would justle the Almighty out of the Throne" and "be above him." Sin "smites at the Essence of the Almighty and the desire of the sinner, is not only that God should not be supream but that indeed he should *not be at all.*" The problem that arises here tends to plague all deterministic philosophies of history. The Puritans succeeded in developing a theory that explained all events, banished contingency, and supported the supremacy of God's will, reducing human efficacy to the role of secondary, mediating agency. But they were left with the problem, over which they expended great energy and ingenuity, of reconciling providential determinism with the origin and presence of evil and with a theory of human responsibility.[13]

History was for the Puritans *God's* history. Even if historical writings chronicled events in human time, their purpose was to record the track of God's will. God was the author of history, man was His instrument and chronicler. "It is our great duty to be the Lords *Remembrancers* or *Recorders,*" wrote Urian Oakes in 1673, "that the mercies of the Lord . . . may be faithfully registred in our hearts, and remembred by us." Writing history was thus in itself an act of piety for it was the study of God's revelation.[14]

Puritan theorists painted two complementary images of providence: God's foreordination of events, His grand design for all of history, in which God was depicted as the creator and sustainer of the whole historical process; and God's use of "special providences," His intervention into history on particular occasions in order to alter the course of events either by acting directly or (more usually) by using means or second causes. In both cases, though it is more conspicuous in special providences, God was depicted as the locus of causation and meaning in history. *"The Lord in Heaven knows all that is done upon the Earth,"* wrote Mather. "He knows all things long before their accomplishment." God declared *"the end from the beginning, and from ancient times the things that are not yet done,"* sometimes mentioning specific people and events long before they appeared on earth precisely so that people would realize vividly that God knows not only "the general concerns" of the world but also its most particular details. Thus, "whatever things happen in the world, could not but be so."[15] Foreordination, like the covenant itself, served as the ground of surety in Puritan historical theory. It guaranteed order and regularity in history by presenting a transcendent standard of truth against which finite man could measure his actions and interpretations. As the locus of causation, moreover, it was the ultimate source from which events derived their being as events.

Special providences, as the name suggests, were "events of

providence in which there is *a special hand* of Heaven ordering them." Almost always concerned with unexpected deliverances and punishments, the doctrine of special providences was a means of locating causation for events which appeared to be inexplicable by human reason. Although "emperours and all the world with them were resolved to be [the] death" of Athanasius, for example, "yet they could never accomplish it, because a *special providence* of God was ingaged for him." This was always true in such cases, Mather insisted, "and the like is to be said concerning eminent Judgements which befal men in this world." Indeed, great events were the fulfillments of supernatural judgments even when they were obviously the results of natural means. "When there are ... amazeing changes either as to the world in general, or as to particular Nations and Countreys, he that sitteth in Heaven upon the throne hath a special hand in those great alterations of the state of affairs. . . . When the scene of affairs in a whole Kingdome is turned quite upside down, there's a special hand of Heaven in bringing about such changes." "Great commotions" always revealed a special providence, though man tended to appreciate God's hand in them "most of all when they are brought about suddenly and unexpectedly."[16]

Foreordination and special providences were in theory complementary formulations which operated together to constitute an overarching explanatory grammar for history. Both pointed to an active God who ordered history and made it meaningful, for all that happened, "disaster as well as triumph, the minutest event as well as the greatest, has been under divine control." To the question why the Puritans required a doctrine of special providences when the concept of foreordination should, presumably, have disposed of all special occurrences, Increase Mather responded that special providences merely evidence more emphatically God's foreordination: *"Many things come to pass at such a nick of Time, as that 'tis from thence evident that there is an hand of Heaven over ruling all."*[17]

The Activity of Providence

Puritan providential history required an active God. A century before New Englanders started to emphasize means or second causes in history, English historians, though reluctant to abandon the notion of providential causation, nevertheless began to look behind the ways of God in order to understand better the ways of man. At the turn of the seventeenth century, English historians were beginning to assume "that in a rational universe God acted rationally, and so the operations of the first cause might be taken as a precondition but otherwise ignored." Between 1580 and 1640, argues F. Smith Fussner, English historical writing "was no longer the submissive servant of faith."[18] Thus, long after English writers had shifted their attention from primary to secondary causes—indeed, decades after they had driven a wedge between God's providence and human action and already had begun to debate the status of miracles— American Puritans continued to insist on an active deity. They did so because providence still played vital theological and social roles that rested on a commitment to providence as the guarantor of the divine order of history in a world that appeared to be contingent and precarious.

Puritan history was jeremiadical; it served as a means of exhorting people whom the ministers saw declining in vital piety to witness God's tests and punishments as well as His deliverances and to reform their ways in the hope that God would again deliver them from iniquity. Ironically, the histories, like the jeremiads, emphasized the ruthless, unpredictable, active God that Puritan thought apparently had begun to minimize during the last quarter of the seventeenth century. Kenneth Murdock has argued that second- and third-generation Puritan historians played on God's activity in order to revivify the image of the God of the first generation. Partly as a response to scientific advances which increasingly brought historical phenomena into the category of "normal operations under some natural law," and partly

33

because the pious saw a waning of traditional spirituality in New England, Puritan historians hoped that by emphasizing God's special favor to His chosen the people might be excited to "greater efforts toward righteousness."[19]

Throughout the latter decades of the seventeenth century and well into the eighteenth, Puritan thought manifestly shifted in emphasis toward the "naturalness" of the natural order. The shift is evident, for example, in political theory. While in 1630 John Winthrop argued in the "Model of Christian Charitie" that government was necessary because man since the fall was corrupt, William Hubbard wrote in 1676 not only that God's political and social order represented "a sweet subordination of persons and things, each unto other," but that in creating His order God "consulted the good of humane nature" as well as "the glory in his own wisdome and power." Two decades later Samuel Willard went a step further, referring to a concept of "the Law Natural" which was accessible not only to the regenerate but even to "such as are strangers to Scripture Revelation." By 1717 John Wise had expanded the Natural Law thesis, arguing that "Reason is Congenate with [man's] Nature," and that "Right Reason" with respect to proper conduct was "founded in the Soul of Man." And by 1734 John Barnard had so inverted Winthrop's understanding of the necessity of government that he thought it "very evident, [that] the Nature of Man is formed for Government, and necessitated to it, from that Power of Reason and Understanding that is in him, his fixed Bent to Society, and the many Weaknesses and Imperfections that attend him." Neither Hubbard, Willard, Wise, nor Barnard would have challenged Winthrop's formulation. But in the century between Winthrop and Barnard not only was human nature seen to be more benign and educable, but the political order itself was understood to be more naturally and intrinsically regular and reasonable.[20]

Perry Miller and Kenneth Murdock have pointed to a similar shift in historical theory and writing, arguing that by the last decades of the seventeenth century Puritan historians had begun gradually to de-emphasize special providences and to rely increasingly on the notion that God had ordered all events to operate naturally and thus without the need to see His direct intervention in specific historical occurrences. This is to say that they began to emphasize means or second causes in history. In 1677, for example, in a sermon given at Cambridge, Massachusetts, Urian Oakes preached that "though God is *able* to give Being to things in an immediate way, yet it is his *pleasure* in the course of his Providence to use Means," for by making events occur through the "mediation and Agency" of second causes He gives means a *"causal virtue"* in producing particular effects. Indeed, Oakes argued that second causes were efficient (though not sufficient) causes, and to deny that "were to deny and destroy their *causality,* and to make nothing of their *efficiency.* Second causes have their peculiar Influence into their *Effects,* and contribute something to their *Existence:* and to assert the contrary, were to say that Causes are no Causes, and to speak a flat Contradiction."[21] Statements like these, which clearly suggest an expansion of the role of means, prompted Murdock to see in William Hubbard's *General History of New England* (1682) and in his *Narrative of the Troubles with the Indians* (1677) a slight shift away from God's direct intervention and toward a more naturalized view of history. Thus Hubbard appears at times to explain events in terms of their immediate material causes, implying that natural explanations were as valid as supernatural ones. And this, claimed Murdock, "was not the method of the historian who was convinced that history was chiefly valuable as a record of God's providence."[22]

Murdock's analysis is a subtle one and it points us in the right direction. But judicious and careful as he is, he overstates the case and identifies the alteration in historical theory too early. For even as Urian Oakes insisted upon the efficiency of second causes he cautioned his auditors not to carry the idea too far. For "no man hath the absolute command of the Issue & success of his own Undertakings. He may be sure of this or that Event, if the Lord *Promise* it to him, or *Reveal* it to be *His Pleasure* to give such Success to such Endeavors: but he cannot be secured of it from, or by any *Sufficiency* of his own." According to this notion man is a second cause which gained its causal efficiency only because God *"out of the abundance of his goodness*... communicate[d] causal power and virtue to his Creatures, & to honour them with that Dignity that they may be his Instruments, by which He will produce these and those Effects."[23] Thus, whether Puritans emphasized the first cause or second causes—God's supernatural role or His ordering of events through natural means—the essential theory remained unaltered: since God made things happen *"either with or without means* as it appears good to him," He was the necessary and sufficient cause of all events. To this point Puritan historians, Hubbard included, would always return.[24]

Equally important, at precisely the time to which Murdock would point to support his notion that a shift was occurring, Puritan historians were still writing of "extraordinary providences [which] cause wonderment in the world." Indeed, they were still using the language of miracles, despite the fact that in theory miracles had been abandoned. Extraordinary providences caused even greater wonder, wrote Increase Mather in 1684, "especially when they are of a *miraculous* nature. . . . *Works which are above and beyond the Constituted order of Nature."*[25] Even when they emphasized means or second causes—in fact, in a certain sense even more when they emphasized means—Puritan historians and theorists pointed to the workings of an active God in history. There was no escape from the logic: special providences and events above, beyond, and even against the common course of nature were obviously the work of God; but to see in history the order and regularity of events operating naturally and without direct intervention was to glorify God for having infused in history the unalterable laws according to which it operated.

The Indian Wars

Nowhere was God's active role in history more clearly evidenced than in the Indian Wars. Here we see not only the God who delivered but the God who tested and punished His people for their neglects and transgressions—the God who "ordereth all events Prosperous *and adverse.*"[26] Written at a time when we should expect a greater emphasis on natural means and second causes, the narratives of William Hubbard and Increase Mather were explicitly aimed to reassert the primacy of God's will by being "the faithful *Records* of [God's] Providential Dispensations."[27] Hubbard's and Mather's intention was avowedly to chastise New Englanders for neglecting their duty to convert the Indians. "I know not," wrote Mather, "but that the Lords holy Design in the *War* which he hath brought upon us, may (in part) be to punish us for our too great neglect in this matter."[28] While Mather was reluctant to say decisively what God's ultimate purpose was, he hesitated not at all to identify God as the cause of the war.[29] After the fashion of the jeremiad, Mather pointed out to his readers that the wars came in full force only after the passing of the first generation, making clear that God (like Mather) saw a waning of piety and was testing the faith of a complacent people.[30]

The narratives are, as Perry Miller has written of Puritan histories generally, "not only philosophy teaching by example, but theology exemplified." They are practical illustrations of Mather's *Doctrine of Divine Providence,* built upon a tissue of providential interpositions, and intended to identify providence as the cause of all causes located in the "transmundane." They are from the outset cast in cosmic terms: King Philip was led to hate the settlers at "the instigation of Satan"; it was "the Devill" who filled his heart with murder.[31] Against Satan's will God worked His providences, but not until He tested His people and punished them for their neglects and omissions.

It is obviously to be expected that Puritan historians saw the Indian Wars as a proof of God's design to deliver His people. It is less obvious that they were able to portray providence acting "negatively" (negatively, that is, from their standpoint). Not only were the wars a punishment to begin with, but during the wars the settlers continued to experience God's judgments. On July 19, 1675, for example, the colonists were hot on Philip's trail, following his forces into a dismal swamp. But they had to withdraw before capturing him because, unable to direct their fire accurately, they found themselves shooting at anything that moved, including one another. From this Mather gleaned: "It is a sign God is angry, when he turns our weapons against ourselves."[32] As they later learned from the Indians they had pursued into the swamp and eventually captured, if they had followed the Indians a half hour longer, Philip would have surrendered. But the settlers did not pursue the Indians even the necessary half hour more because "God saw that we were not yet fit for Deliverance, nor could Health be restored unto us except a great deal more Blood be first taken from us." Philip eventually left the swamp and the colonists chased him. But this pursuit also failed, though "had the *English* pursued the Enemy they might easily have overtaken the Women and Children that were with *Philip,* yea, and himself also, and so have put an end to these tumults: but though Deliverance was according to all Humane probability near, God saw it not good for us yet." God not only punished His people, He also interposed at times to help their enemy—the Puritan historians were willing to use the doctrine of divine providence even-handedly.[33]

At the heart of the Indian narratives is a sense of the appropriateness of God's relationship to worldly, historical affairs. Whether events were prosperous or adverse, the Puritans saw God acting with complete justice. When adversity was the fare, they pointed to the people's failure to live up to the law. Thus Mather cautioned, jeremiadically: "We have often carried it before the Lord as if we would *Reform* our ways, and yet when it hath come to, we have done nothing: So hath the Lord carried toward us, as if he would deliver us, and yet hath deferred our *Salvation,* as we our selves have delayed *Reformation.*"[34]

The colonists' ultimate deliverance from the Indians, like all events during the war, was God's doing—not *because* the people had reformed their ways but because God acted justly. To underscore this point Mather reiterated the either/or he stated in the *Doctrine of Divine Providence.* The colonists were victorious, to

be sure. But "God hath let us see that he could easily have destroyed us, by such a contemptible enemy as the Indians have
been in our eyes; yea he hath convinced us that we ourselves
could not subdue them. . . . So that we have no cause to glory, for
it is God which hath thus saved us, and not we our selves."[35] In short,
regardless of how He ordered the colonists' deliverance,
whether by means or by direct intervention, "nevertheless, the
supream cause must not be disacknowledged. The Eternal himself has a mighty hand of Providence in such works."[36]

The Limits of Historical Knowledge

Designed for both theological and social reasons to point to
the hand of an active deity, Puritan histories always threw man
back upon the limits of his rationality and efficacy. Faced with
the unexpected, inexplicable event that defied human probability and rational conjecture, the Puritan's response was properly
awe and wonder, prompting him to seek its cause and meaning
in God's providence, a search that would yield the ultimate
ground of historical order. But at the same time, when he perceived order and regularity in the historical world, when he
perceived a process intrinsically suffused with meaning, he was
constantly reminded that finite man always stood in the face of
the infinite, that whatever order he discerned was the product of
God's will, and that history was thus precarious because "the
frame of nature would be dissolved the next moment, if there
were not an hand of Providence to uphold and govern all."[37]
God, paradoxically, was both the source and the resolution of
the problem of contingency.[38] Confronted with an absolutely
sovereign God at every turn, the Puritan could only conclude
that the historical and natural worlds were, ultimately speaking,
unfathomable mysteries. He could feel that he lived in a natural
world, in which natural causes produced natural effects, only as
long as he never lost sight of the fact that God's supreme authority entailed that he face the world's precariousness.

Early in the eighteenth century, Puritan intellectuals began to lose sight of that fact (or at least began to de-emphasize it). The historical and natural orders were, for Cotton Mather, more orderly and rational than ever before, precisely as the social-political world had become for Puritan political theorists. Mather was no more willing than his contemporaries to abandon the traditional emphasis on God's supremacy and therefore on the restricted status of human rationality and efficacy. Indeed, his aim was to reassert the traditional emphasis by widening its sphere of influence. But even as he assumed the fundamental division between God's revealed will and His concealed will (the source of Puritan epistemological dualism) Mather began to expand the domain of the revealed will. If God's concealed will remained utterly beyond human penetration, His revealed will was open to human rationality. If God's concealed will demanded faith, His revealed will was accessible to reason, indeed even to natural, unassisted reason. God "may still be essentially unknowable," wrote Perry Miller, "but He has told enough about Himself, and betrayed enough of His character, so that He is not an utter blank. His eternal purposes are still 'sealed secrets,' but in the covenant He has given us more than a glimpse of their direction."[39]

Mather's project was to bind together what he saw being pulled apart: reason and faith, the demands of the human intellect and the requirements of piety. Thus, he intended to demonstrate in his *Christian Philosopher* (1721) "that *Philosophy* is no *Enemy,* but a mighty and wondrous *Incentive* to *Religion.*" But even as he spoke them the words revealed his anxiety that the task might be impossible. In this relatively neglected work, addressed to the members of the British Royal Society, Mather argued that God had revealed His will in two basic forms: in Scripture and in Nature. Mather would guide us through the latter book, taking all of nature as God's revelation, for doing so would help our reading of the book of Scripture. There is already present here a shift away from traditional formulations; by taking nature as his text, and by suggesting that reading nature assists one in reading Scripture, Mather implies the equality of reason and revelation. For although he argues that nature *is* revelation (and thus, astonishingly, anticipates the Transcendentalists' notion that the natural world is to intuition miraculous) he explicitly argues that nature is accessible to *all*: "Here is reading easy for everyone even though they have not learned to read, and it is open to all, and set out before everyone's eyes."[40] Indeed, even a "Mahometan," a Puritan symbol of unregenerate man, not only unlearned in science but unjustified in the sight of God, "will shew thee one, without any *Teacher*, but *Reason* in a serious View of *Nature*, led on to the Acknowledgement of a Glorious GOD." Thus, man's natural, unassisted reason, operating in fact through "the *Senses* of all Men," can deduce God from His creation, a notion quite far removed from the early Puritan idea that the genuine apprehension of God required regeneration.[41]

Mather's strategy in *The Christian Philosopher* was that of inclusivity. Faced with what he saw as an increasingly exclusive religion—one based fundamentally on the conversion experience and, as a result, declining in the number of full church members—he sought to present nature in effect as a converting ordinance. By appealing to their intellects, he hoped to prompt unregenerate and secular scientists to reaffirm "the grand End of [man's] Being, which is, To glorify GOD," by showing them that the principles of Puritan theology lay at the end of their scientific quest.[42] Brilliant as it might have been, however, his strategy, and ultimately his project, were tragically doomed. For by adopting the voice, the methods, and the conventions of the scientist he found himself emphasizing reason at the expense of faith. In the section "Of Magnetism" for example, Mather wrote a lengthy empirical description of what had been observed about the properties of magnets and the various phenomena associated with them. With great concern for detail he adduced fact upon fact until he interrupted himself in mid-thought in a burst of uneasiness and wrote: "But it's time to stop, we are got beyond *Human Penetration*; we have dug as far as 'tis fit any *Conjecture* should carry us.... Once for all; *Gentlemen*

Philosophers, The Magnet has quite *puzzled* you." The next step was obvious: impenetrable natural facts prompted the same response that special providences did, to "glorify the infinite Creator of this, and of all things, as *incomprehensible.* You must acknowledge that *Human reason* is too feeble, too narrow a thing to comprehend the *infinite* God.... I will now single out a few plain *Mathematical Instances* wherein, Sirs, you will find your finest *Reason* so transcended, and so confounded, that it is to be hoped a *profound Humility* in the grand Affairs of our *holy Religion* will from this time for ever *adorn* you."[43]

The problem, of course, as Mather knew full well, was that the Gentlemen Philosophers did *not* have to acknowledge the feebleness of human reason. Mather's scientific insight and method (if not state of the art, at least worthy of a member of the Society) demonstrated just how much rationality could accomplish.[44] His insistence upon the inextricability of reason and faith could be read by his audience as an afterthought—a profound commitment on Mather's part, but by no means a proven or self-evident proposition. To the contrary, calculated to call the unregenerate back to the covenant, *The Christian Philosopher* dramatized better than almost any contemporary document just how fragile was the hyphen that held together the Puritan ideal of Reasoned-Faith.

Mather's *Magnalia Christi Americana* (1702) reveals the same sort of tensions, though in different terms. Until Mather's great historical work, Puritan histories were narrated essentially by one voice, Urian Oakes's "the Lords Remembrancer." The narrator of Puritan history, like that of spiritual autobiography, was self-effacing: God *wrote* history, the historian merely recorded it.[45] Thus even though the narrative voice spoke in several inflections—that of the minister, chronicler, even prophet—the "I" that narrated seventeenth-century Puritan histories sought anonymity; indeed, it sought to create its own absence from the narrative (and thereby becomes all the more conspicuous for the modern reader) as if to suggest that God's history speaks for itself.

Mather, on the other hand, in the *Magnalia* identified himself with a variety of narrating personae (though he did not attempt to execute them all in his narrative). In the General Introduction alone he adopted roles ranging from "one poor feeble *American*" (the American provincial which Benjamin Franklin elevated into a native art form), to an American Vergil writing the epic of the Reformation in the new world, to an entertainer as well as an instructor of man, to a classical historian like Thucydides, Livy, Tacitus, or Polybius. More important than this ostentatious (some would say obnoxious) display of American erudition, however, is the fact that his play with narrating personae (as well as his puns and other devices) called attention to himself as historian, as the *author* of his work. Mather explicitly and self-consciously refused to hide behind a pseudonym and also refused to adopt an anagram of his name. Instead, "I freely confess, 'tis COTTON MATHER that has written all these things."[46] This is more than a display of vanity (for which Mather in any case excused himself); it is also more than an evidence that modes of narration were changing in English literature (and that Mather was announcing that he, a mere provincial, was well aware of the changes).[47] To say that he has "written all these things" implies that the historian participates in the history he narrates, that he *creates* history in some crucial sense; in short, it subtly alters the notion that God, not man, is the author of history.

Yet despite these important movements away from earlier Puritan historical formulations (and a comprehensive study should point up their richness and complexity) Mather's *Magnalia* no more than his *Christian Philosopher* sought to abandon the traditional providential synthesis. The *Magnalia* was decisively providential history operating on the same fundamental principles that motivated and validated his father's works. Mather recoiled from the audacious "I" that would presume to author history much as in *The Christian Philosopher* he drew back from the possibility that reason might actually constitute, not merely discover, the natural world. If a later New Englander was "glad to the brink of fear" at intuiting reason's constitutive power, Mather, horrified at the thought (though strangely attracted by it), reaffirmed the traditional idea that history and nature were works of God and therefore came under the purview of theology. Although in the *Magnalia* people seem to act efficaciously in the world, although events seem to follow one another in natural causal sequence, although political, economic, and rational concerns appear to motivate people as much as do spiritual factors, Mather reminds his readers that God governs all and that writing history is an act of piety: "To Regard the illustrious Displays of that PROVIDENCE, wherewith our Lord CHRIST governs the World, is a Work, than which there is none more *Needful,* or *Useful,* for a *Christian:* To *Record* them is a Work, than which, none more proper for a *Minister.*"[48]

Among eighteenth-century transformations of Puritan historical theory, none is more important than that of Jonathan Edwards, whose only historical work, *A History of the Work of Redemption,* remained unfinished.[49] Edwards reaffirmed the providential historical synthesis by grounding it philosophically in the principle that contingency and free will (as it was being interpreted particularly in Europe) were utterly inconsistent with *any* concept of historical order. Yet by developing a theory of "moral necessity" Edwards expanded and made more coherent and systematic the movement toward a history of means or second causes that had started at the beginning of the eighteenth century. In fact, Edwards's theory of moral necessity, concerned with the "law or constitution of nature" and based upon "the continued, immediate efficiency of God," made it possible to see history as a virtually immanent process, one containing *within* itself the motive forces that empower the whole chain of historical events.[50] Since for Edwards the causal-temporal relationship between events "is established by previous necessity, either natural or moral," there was no need to identify the hand of God in each historical event.[51] Once one acknowledged that God "was both the efficient and final cause of history—and, indeed, its formal and material cause as well," one could view history as a process containing its own *interior* logic, a logic predicated upon God's creation of all agents to obey by moral necessity their own essential natures. History could thus be seen as "a grand conception, a design, a chain of events within a scheme of causation."[52]

Emphasizing the idea, later elaborated by Samuel Davies, that it is God's "hand that sustains the great chain of causes and effects, and [that] his agency pervades and animates the worlds of nature and grace," Edwards's historical theory practically did away with the need to distinguish special providences from the normal workings of history. Indeed, Alan Heimert has argued that, instead of merely refining the earlier distinction between primary and secondary causes, Edwards and his followers "all but obviated the need for such a distinction by making the Deity the efficient cause of all phenomena."[53] Edwards did not repudiate the idea of special providences (he refers to interpositions of God "after the world was created"),[54] but his philosophy of history comes closer to that of any American Calvinist to being a theory of immanence.

Edwards's theory was potentially liberating, for by relocating God to the beginning of the historical process he returned history to the study of the mundane world. Nevertheless, his philosophy remained providential, transcendent, and rigorously deterministic. To speak of causation was still to speak of God's "universal determining providence" as necessary *a priori* for the existence of historical order at all. While he carefully distinguished between physical necessity and moral necessity (in order to avoid the logic of fatalism), moreover, he insisted that moral necessity "does as much ascertain the futurity of the event, as any other necessity." It was manifest to Edwards "that the sovereign Creator and Disposer of the world has ordered this necessity, by ordering his own conduct, either in designedly acting or forbearing to act. . . . And therefore every event which is the consequence of anything whatsoever, or that is connected with any foregoing thing or circumstance, either positive or negative, as the ground or reason of its existence, must be ordered of God." Edwards's logic was inescapable, given his assumption of

God's efficacy and man's instrumentality. One could view history as an immanent process of causes and effects as long as one realized that God was necessary to empower the whole: "It follows therefore, that the whole series of events is thus connected with something in the state of things, either positive or negative, which is *the original in the series*; i.e., something which is connected with nothing preceding that, but *God's own immediate conduct,* either his acting or forbearing to act." Although Edwards's formulation was much more rigorous and elegant, this was the point that Increase Mather had made seventy years earlier: God willed or nilled the very being of things. It followed, wrote Edwards, "that as God designedly orders his own conduct, and its connected consequences, it must necessarily be, that *he designedly orders all things.*"[55]

Edwards's mode of argument is regressive: given the fact that all events are causally sequential, and that "it is indeed ... repugnant to reason, to suppose that an act of the will should come into existence without a cause,"[56] there must be some *original* cause that empowers the first cause in the series. The same is true of the will itself (and this was the great burden of *The Freedom of the Will*). It was easy enough to argue (as he accused the Arminians of doing) that historical events depend upon man's will. But it was quite another thing to argue (as he also accused the Arminians) that the will wills its *own* being. It was absurd to believe in the self-determination of the will because the belief caught one in an infinite regress: what was the cause of the will that willed itself? the will? Doubtless the origin of the will and the source of its (limited) efficacy was some cause, not the will itself, that was prior to it and transcendent of it, namely God. The human will, like all historical instruments, was comprehended by the moral necessity of the universe which God created to inhere "in the state of things."[57]

At the heart of Edwards's concern—and of all Puritan historical theory—is a concept of divine order that required the annihilation of contingency and self-generated human efficacy. "For Edwards as a theologian the issue is a simple one," Paul Ramsey

has noted: "either contingency and the liberty of self-determination must be run out of this world, or God will be shut
out." Contingency and the freedom of the will were absolutely
inconsistent with God's providence. And the stakes could not
have been higher, for "the consequences of a single human volition, when traced out, are so immense as to destroy the providence of God if the will determines itself."[58]

From "Will He, Nil He" to "Willy-Nilly"

From William Bradford's *Plymouth Planation* to the writings
of Jonathan Edwards and Thomas Prince in the middle of the
eighteenth century, providential concepts constituted a paradigm of American historical theory and writing. New Englanders shaped this historiographical tradition in part because
they wrote many more narratives in all periods of early American history than did the people of any other region. Perry Miller
has argued, however, that Southerners, too, produced a literature that reflected providential assumptions—though less rigorously and consumingly so than those of the Puritans. More
important, since the principles of providential history were suffused with the theology that generated them, providence was the
philosophical concept that not only integrated theology and history but formed the central unifying principle of a coherent,
continuous, and consistent set of conventions that governed historical discourse until the era of the Revolution.[59]

During the century or so that the providential interpretation
dominated American historical writing, Puritan historical theory
remained fundamentally unaltered. Despite subtle and important changes *within* the paradigm—the increasing emphasis on
means and the naturalization of the historical process, for
example—the Puritans consistently employed the same
theological-historical categories. Throughout the period of its
dominance, the doctrine of divine providence served four related purposes as a philosophy of history (leaving aside, that is,
its possible psychological and ideological values): first, it located

in the transmundane the cause of history itself and of all events in history, thereby providing an infallible grammar of historical explanation—all events had their source outside the historical process and all were the doing of God; second, it guaranteed that all events were meaningful by rejecting the notion that contingency—chance, or (as the Puritans saw it) the uncaused—was a feature of historical reality; third, it maintained God's active role in history by denying the efficacy of the human will except insofar as the will was an instrument of divinity; fourth, and perhaps the governing point, it guaranteed that history had an overriding purpose and shape because the order of human affairs reflected the divine order.

But if in the middle of the eighteenth century the providential interpretation continued to pervade American historical consciousness, within three decades it was absent as a structure of explanation (though, I will show, it persisted as a highly charged ideological and cultural metaphor). The historical revolution generated by events of the Revolutionary era left the providential theology of history decisively behind. And this dramatic transformation of historiography seems to have had no clearly identifiable roots, for if the change had been gradual, reflecting alterations that had begun *within* the providential synthesis, it cannot be traced through narrative histories or theoretical writings. The histories of the Revolution, in short, appear to have arisen *sui generis,* begetting in a burst of creativity a cohesive group of narratives (though not theoretical studies) that simply no longer obeyed the imperatives of providential history.[60] My project here is not to account for the historical origins of revolutionary historical writing. I am content to observe that the providential interpretation had been paradigmatic and that this group of fundamentally secular narratives appeared, and to explore the significance of the revolutionary histories in philosophical, ideological, and formal terms. Nevertheless, in light of some important recent studies of eighteenth-century theology, it is worth speculating on what happened to providence in the Revolutionary era.

The language of providence did not suddenly disappear in the late eighteenth century. To the contrary, it has been argued that from the 1740s and fifties—when "an unprecedented outpouring" of apocalyptic, millennialist sermons were published—to the 1780s, more significant eschatological writings founded on traditional providential concepts were published than in any comparable period since the time of the Puritan founders. Moreover, several historians have discussed these sermons in terms of historical consciousness.[61] More pertinent to my purposes, the revolutionary historians themselves used the language of providence, prompting Arthur H. Shaffer to suggest that the historians "set out to demonstrate that from its inception the nation's history was part of a Providential plan to expand the boundaries of knowledge and liberty."[62]

The issue is not, then, whether the language of providence persisted, or even whether it remained "vital" in the Revolutionary era, as John F. Berens contends. It is clear from these studies that providential language persisted with great vitality in Revolutionary-era theology; indeed, it may have been reinvigorated in that period, as Nathan O. Hatch has argued. The question is what providential language meant; and, more specifically, whether it continued to function as a philosophy of history, that is, as a theological-historical structure of explanation, as it had for the Puritans. On this issue the theological waters are muddy, in part because most historians have too readily assumed that the meaning of providence remained consistent throughout the eighteenth century. Thus, instead of questioning how the concept of providence functioned in sermonic literature, they have assumed that where the language of providence appears, there is a Puritan set of meanings.[63]

While historians of religion in the Revolutionary era continue to work toward a synthetic approach to the relationship between theology and ideology, two interpretations seem most consistently to emerge in their writings. One, most recently represented by John F. Berens (and following several avenues opened by the pioneering work of Alan Heimert), sees providential thought as fundamental to the American mind through and beyond the Revolutionary era. Traditional providence as outlined by the Puritans remained essentially unchanged, serving as a source of conviction and hope and as a mode of explaining historical reality. According to this view, providential thought was the most finely ground lens through which American experience and republican ideology were filtered and refracted. A second interpretation—by no means the first's opposite, which would, presumably, deny the continued vitality of providence altogether—is most ably represented by Nathan O. Hatch, who contends that, far from remaining static or intact, theology was significantly altered during the Revolutionary era. Outlining a more complex relationship between theology and ideology, Hatch suggests that theology was politicized and that theologians concerned with worldly affairs (as well as with the status of religion and the clergy in the emerging political order) used religious ideas to sanctify the Revolution and its ideological underpinnings. Precisely by being used in the service of politics, theology was profoundly altered; at the same time, the pressure of events and ideology effectively rescued theology from threatened ossification.

Did the language of providence continue in the Revolutionary era to articulate an encompassing constellation of ideas and values that assimilated ideology and both explained and sanctified contemporary events? Had it become merely the servant of politics, providing a convenient and attractive rationale for partisan political activities? Agreement on these and other questions concerning eighteenth-century theology is not likely to occur until historians address the deeper question on which they rest: what does the language of providence mean in historical and sermonic literature of the Revolutionary era? Only by examining providential language can we begin to determine whether providence continued to reveal emotional and intellectual commitment, or whether it had become so thoroughly conventional a vocabulary that its absence would have been more significant than its presence. In short, it is clear that providential language persisted in late-eighteenth-century sermons, that it was enlisted by ministers in the service of the Revolution, and that the clergy used it to blur the distinction between sacred and profane history by wedding events of the Revolution to the history of redemption. It is unclear, however, whether providence continued to be a principle of historical explanation even in the writings of theologians, assuming that it retained its traditional function in sacred philosophy of history at all.

The revolutionary histories present a somewhat different though parallel set of problems. Most of the historians who wrote them were lay people, and one might reasonably assume that they used providential language more like congregants than ministers—less rigorously and consistently, more rhetorically. But several ministers who championed independence in their sermons also wrote histories of the Revolution, and the providence that appears in their histories is indistinguishable from the lay historians'. Problems arise, in fact, not in comparing both groups' histories, but in comparing the providence in the ministers' sermons with the providence in their narratives: the active, interceding, causal deity that appears in their sermons is strikingly absent from their histories.[64]

While this complicates matters somewhat, it also points to a way through the difficulties. Simply stated, theology and history split apart from one another in the Revolutionary era. If we can rely on recent interpretations of religious writings, providence was now beginning to function differently in sermons than in historical narratives, and the difference was as apparent— probably more so—to the ministers who wrote history as it was to the lay historians. Or, to use language that will be more important later, whereas a single complex set of literary conventions had long governed both religious and historical discourse, it broke down in the Revolutionary era so that, as far as providence was concerned, historical narratives and sermons no longer participated in the same set of conventions.

The reasons for this shift in language and forms are not completely clear, and explication of them would carry us deep into the social history of the eighteenth century and therefore beyond the scope and competence of this study. It is possible, however, to point to several reasons which will be pertinent later. First, historians have long been interested in the influence of European, particularly English, ideas on eighteenth-century America, and, tricky as the question of historical influence may be, English historical ideas were clearly important to the revolutionary historians. Indeed, while with few exceptions (and these are confined to the ministers' works) the historians rarely mentioned early American histories, they frequently cited the contemporary English works of Gibbon, Hume, Bolingbroke, Robertson, Macaulay, and Goldsmith, as well as those of the classical historians Livy, Tacitus, and Polybius. This is not, of course, to say that because late-eighteenth-century English historians had abandoned providence the Americans suddenly became skeptics. It is to suggest, however, that the available models of historical scholarship—works whose conventions were generally accepted as proper for historical writing—failed to contain a serious providential dimension. Second, while Nathan Hatch and Sacvan Bercovitch are surely correct in contending that providential and republican ideas had strong mutual affinities, republican ideology rested on crucial philosophical assumptions that were incompatible with traditional theology. The concepts of political liberty and self-government, I will argue, necessarily involved prior philosophical assumptions about human freedom, efficacy, and self-determination, which may or may not have been consistent with what may have been a transformed *Revolutionary* theology, but can hardly be squared with traditional *Puritan* views.

Finally, and most important, providential language simply made no sense to the revolutionary historians as a language of explanation: it was not merely inadequate, but irrelevant. The historians said with Mercy Otis Warren: "Religious discussions we leave to the observation of the theologian, who . . . traces the moral causes and effects that operate on the soul of man." They would limit themselves to phenomenal reality where "the effects only are level to the common eye."[65] I will argue in Part I that the providential language of the histories was a strategic language that no longer reflected its theological origins. Thus, no longer a language of historical explanation, providential language actually belied the historians' attitudes toward chance, historical order, human character, and human freedom, all of which ran counter to the providential tradition.

While in Part II it will be shown that the revolutionary histories continued the didactic and ethical tradition in which Puritan history participated, Part I should make clear that revolutionary didacticism and ethicality were no longer based on a theological conception of history. Most important in the philosophical discussion, the revolutionary historians sought to reinfuse into history what the Puritans sought to banish: the principle of contingency and the notion that man creates his own historical order and destiny. This radical reorientation in historical theory was a movement from determinism to relativism, and can be captured in phrases characteristic of each historical mode. For the Puritans events happened only because God willed or nilled their very being as events—events happened "Will He, Nil He." For the revolutionary historians, for whom chance played a genuinely important role in history, events sometimes happened "willy-nilly."

PART I

PROVIDENCE TO IMMANENCE:

PHILOSOPHICAL ASSUMPTIONS

Every man with self-respect enough to become effective, if only as a machine, has had to account to himself for himself somehow, and to invent a formula of his own for his universe, if the standard formulas failed.

—Henry Adams, *The Education*

2

The Invisible Hand:
Providence, Chance, and Politics

Burgoyne was effectively trapped. Encamped across a shallow creek from a superior American force, he and his troops had faint hope of escaping through a forest to their rear and of reaching Fort Edward. Improbable or not, such an escape was their only chance to avoid decimation or surrender, and Burgoyne decided to risk it. At least that is what General Horatio Gates, commander of the American force, believed. On the morning of October 11, 1777, Gates acted on a report which said that Burgoyne had begun a retreat and had left only a token detachment behind. That detachment, the report said, was designed to deceive the Americans into thinking that the whole British force was still there, and then harrass the Americans once Gates discovered the deception and pursued.

But the report itself was false. Burgoyne had planted it in order to lure the rebels into a well-laid ambush. He had not evacuated Saratoga for Fort Edward but remained in full force on the opposite shore. Not knowing this, Gates ordered the Americans to chase Burgoyne, giving the honor of leading the pursuit to General John Nixon and his brigade, which began to ford the creek. Following Nixon's men, General Glover's brigade entered the water when Glover saw a British soldier making across from the opposite shore. Quickly interrogating the man Glover learned that he was a deserter seeking refuge with the Americans. To the crucial question how Burgoyne's army was deployed, the deserter responded with the dreadful news: "it is encamped the same as days past." Deciding to trust the deserter, Glover immediately sent word to Nixon to turn back. Nixon received the message just in time successfully to recross the creek with virtually all his brigade intact.

Heightening the drama of this crucial event, William Gordon wrote, "Glover's message was received by Nixon in the critical moment; a quarter of an hour later would probably have proved fatal to his whole brigade, and given a turn to affairs in favor of the royal army." Indeed, as if to emphasize how the apparently trivial event often proves to be of the utmost significance in history, he added, "On incidents of this kind may depend the rise and fall of mighty kingdoms, and the far distant future transfer of power, glory and riches, of arts and sciences, from Europe to America." Expanding to cosmic dimensions, he concluded with this question: "Are [incidents of this kind] blind unmeaning casualties? Or are they the direct orderings of a Divine Being, for the establishment of his own purpose, by a superintending Providence, amid the jarring devices of mortals?"[1] The question is a momentous one and, since Gordon posed it as a clear-cut choice between mutually exclusive alternatives, an answer to it must be decisive. Blind unmeaning casualty or superintending Providence? Perhaps perversely, neither Gordon nor the other revolutionary historians attempted to answer it, for the question, as posed, had become irrelevant.

Since Gordon was a dissenting minister of considerable knowledge and skill, it is possible that he was aware of entering an important theological debate when he posed his question. No less a theologian than Jonathan Edwards had engaged the same question as recently as 1757 when he addressed Lord Kames's *Essays on the Principles of Morality and Natural Religion* (1751). Kames, wrote Edwards, "supposes that the liberty without necessity which we have a natural feeling of, implies *contingence:* and speaking of this contingence, he sometimes calls it by the name of 'chance.'" But, Edwards continued, "what he says about it, implies things happening 'loosely,' 'fortuitously,' by 'accident,' and 'without a cause.'" Kames's position was, for Edwards, absurd, for it suggested that effects can be causeless, that people's actions are "altogether contingent, fortuitous and without a cause."[2]

Edwards had revealed the flaw in Kames's argument, for although Kames vacillated on this issue, he had in fact argued that chance was absolutely inconsistent with causation (a point with which Edwards agreed) and that chance was a feature of the objective world of nature and history (a notion with which Edwards vigorously disagreed). The position was incongruous as Edwards saw it because it involved locating the uncaused in the very domain of the causal, the chance event in objective reality. By the third edition of the *Essays,* however, Kames had adopted the same position as David Hume's, writing "that there is no such thing in nature as a sense of chance or contingency." While this statement would in itself have satisfied Edwards, Kames revealed that he had altered the terms of the debate, arguing that, although chance had no place in *nature,* it was a phenomenon of *mind;* it signified not the uncaused occurrence but merely "that we are ignorant of the cause, and *for ought we know* the event might have happened, or not happened."[3]

Gordon's question involved the same issue: "blind unmeaning casualty" implied that something had happened without a cause, without reason, and ultimately without meaning, leaving only providence as a viable mode of explaining causation. Yet nowhere in his historical writings (or in his personal correspondence) does Gordon indicate that chance meant the uncaused. To the contrary, he and the other historians used the language of chance precisely as Kames and Hume used it, viewing chance as a problem of epistemology rather than ontology, and thus indicating that statements about chance concerned what people knew and did not know, could and could not know, rather than the presence or absence of causation itself.

In practice, the historians destroyed the traditional concept of providence by blurring the line between providence and chance.

They used the terms interchangeably and they used both descriptively to suggest only that the improbable, unexpected, inexplicable event had indeed occurred. In addition, they used both the language of providence and the language of chance not as modes of historical explanation but precisely to reserve judgment about causes when they were unknown. By destroying the distinction between providence and chance, the historians made clear that providence was no longer for them an adequate mode of historical explanation. The history they narrated was, as they saw it, both contingent and free, and the logic of contingency and freedom could no longer be explained in terms of the theologic of providence. At the same time, the mere persistence of the language of providence in the histories of the Revolution indicates that providence remained a highly charged, culturally attractive metaphor that was enormously useful for ideological and aesthetic purposes.

The Invisible Hand

"There have been various special providences in our favour," wrote William Gordon in 1775, "which I have a design of minuting down, to be thrown in order when time and circumstances will admit of it." Benjamin Trumbull hoped to be even more systematic, designing his *General History of the United States* (1810) as "Sketches of the Divine Agency," and stating at the outset that his purpose was to trace "the exertions of Providence" in the discovery, growth, and maturation of the colonies and to transmit them to succeeding ages, as a tribute to their great and beneficent AUTHOR."[4] Gordon's and Trumbull's stated intentions invite comparison with those of the Puritan historians who presented history as the track of God's will. But, unlike their clerical forebears, who wrote not only historical narratives but theological discourses on the nature of history and of historical explanation, Gordon, Trumbull, and the other revolutionary historians wrote only narratives. In the absence of theoretical statements, one must turn to the narratives themselves in order to understand their underlying philosophical assumptions. Specifically, the language of providence appears in virtually all the revolutionary histories: what does that language mean?

In the revolutionary histories, much as in Puritan historical writings, providence appears in two basic forms: as a long-range program for all of human history, according to which American independence was understood to be the inevitable product of God's preconcerted design; and as an active causal agency or force, suddenly intruding into human affairs and bringing about changes in the course of events contrary to people's expectations. These two formulations echo Increase Mather's. As a preconcerted design for all of history, providence was analogous to the Puritan concept of foreordination. As an active, intrusive force it was similar to "special providence." Despite the fact that the providential interpretation had declined during the half century prior to the Revolution, the language of special providence frequently appears in the revolutionary histories. Deliverances in the nick of time, sudden alterations in natural conditions, unanticipated difficulties that arise to thwart the best calculations of soldiers and statesmen abound in the histories, and the historians sometimes used the language of providence to describe such "untoward events."[5]

It is useful to begin with an event that practically every historian discussed in order to focus on the language and mode of description. The facts surrounding the battle of Cowpens, South Carolina, in the middle of January 1781, are undisputed by all the revolutionary historians. Under the command of General Nathanael Greene, American troops engaged Lord Charles Cornwallis's forces led by Lieutenant Colonel Banastre Tarleton on January 17, and in a grand battle decisively defeated the British and captured some five hundred prisoners. Although the Americans effected a splendid victory, British reinforcements applied such pressure in the aftermath of the battle that the Americans were forced to retreat from Cowpens, prisoners in tow, toward Guilford Courthouse, North Carolina. General

Daniel Morgan led the retreat and Cornwallis himself pressed the pursuit. David Ramsay wrote the earliest narrative account and provided the other historians with a model.

Setting out in inclement winter weather, Morgan had only a half-day's march on Cornwallis. As Ramsay described it:

> The British had urged the pursuit of general Morgan with so much rapidity, that they came to the ford of the Catawba on the evening of the same day that the Americans had crossed. Before the next morning a heavy fall of rain had made it impassable. The Americans, confiding in the protection of Heaven, considered this event as a special interposition of Providence in favour of their righteous cause. It is certain that if the rising of the river had taken place a few hours earlier, general Morgan, with his whole detachment, and five hundred prisoners, could have scarcely had any chance of escape.[6]

The frustrated Cornwallis had to wait until the river subsided, giving Morgan and his troops time to move farther ahead. Finally, Cornwallis remounted his pursuit to the shores of the Yadkin River, where fresh rains again impeded his progress by making the river impassable. Writing of this later deliverance Ramsay tells us:

> This second hair-breadth escape was considered by the Americans as a fresh evidence that their cause was favoured by Heaven. They viewed it in every point of light with pious gratitude, and frequently remarked, that if the rising of the river had taken place a few hours earlier, it would have put General Morgan's whole detachment in the power of a greatly superior army; if a few hours later, that the passage of it would have been effected by lord Cornwallis, so as to have enabled him to get between the two divisions of the American army [i.e., Morgan's and Greene's], a circumstance which might have been of fatal consequence to both.

And he concludes:

> That the Americans with their prisoners should, in two successive instances, effect their passage, while the British, whose advance was often in sight of the rear of their retreating enemy, seemed to be providentially restrained, affected the devout people of [Guil-

ford Courthouse] with lively thankfulness to Heaven, which added fresh vigour to their exertions in behalf of their country.[7]

The biblical metaphor is striking, if obvious, and Ramsay clearly found it irresistible. The rain and the rising of the rivers before the British could pursue, and the dramatic narrowing and widening of the gap between the pursuers and pursued, completed the analogy to the opening of the Red Sea by Moses as God's instrument and its abrupt closing upon the Egyptians.

John Lendrum, Abiel Holmes, and Mercy Otis Warren all agreed with Ramsey's portrayal of the facts. What is important in their descriptions is the language they used to narrate the events. Lendrum wrote:

> The Americans met with very providential escapes in this hot pursuit. The British reached the Catawba on the evening of the same day on which their fleeing adversaries had crossed it: And it is certain that if the rising of the river had taken place a few hours earlier, general Morgan with his whole detachment and 500 prisoners would have scarcely had any chance of escape. The same good fortune, attended with similar circumstances, protected them on passing the Yadkin.[8]

Abiel Holmes, Congregational minister of Cambridge and a co-founder of the Massachusetts Historical Society, described the events as follows:

> In this retreat the Americans endured extreme hardships with admirable fortitude. The British urged the pursuit with such rapidity, that they reached the Catawba on the evening of the same day on which the Americans crossed it; and before the next morning a heavy fall of rain rendered that river impassable. A passage at length being effected, the pursuit was continued. The Americans, by expeditious movements, crossed the Yadkin on the second and third days of February, and secured their boats on the north side; but the British, though close in their rear, were incapable of crossing it, through the want of boats, and the rapid rising of the river from preceding rains. This second remarkable escape confirmed the Americans in the belief, that their cause was favoured by Heaven.[9]

Mercy Otis Warren, poet, playwright, and historian, wrote of the retreat from Cowpens that the Americans

> remarkably escaped a pursuing and powerful army, whose progress was, fortunately for the Americans, checked by the same impediments, and at much less favorable moments of arrival. Though we do not assert, a *miracle* was wrought on the occasion, it is certain from good authority, that the freshets swelled, and retarded the passage of the British, while they seemed at times, to suspend their rapidity in favor to the Americans: and the piety of general Greene in several of his letters, attributed his remarkable escapes, and the protection of his little army, to the intervention of a superintending Providence.[10]

Although all these descriptions appear to embrace a straightforward providential interpretation, a careful reading reveals that in no case does a historian use providence as an explanatory concept. Indeed, Lendrum excepted, the historians refused to own the language of providence at all. Instead, Ramsay, Holmes, and Warren attributed the providential interpretation to others, limiting themselves to reporting the events of the retreat and to the fact that others viewed the events as providential. Thus, according to Ramsay, "*The Americans* considered this event as a special interposition of Providence"; the "second hair-breadth escape *was considered by the Americans*" as providential; and "*the devout people*" of Guilford Courthouse thanked heaven for the deliverances. Ramsay narrated in his own voice only what he believed were certainties: "It is certain" that if the rivers had not swelled at precisely the opportune moment the Americans "could have scarcely had any chance of escape." Even the Congregational minister, Holmes, refused to explain the events as the work of providence, observing only that the second "remarkable escape confirmed *the Americans* in the belief, that their cause was favoured by Heaven."

Mercy Warren, perhaps uneasy about the possibility of seeing her account misconstrued, carefully dissociated herself from a providential explanation, insisting that "we do not assert a *miracle* was wrought on the occasion." She limited herself to what could be taken as "certain from good authority" (namely, the letters of Greene and other officers): "that the freshets swelled, and retarded the passage of the British." But even when it came to suggesting that the swelling freshets suspended their rapidity "in favor to the Americans," Warren was willing to state no more than that they "seemed at times" to do so.[11] This is consistent with Warren's treatment of events in South Carolina after the British had captured Charleston in 1780. Despite their awesome difficulties the Americans' morale remained firm.

> A confidence in their own good fortune, or rather in that Providence, whose fiat points out the rise and marks the boundaries of empire, supported *the more thoughtful;* while a constitutional hardiness, warmed by enthusiasm, and whetted by innumerable and recent injuries, still buoyed up the hopes of *the soldier, the statesman, the legislator,* and *the people at large,* even in the darkest moments.[12]

Again, Warren carefully avoided a providential explanation here, insisting upon the complexity of causation and motivation. She described a rough division of Charlestonians into two groups: "the more thoughtful," who relied upon providence as a bulwark against despair; and the soldier, the statesman, the legislator, and the people at large, who depended upon their toughness, their enthusiasm, and a kind of vengeance.

In all these accounts the historians' refusal to adopt a providential interpretation indicates that providence was no longer viable as a mode of historical explanation, although it remained an attractive descriptive metaphor. In part the issue here involves the historians' sensitivity to their own credibility. As Abiel Holmes wrote in another context: "In relating facts without comment, we become not responsible for the *principles,* which they involve."[13] Warren's uneasiness underscores Holmes's point. At the same time, it reveals her intuitive insight into David Hume's famous observation on miracles: "that no testimony is sufficient to establish a miracle unless the testimony be of such a kind that its falsehood would be more miraculous than the fact which it endeavours to establish."[14] The problem with miracles, Hume believed, resides in the *report,* not the *event.* Because miracles are not manifestly credible, when one hears about a miracle one's attention is directed not toward the objective world where the miracle is reported to have occurred, but toward the credibility of the reporter himself. Thus, in those cases in which the language of special providence might have been construed as a historian's report of a miracle, the historians scrupulously avoided the language of providence altogether.

John Lendrum was the only one of the four historians who narrated the events at Cowpens using providence in his own voice: "The Americans met with very providential escapes in this hot pursuit." But Lendrum's language raises additional problems. Not only may we suspect that providence has lost a great deal of its traditional authority when it is modified by an adverb—"*very* providential," indeed—but, more important, Lendrum identifies providence with "good fortune" two sentences later. To use providence as a synonym of fortune, which all the historians did, is to demonstrate that providence could not account for historical causation, for fortune—like chance and accident—is an acausal concept; it signals the historian's intention not to explain but to reserve judgment about causation. Providence as fortune, moreover, is self-referential and judgmental language: it points to the values and attitudes of its speaker rather than to the nature of the events spoken of. Whereas the Puritans used the language of providence to explain causation and signification in the objective world of nature and history—and precisely by using it as an explanatory grammar revealed their belief in it as a language of objectivity— the revolutionary historians used providence descriptively and valuatively, revealing more about their feelings and perceptions of the significance of some events (and about their notions of narrative technique), than about the nature of the events themselves. In short, for the historians to write that an event was "providential" was to say something about their attitudes toward the event rather than to say something about the event itself. And, to anticipate a later discussion, the historians' judgmental use of providence indicates that the language of providence was ideologically charged, for in every case in which it was used it described a situation in which the patriot cause was furthered.

All four historians narrated the events at Cowpens in the same terms. Contrary to anyone's expectations, a natural event occurred in the nick of time, transforming a situation filled with danger into a signal victory for the Americans. To heighten the feeling of momentousness the historians also speculated on what could have happened had the rains not swelled the rivers, leading one to affirm Marc Bloch's insight that might have been questions are "simple rhetorical devices intended to illuminate the role of contingency and the unforeseeable in the progress of mankind."[15] And they concluded that only such a unique concatenation of events could have conspired to effect the American retreat. If the language of providence was appropriate at all, it was appropriate only in enhancing the dramatic intensity of a complex coincidence of events, and in identifying the American cause with the cause of heaven, not in locating the cause of the rains, of the rising rivers, of Cornwallis's want of boats—of, in short, the successful American escape.

One may speculate that the historians' use of providential language was essentially idiosyncratic—that such ministers as William Gordon, Abiel Holmes, Jeremy Belknap, and Jedidiah Morse would naturally have used providence not only more frequently but with greater theological rigor than, for example, the physician David Ramsay, the poet-playwright Mercy Otis Warren, or the jurist John Marshall. But that appears not to be the case. Although providence seems to function forcefully in their *sermons,* the ministers, like the other historians, wrote *history* according to a newly emerging (for America) set of explanatory conventions in which providence played no causal role. It has been argued that Gordon, Holmes, Belknap, and Morse preached sermons that resounded with providential deliverances, millennial hopes about the new nation and its sacred cause of liberty, and images of America as God's New Israel, in the same style that characterized sermons delivered by Ebenezer Baldwin, Samuel Sherwood, and scores of other ministers. But these themes and their implication of God's active involvement in history are absent from their narratives.[16]

Indeed, Jeremy Belknap ridiculed Cotton Mather's *Wonders of the Invisible World* because in it Mather so relentlessly emphasized the causal role of forces external to human history, particularly the devil. "I wish you were here to laugh with me" at the book, he wrote to Ebenezer Hazard, and Hazard rejoined, "It was well for Mather that he was in good keeping, or the devil would have paid him for abusing him so. What a charming philosopher he was!"[17] And William Gordon was maddeningly inconsistent with respect to the meaning of providence. The minister who would minute down the "various special providences in our favour" also wrote to his frequent correspondent General Horatio Gates that "I still expect that we shall be saved by Providence and not by luck," implying that "luck" could conceivably be understood as being as significant a historical construct as providence.[18] Or, the minister who wrote that "Heaven may leave men to blunder, that the positive interposition of Providence in extricating us out of our difficulties may be the more conspicious," also wrote that "good and bad success are often tho' not always accidents."[19]

Although it appears to be the case that the minister-historians used the language of providence more frequently than, say, John Marshall (who avoided it almost completely in five lengthy volumes), the historians' personal religious opinions seem to have been outweighed by the need to conform to the imperatives of narrative historical conventions. Historians, perhaps too readily assuming that ministers' religious convictions consistently found their way into everything the ministers wrote, have tended to pay too little attention to genre, form, and sets of governing conventions, and thereby have lost sight of the particular mode of discourse in which certain ideas must be formulated in order to attain coherence and fulfill readers' (or auditors') expectations about the *kind* of ideas they may properly anticipate. As Roland Barthes remind us, "it is not granted to the writer to choose his mode of writing from a kind of non-temporal store of literary forms. It is under the pressure of History and Tradition that the possible modes of writing for a given writer are established." And Jonathan Culler argues that a mode of writing is "a set of institutional conventions within which the activity of writing can take place."[20] Thus, regardless of their religious convictions (which concern me here almost not at all), the historians *could* not express the same ideas in both historical and sermonic discourse once the conventions governing those modes split apart.[21]

Abiel Holmes's treatment of an episode in the history of colonial Latin America underscores these points. In discussing Cortés's conquest of Mexico, Holmes raised a question that for centuries had puzzled historians: why did Montezuma admit Cortés into his fortified city without a struggle and even accede to his own assassination with hardly a protest when his forces were clearly superior to the invaders'? Holmes adopted a surprising line of argument to answer the question. First he recounted the answer of the Spanish historian Antonio de Solis:

> The very effects of [Cortés's conquest] have since discovered, that God took the reins into his own hand on purpose to tame that monster [i.e., Montezuma]; making his unusual gentleness instrumental to the first introduction of the Spaniards, a beginning from whence afterward resulted the conversion of those heathen nations.

De Solis offered a providential explanation, resounding with echoes of Increase Mather or William Hubbard relating the history of the Indian Wars, that God used both Montezuma and Cortés as "instruments" in His grand design to spread Christianity (and, of course, Spanish civilization).

But Holmes, in a burst of vehemence, rejected De Solis's explanation *because* it was providential and offered in its place a "natural causal" explanation. He argued:

> We ought to adore that Providence, which we cannot comprehend; but it is impious to insult it by assigning such reasons for its measures, *as are contradicted by facts. The natural causes* of the abject submission of Montezuma may perhaps be traced to a long and traditionary expectation of the subjection of the Mexican empire to a foreign power; to the predictions of Soothsayers, with their

expositions of recent and present omens; to the forebodings of a superstitious mind; to the astonishment, excited by the view of a new race of men with unknown and surprizing implements of war; and to the extraordinary success of the Spanish arms from the first moment of the arrival of Cortés on the Mexican coast.[22]

Holmes's vehemence doubtless owes something to ideological motives: to his abhorrence of a "popish" interpretation of providence. It is also arguable that Holmes rejected De Solis's account in the interest of piety for, since natural causes could explain the events, the use of providential language might tend to trivialize a providence that ought to be adored as transcendent.

Yet despite these possible qualifications, Holmes rejected De Solis's account precisely because it was a providential explanation which was "contradicted by facts." And this in itself represents a significant alteration in the understanding of providence, for to set "facts" against "providence" was at minimum to suggest the explanatory *priority* of rational historical analysis to revelation. Holmes did not reject providence as such, and he said so at the outset. But he did reject the kind of historical explanation that pointed outside the historical process itself to locate the cause of "natural" events. He argued that providence ought never to be employed to explain causation when one could identify natural causes at work. But the practical effect of his injunction was *never* to use providence to explain events, for the historians, Holmes included, never seemed to find an event that defied the assumption that natural causes operated.

To the contrary, even when the historians confronted an apparently inexplicable event, instead of turning to providence to explain it they reserved judgment about its causes, choosing to live with the mysteries of historical causation rather than to reduce meaning to a single explanation. Thus Mercy Warren puzzled over General William Howe's behavior after he had dogged the heels of Washington's ragtag army from Long Island all the way across New Jersey during the fall and winter of 1776. Although he knew that Washington's army was in dire straits, Howe allowed him to encamp on the Pennsylvania side of the Delaware River, failing to deliver the decisive blow. "Why this was not done," she wrote, "remains involved among the fortuitous events, which often decide the fate of armies, or of nations, as it were by accident." As if searching for an adequate explanation of the inexplicable she continued:

> The votaries of blind chance, or indeed the more sober calculators on human events, would have pronounced the fortune of the day was in the hands of the British commander. Why he did not embrace her tenders while it was in his power, no one can tell; nor why he stopped short on the borders of the river, as if afraid the waters of the Delaware, like another Red Sea, would overwhelm the pursuers of the injured Americans, who had in many instances as manifestly experienced the protecting hand of Providence, as the favored Israelites.[23]

This, like the accounts of Cowpens, is explanation by metaphor, if it is explanation at all. Virtually exhausting the historians' lexicon of words describing the occurrence of the unexpected, improbable, inexplicable event—"fortuitous," "fate," "accident," "blind chance," "fortune," "providence"—Warren finally answered the causal question "Why?" But instead of answering with a "because," she wrote simply: "No one can tell."

Warren's answer was perfectly consistent with her notion, clearly shared by the other historians, that the domains of history and theology had been torn apart. They would leave religious interpretations to theologians, who concerned themselves with moral causes and effects, and confine themselves to discussions of empirical historical reality. And when their analyses carried them to the brink of inexplicable causes and the unknown, they would refuse to take the next step into faith or into the abyss.[24]

The Language of Chance

Warren's discussion of Howe's failure to pursue Washington's army, like Holmes's rejection of De Solis's providential explanation, suggests that the historians viewed historical causation as a complex problem. Monistic interpretations, like the providential, simply could not capture and convey the richness of historical experience. At the same time, Warren's discussion of Howe and the four accounts of the escape from Cowpens demonstrate that the whole question of causation had become secondary in importance to the question of consequences. For the most important practical difference between writing that an event occurred "accidentally" and that it happened "providentially" is that one locates the meaning and significance of the event in different places. When Increase Mather wrote that Nebuchadnezzar's capture of Jerusalem was "providential," he emphasized the *cause* of that "Great Revolution": it derived its meaning and significance as event from the fact that God had interceded on behalf of Nebuchadnezzar. Mather's narrative showed that the meaning and significance of providential events resided in the fact that they were, precisely, providential, that they were caused by God's actions. But the meaning and significance of the chance or accidental event lie in its consequences. The import of the escape from Cowpens was that the escape succeeded: it preserved an American victory, maintained the American possession of five hundred prisoners, boosted American morale, served to lower British esteem for Cornwallis and Tarleton, and elevated Greene and Morgan into national heroes. The significance of Howe's failure to pursue Washington across the Delaware was that it gave the Americans time to regroup and, soon after, to make a daring crossing of the river late in December, surprise the Hessians at Trenton, recapture Princeton, and solidify a foothold in New Jersey.[25]

But the historians treated the providential event precisely as they treated the chance or accidental event, shifting concern from its causes to its consequences and thereby indicating that what made an event "providential" at all was the fact that its *ramifications* were significant. Mercy Warren addressed this shift in focus in a comment typical of the historians. She wrote of the Boston Massacre (March 5, 1770) as an "accident" that "arose from a trivial circumstance; a circumstance which[,] but from the consideration that these minute accidents lead to the most important events, would be beneath the dignity of history to record."[26] This is reminiscent of William Gordon's narrative of the momentous events at Saratoga, in which the significance of the British soldier's desertion in the nick of time lay in the future—in the successful retreat of Nixon's brigade—and even in the imaginative, hypothetical future—in "the far distant transfer" of power, culture, and knowledge from Europe to America.

Clearly, Warren did not view the Boston Massacre or Howe's failure at the Delaware as causeless events, "blind unmeaning casualties," as Jonathan Edwards would have understood the phrase. To the contrary, such events had causes, but the historian was properly less concerned with causes when "no one can tell" what they might have been than with discussing the meaningfulness of the events' future consequences. The historians' notion that significance resided in the future of events, not in their past, implies a re-vision of the concept of historical meaning. But for the implications of the escape from Cowpens or of hundreds of similar incidents, the "trivial" circumstance producing the event would have remained precisely that—receding into obscurity where all other inconsequential causes resided, never noticed or remarked by historians. As the historians understood it, in narrative history, unlike in experimental science, causation is constituted retrospectively: effects generate causes in their wake.

As Warren pointed out, trivial, accidental events often generate momentous consequences. According to John Lendrum's account, America's most important military victory, Yorktown (October 1781), hinged on what Lendrum called an accident. Lendrum set the scene for this critical encounter by describing how Lord Cornwallis fortified his positions at Yorktown and Gloucester Point, on the James River, as early as July 1781. Meanwhile, George Washington was meeting with his officer corps at Wethersfield, Connecticut, to determine whether or not to risk an attack against General Henry Clinton at New York City in order to recapture the bastion of British occupation. Washington decided to attack New York and called upon the Continental Congress for a major reinforcement of troops. Congress, in turn, sent out requests for more troops to the states.

But the states acted slowly on Congress's request, failing to send the needed men to support Washington's planned invasion.

Echoing myriad statements about the chance event transforming disadvantage into advantage (and vice versa), Lendrum wrote of the states' reticence: "The tardiness of the states, which at other times had brought them to the brink of ruin, was now accidentally of real service." For if the troops had arrived in time Washington would have attacked New York with undetermined success. But in the interim, while waiting for the reinforcement, Washington learned that Cornwallis was busy during the summer fortifying his positions in Virginia. This information, plus the news that the French Count de Grasse would sail for the Chesapeake, prompted Washington to change his plans.[27]

As Lendrum described the events, had Washington attacked New York as originally designed he would have marched into the teeth of Clinton's forces, for Clinton had received intelligence of Washington's Wethersfield plan and had prepared for it by keeping all of his troops in New York, instead of sending Cornwallis the reinforcement he had requested. Washington thus retained his original plan only as a subterfuge, keeping Clinton's forces tied up in New York. He marched south from Connecticut but instead of attacking New York he slipped by the city and raced for Virginia, where in October the siege of Yorktown virtually ended the Revolutionary War. All these twists and turns of the fortunes of war were, if we take Lendrum seriously, the products of a pivotal "accident," trivial in itself, but so filled with important consequences (indeed, potentially catastrophic) that the historian was compelled by its significance to record it.

When the historians stepped back and viewed history from a wider perspective they recognized how crucial the implications of the chance occurrence could be. Were it not for the delay of the states which was "accidentally of real service," or for "a mistake, fortunate for the Americans" in the winter of 1776, or for a "series of adverse accidents," or for a "lucky moment" seized on by some officer, or for hundreds of other "accidents" and "trivial manoeuvers" that arose from time to time, events of the most far-reaching consequences might have turned out differently.[28] That these were chance occurrences rather than providential ones, is evidenced by the simple fact that both chance and providence were available concepts and the historians chose to frame their observations in terms of the former.

The language of chance served to heighten the dramatic import of the trivial-become-momentous. Most of the historians mentioned the discovery and publication of some particularly damning letters written by Thomas Hutchinson and Andrew Oliver during the Stamp Act crisis. Referring to two sets of letters found in 1769 and 1775, Timothy Pitkin pointed out how valuable the discoveries were. For Pitkin, as for John Lendrum, the letters were discovered by chance: "If the letters of the governor [Hutchinson], transmitted by Dr. Franklin, did not prove the allegations in the petition, those he afterwards wrote to the ministry and others, at various times, from 1770, to the close of 1773, substantiated them, beyond all doubt. His letter book was accidentally found in the spring of 1775, at his house in Milton, in an old trunk, among some useless papers."[29] The ending—"in an old trunk, among some useless papers"—is designed to underscore the fortuitousness of the "accident." The discovery of the letters was vital, for while the letters were false and erroneous as far as Pitkin was concerned, yet "the ministry were led to believe, though in the face of the almost unanimous representations of all the colonial assemblies, that opposition to their measures, in America, was confined to a comparatively few *demagogues without property;*' and that *unanimity* and *resolution* in Great Britain, would soon make all things 'quiet' in the colonies."[30] While Pitkin would not go so far as to argue that Britain instigated a hard-line policy on the strength of Hutchinson's letters alone, he recognized how important it was for the colonists to have discovered the letters in the critical year 1775, for the letters helped to push them over the brink of decision for independence.

Why were these "fortunate accidents" rather than providential deliverances? It is generally true that the historians used providential language only with respect to the most significant situations, for providence had become for them a dramatic rather than a theological construct (although even this vague rule was observed almost as often in the breach). What is difficult to deal with is the sense that providence is somehow *missing* from a narrative in which it seems to belong. When a fifth historian, John Marshall, described the American retreat from Cowpens, for example, he avoided the language of providence altogether, writing that General Morgan's "good fortune interposed to save him," that the rising rivers were a "favourable circumstance," and that the success of the escape "is an evidence of the judgment with which every favourable circumstance was improved." Marshall's failure to use providence—even to the point of neglecting to mention that *others* saw the event as providential— owes less to a lack of piety than to a deficiency in his dramatic sensitivity. His account is flatter and less exciting than the others in great part because he failed to play upon the obvious dramatic possibilities of the escape by using the providential metaphor.[31]

Yet Marshall recognized that historians used both chance and providence to best dramatic advantage when a situation arose that thwarted people's expectations—when, for example, "a variety of accidents had defeated plans judiciously formed, having every probability in their favour." About these he observed: "So much are the best laid plans, and the most important human transactions dependent on fortune, and the judicious use of occurrences, in themselves apparently indifferent."[32] Here Marshall voiced what was clearly implicit in all the historians' accounts: that the occurrences were "in themselves apparently *indifferent*," thus emphasizing the self-referentiality of the language of chance and of providence.

Even when the historians employed the language of providence, and spoke it in their own narrative voices, they made clear that providence no longer retained its traditional authority as a theological-historical principle of causation and explanation. John Lendrum, for example, described the events at Long Island in August 1776. The Americans under Washington's command found themselves backed up against the East River after the British had successfully effected a landing on the island and had penetrated General Israel Putnam's lines and forced the Americans to retreat. Backs to the river and confronted by an enemy on three sides, the Americans could either surrender or face certain annihilation if they resisted. But during the night of August 29 they actually retreated across the East River to Manhattan. As Lendrum depicted it:

> Providence seems to have ordered every circumstance so as to second the skill and conduct of the American commander. The wind, which seemed to prevent the troops getting over at the appointed hour, afterwards shifted to their wishes. Towards morning, an extreme thick fog came on, which is very unusual at that time of the year, which hovered over Long-Island, and by concealing the Americans, enabled them to complete their retreat without interruption, though the day had begun to dawn some time before it was finished.[33]

This is one of dozens of examples of uncommon natural occurrences which the historians narrated in providential terms: shifting winds that allowed vessels to pursue a desirable course, sudden freezes which rendered muddy roads "firm and smooth as pavement," fogs that concealed important activities.

Rather than a straightforward affirmation of providential deliverance, however, Lendrum's description of the escape from Long Island, while marvelously dramatic, is confused. For Lendrum *reversed* the traditional meaning of providence by portraying providence *seconding* Washington's skillful actions, inverting the theological concept of instrumentality. It is also noteworthy that Lendrum characterized the whole affair at Long Island, from the British landing to the American evacuation, as an "unfortunate engagement."[34]

Providence and Politics

Philosophically, the historians used the languages of chance and providence interchangeably. They used both to reserve judgment about causation when causes were apparently inexplicable, and to heighten the dramatic import of a series of events when it was clear to them that the events' consequences were of greater political or military (or theatrical) significance than their causes. But because the historians believed that it tapped a well-spring of traditional cultural values, the language of providence was useful ideologically in ways that chance was not.

In one of the many contemplative digressions in her history, Mercy Warren reflected on England's preparation for war with the colonies. England's activity simply did not make sense. "[I]t is difficult to account on any principles of human policy, for the infatuation that instigated [Britain] to the absurd project of conquering a country, already their's on the most advantageous terms. But," she continued, making clear her intention to wed politics and traditional religious beliefs, "the seeds of separation were sown, and the *ball* of empire rolled westward with such astonishing rapidity, that the pious mind is naturally excited to acknowledge a superintending Providence, that led to the period of independence, even before America was conscious of her maturity."[35] Like Increase Mather, Warren questioned human knowledge, though she arrived at a very different and, for her purposes, more useful conclusion. However industrious man may be in his pursuit of wisdom, he "yet discovers a deficiency of capacity to satisfy his researches, or to announce that he has already found an unerring standard on which he may rest." Lacking any absolute source of insight, even virtuous people operate in a "narrow sphere of comprehension." Because of their fundamental limitations they will simply have "to wait, in a becoming manner, [for] the full disclosure of the system of divine government."[36]

But Warren's epistemological misgivings allowed her to carry her ideological point. In the absence of a full disclosure of the divine plan, Americans could adopt the most optimistic interpretation of historical possibilities, an interpretation by no means limited to "the pious mind": that independence was part of God's program for human history. What Warren artfully implied, William Henry Drayton bluntly stated: "the Lord of Hosts is on our side!" It was apparent, Drayton said to the South Carolina grand jury, that "the Almighty Constructor of the universe, having formed this continent of materials to compose a state pre-eminent in the world, is now making use of the tyranny of the British rulers, as an instrument to fashion and arrange those materials for the end, for which, in his wisdom, he had formed them." The words are those of Chief Justice Drayton, but the fact that David Ramsay and Timothy Pitkin quoted them testifies to the appeal and evocative power of Drayton's language.[37] In his charge to the jury Drayton used the language of instrumentality and wrote of God's appointed means and ends in a way that is reminiscent of Increase Mather and William Ames. God created America for a specific end, and British tyranny—replacing Mather's Indians—was an "instrument" God was using to bring about that end.

To underscore these points Ramsay and Pitkin quoted further from Drayton's speech: "The Almighty created America to be independent of Great Britain: let us beware of the impiety of being backward, to act as instruments, in the Almighty Hand, now extended to accomplish his purpose. . . . In a word, our piety and political safety are so blended, that to refuse our labors in this divine work, is to refuse to be a great, a free, a pious and a happy people."[38] Drayton's language could be heard almost anywhere in America, in the sermons preached by patriot ministers on public occasions as well as in church meetings. He was merely more explicit than most when in his key phrase—"our piety and political safety are blended"—he, like the clergy, attempted to harness the Revolution to the millennium.

Although in these examples Warren's and Drayton's providence is a superintending, programmatic providence, it is clear that the historians used special providence in the same way. For unlike the Puritans, who saw the hand of God in all events "prosperous *and* adverse," the revolutionary historians used providence in a strictly partisan way. They did, of course, narrate events in which the patriot cause was not advanced; the

British did win battles and the Americans suffered crucial defeats. But the historians uniformly attributed such events to blunders and miscalculations, to superior British strategy and tactics, or, when the causes were neither readily apparent nor sufficiently interesting, to chance, accident, or fortune. If the minister-historians used providence evenhandedly to emphasize God's tests and punishments as well as His blessings, they did so only in their sermons; as historians they used the language of providence in their narratives to make political judgments. Wrote William Gordon to John Adams in 1782: "I am a Protestant in politics as well as in Divinity."[39]

The historians recognized that anyone could use providence to justify almost any political bias, and this helps to explain why they were reluctant to use it in many instances. John Lendrum, for example, pointed to the political dimension of the sermons of patriot clergymen, observing that "they represented the cause of America as the cause of heaven."[40] They also recognized that the partisan use of providence could backfire. The incisive ridicule of one articulate opponent could turn the providential interpretation into a liability. Joseph Galloway, the Maryland Loyalist, was just such an opponent. Writing five years before the first patriot history was published, Galloway used the revolutionaries' own arguments about how the religious ideas of the seventeenth-century settlers inexorably led to the political views of the revolutionaries. Elevating the conspiracy theory almost to an art, and hinting at what is now recognized as a strong prophetic and millennialist theme in early philosophy of history, he argued that the Puritans themselves had used providence ideologically. The Puritan view that God favored American independence was still being advanced during the Revolution, and a thinly disguised political ploy it was. The revolutionaries were merely a later group of "democratic sectaries" playing upon the tradition of providence to support their political ends.[41]

Yet despite their recognition that providence could be construed as being no more than a partisan political judgment, the historians used it in a partisan way. And while this use is further evidence that providence had lost authority as a principle of historical explanation, it also suggests that the historians continued to find providence useful as a culturally charged ideological principle. In September 1780, for example, Benedict Arnold, commander of West Point, conspired to betray the fortress. Arnold's accomplice was a young British major, John André, who had disembarked the *Vulture*, a sloop of war lying at anchor off West Point, and had met Arnold to receive the plans of the fort. After receiving these valuable papers André was unable to return to the *Vulture*. In civilian clothing, and therefore subject to treatment as a spy, and carrying a pass from Arnold, André left West Point on horseback, hoping to reach New York City, the headquarters of British troops in America. On the second day of his journey through enemy territory, according to John Lendrum, "he travelled without any alarm, and began to consider himself out of danger; but unhappily for him, though providentially for America, three of the New-York militia were with others on a scouting party between the outposts of the two armies." The New York militiamen, later immortalized in the song "John Paulding," captured André, foiling the scheme to take over a major military installation and a key strategic point along the Hudson River. André, though a sympathetic figure for many Americans, was hanged as a spy. After his detailed description of the capture, Lendrum again referred to America's "providential escape from the deep laid scheme against West Point."[42]

Lendrum's narrative is obviously partisan and his partisanship helps to illuminate what has happened to providence when it is used for political purposes. The phrase, "unhappily for him though providentially for America," indicates that "providentially" was no more than a synonym for "happily." But the cultural and psychological differences between the two words are enormous, even if philosophically they are synonymous. For the language of providential deliverance implicitly associated the Revolutionary generation with their seventeenth-century forebears and with the Hebrews, models not only of perseverance and virtue but of God's chosen people. The historians thus preserved the ideological and cultural values traditionally associated with providence even as they rejected providence as an explanatory concept.

Toward a Theory of Historical Immanence

When William Gordon posed his great question—"blind unmeaning casualties" or "superintending Providence"?—he refused to answer it directly, and not to answer it was a sound strategy. Those readers who thought the question was manifestly rhetorical and that, obviously, such incidents were caused by God's intervention into human affairs were among Mercy Warren's "pious minds" who "naturally" saw America's destiny in terms of God's program for human history. Others might have viewed the question as no more than a minister's sermonizing, a digression characteristic enough of a preacher's bent but of little moment compared with the events narrated. That Gordon did indeed answer his question indirectly almost certainly would have gone unnoticed by his readers. For Gordon referred to the British defeat at Saratoga, which turned on the soldier's desertion, as "a reverse of fortune."[43]

On one level Gordon posed his question correctly, as Jonathan Edwards clearly would have recognized. The assumption of chance in history was incompatible with a theology of providential causation and explanation. For even if chance meant no more than that the historian would reserve judgment about causes instead of assigning causation to the transmundane, then historical explanation had been redirected to the historical process itself. Chance was incompatible with providence, but it was not incompatible with causation.

Leo Braudy has argued that providential explanations "irked" and "concerned" such eighteenth-century writers as Henry Fielding and David Hume. Fielding played with providence in his novels in order to deflate it, showing that the credulous craved simplistic, "monolithic interpretations . . . that flatten the variety of life into harsh paradigms and exempla," when in reality experience revealed complexity.[44] Braudy quotes Hume as saying that among history's uses is that it instructs us "in the great mixture of accident, which commonly concurs with a small ingredient of wisdom and foresight."[45] At the same time, the great English historian Edward Gibbon condemned providential explanation in Eusebius "as a kind of epistemological laziness," a most appropriate insight into Abiel Holmes's condemnation of Antonio de Solis.[46]

Although one cannot attribute these same thoughts and motives to the revolutionary historians in the absence of their critical comment or manifest plays upon the relationship between chance and providence, Braudy's observations are relevant to their performances. For by conflating providence and chance, by destroying the traditional use of providence as a mode of explanation, and by using chance independently of providence, the historians clearly sought to accomplish the same two principal ends as the English writers: to reinfuse history with a sense of contingency, and to present causation as a complex problem.

To accept chance was to accept the contingency in history that providence explicitly denied, revealing a historical imagination more comfortable with spontaneity and the unknown than was revealed in providential history. It is ironic that the Puritans, who so unflinchingly attempted to engage the absolute on its own terms, sought to make history regular and predictable, while the Revolutionary generation, who rarely acknowledged the possibility of the unknowable or attempted to grapple with the absolute, more willingly lived with the accidental. But if the providential explanation made history more regular, more predictable, and, perhaps above all, more meaningful by locating causation in an omnipresent deity, the revolutionary historians' acceptance of chance suggests that for them historical experience no longer required the assumption of transcendent support.

As Braudy has suggested, Edward Gibbon understood "that

what in retrospect may seem certain and necessary in a 'chain' of events was at the time it occurred actually an accident."[47] This is what Warren and the historians understood about those "trivial accidents" that so often lead to momentous consequences. But, as Marshall and others pointed out, the same was true of the providential. Referring to the Arnold-André affair, Marshall wrote: "When the probable consequences of this plot, had it been successful, came to be considered, and the combination of apparent accidents by which it was discovered and defeated was recollected; all were filled with a kind of awful astonishment, and the devout perceived in the transaction, the hand of Providence guiding America to independence."[48] Thus, neither providence nor chance was seen as intrinsic to the event itself; both terms were used retrospectively and bespoke the values of the historian and, equally important, the historian's narrative skill. Both providence and chance became, then, aesthetic terms capable of conveying drama and suspense.

The historians demonstrated a marvelous sense of narrative possibility by using the vocabularies both of chance and providence, each serving purposes that the other could not. Their use of chance reaffirmed the principle of historical contingency, the sense that anything might happen, particularly when people's expectations seemed to be based on the soundest calculation. In addition, because chance signified the historians' refusal to enumerate causes, it simultaneously heightened the sense of mystery and opened causation to a variety of possible interpretations. Moreover, by shifting attention from causes to consequences without resolving the precise relationship between them, chance enriched both the dramatic thrust of a narrative and the feeling of the openness of future possibility.

At the same time, by retaining the language of providence for dramatic purposes the historians preserved a mode of description that complemented the language of chance. Precisely by using providence ideologically (anticipating the nineteenth-century maxim that God was on the side of the heaviest artillery), the historians made the language of providence a mythic one. By "mythic" I mean to follow Georges Sorel's notion that myths are "expressions of a determination to act." Writing under the assumption that the Revolution was as yet incomplete, they used providence to revive and encourage those traditional values, assumptions, and convictions which, they believed, led Americans "to prepare themselves for a combat which [would] destroy the existing state of things."[49]

This is similar to what Perry Miller meant when he wrote that the revolutionary clergy "did not have to 'sell' the Revolution" to the American people, for what they were selling was a constellation of commonly held beliefs. A secular rationalism "might have declared the independence of these folk, but it could never have inspired them to fight for it."[50] Although Miller was guilty of attempting to deduce popular belief from the writings of articulate ministers, and although he greatly overestimated the *theological* significance of providence in revolutionary thought, he brilliantly captured the tension between theology and ideology, the religious and the secular. It was this tension—in the histories, between providence and chance—that the historians exploited. On the philosophical level the case is clear: the historians saw providence and chance as mutually exclusive, and providence yielded its once exalted status as a mode of explanation and became a mode of narrative description. But on another level, the level of historical art where chance and providence were descriptive terms, the historians bridged the tension between them by using both as instruments of ideology.

3

Contingency, Complexity, and the Shape of History

When he wrote of the abortive American campaign to capture Canada in the winter of 1776, John Marshall typified the historians' effort to infuse history with a sense of contingency and to demonstrate that historical causation was a complex problem. The plan to invest Three Rivers, for example, "was well laid, and considerable resolution was discovered in its execution," he wrote, but "the concurrence of too many circumstances were necessary to give it success." As Marshall saw it, however, the American effort might have been successful had slightly different circumstances prevailed. Emphasizing the importance of chance, he surmised: "Had a few incidents turned out fortunately; had Arnold been able to reach Quebec a few days sooner, or to have crossed the St. Lawrence on his first arrival; or had the gallant Montgomery not fallen in the assault of the 31st. of December; it is probable the expedition would have been crowned with complete success." But, of course, such fortunate possibilities did not materialize. Moreover, *the radical causes* of failure, putting fortune out of the question, were to be found in the lateness of the season when the troops were assembled, in a defect of the preparations necessary for such a service, and still more in the shortness of the time for which the men were in-listed."[1] The principle was clear: "In war, the success of the most judicious plans often depends on accidents not to be foreseen nor controlled."[2]

In these passages Marshall strived to accomplish two aims which are not entirely compatible: to explain the causes of the American failure to capture Canada and, at the same time, to affirm the sense that historical situations are contingent, filled with possibilities. While these are by no means mutually exclusive aims, there is a tension between them, for causal explanation tends to limit interpretation, to effect imaginative closure, by suggesting that it exhausts an event, whereas the affirmation of contingency tends to invite interpretation and to open possibilities. Marshall's account is manifestly causal: he writes of the "radical causes" of the failure and enumerates three fundamental factors (and hints at smaller ones) that operated against a successful campaign. But even as he explains the failure he suggests that things still might have turned out differently, indicating his refusal to reduce the event to the sum of its causes.

Marshall and the other historians were ambivalent about the proper mode of explaining causation, and their ambivalence stemmed from their renewed appreciation of history's complexity and from a revitalized sense of the historian's role. While they earnestly sought to ground events as fully as possible in their antecedent conditions and circumstances, they seem to have felt that it was possible to explain *too much*, to make history too neat, to present such an orderly scheme of events that the sense of contingency would be stripped away. They generally sought, therefore, to steer a middle course between rendering history as a mechanical series of interlocking moments and presenting it as a mass of disconnected happenstances. The result was often less than elegant or satisfying: either a tedious enumeration of prior circumstances, conditions, and causes, the connections among which were left to the sheer mass of detail to convey, or a complete avoidance of analysis and a reflexive recourse to chance, mystery, or "no one can tell."

At their best, however, the historians were able to accomplish both their aims. They fairly reveled in history's complexity, and precisely by pursuing their love of variety they affirmed their sense of contingency. For the very effort to list as many factors as could reasonably be thought to have effected an event demonstrated their feeling that history was rich and complex. Indeed, their efforts to exhaust an event—to "fully account" for its causes, as Thomas Condie put it—betrayed the notion that causal explanation *could* exhaust an event.[3] For list-making reveals a kind of playfulness that points more to the historians' own method of analysis and mode of presentation, and therefore to the sense that any number of other causes might also have been operating, than to their satisfaction that they have somehow fully accounted for anything.

In short, the historians did write causal narratives. To abandon the providential mode of explanation was not to abandon causal explanation altogether. To the contrary, the historians' most important achievement was to liberate American history from the monistic and reductionistic providential interpretation, and in doing so to free themselves to engage history's enormous variety and complexity. They presented history in terms of what Abiel Holmes called "natural causes," those which arose in history rather than in the transmundane. And even if the historians failed to develop an adequate theory of historical causation, by viewing history as an immanent process of self-generating events they were able to provide both a sense of the continuity of causes and effects and of the disjunctions which arose by chance, without any reference to forces external to history.

The Quest for Openness

On first inspection the historians' presentation of historical causation appears to be simple and straightforward. Events follow one another in sequential lockstep, the momentum of which is carried by words and phrases that are so obvious to the modern reader that they are taken for granted: "because," "therefore," "as a result of," "as a consequence," "hence," "thus," and so forth, all of which convey the finality of causation.[4] But upon closer examination, their explanations appear to be so complex and ambiguous that one suspects the historians of being almost eager to decompose history into a chaos of "untoward circumstances," "providential [or "accidental"] concurrences of circumstances," "strange and undesigned consequences," and "various unpropitious circumstances," not to mention a welter of fortunate deliverances, unhappy reverses of fortune, chance engagements, and trivial maneuvers.[5]

Viewing this tendency to emphasize the irrational in history as a characteristic of Enlightenment historians generally, R. G. Collingwood concluded with evident disapprobation that their treatment of causation "is superficial to absurdity." Enlightenment historians simply "had no satisfactory theory of historical causation." Instead, "Deep down beneath the surface of their work lay a conception of the historical process as a process developing neither by the will of enlightened despots nor by the rigid plans of a transcendent God, but by a necessity of its own, an immanent necessity in which unreason itself is only a disguised form of reason."[6] Peter Gay has written in similar terms, arguing that Enlightenment historians vacillated widely in explaining causes, sometimes ascribing "great importance to world-historical individuals and the rational plans of statesmen," while other times attributing "large events to trivial causes." But they failed to develop even their impressionistic, "pragmatic" history into a system. "Face to face with great historical questions, the philosophes often seem to be at play; they describe an event, list some plausible causes with an air of confidence, and move on." Gay succinctly concludes: "They had no system."

Gay, however, unlike Collingwood, appreciates the Enlightenment historians' sense of play and even their almost perverse avoidance of system. Gibbon's "list of causes" for the decline and fall of Rome, "scattered through his book and revealed in isolated pronouncements and asides," while "incomplete and uncoordinated" and certainly not systematic, "is impressively diverse." And if the philosophes had too "primitive" an understanding of society to develop a theory of the interaction of causes, and if they moved too easily between presenting causation as "massive impenetrable forces" on the one hand and no more than personal idiosyncrasy on the other, their narratives reveal a sense of openness and possibility, of history as a "spectacle full of pleasure and variety." As Gay sees it, this sense of complexity and variety was the product of a secular historical imagination: "God's disappearance left a vacuum that the secular intelligence was called upon to fill."[7]

This view that history was a rich and complex set of processes was one the revolutionary historians shared with and almost certainly derived from the Europeans. And although the price they paid for their openness was the loss of a satisfactory theory of causation—assuming that they valued such a theory as much as nineteenth-century historians did—the historians' insistence upon contingency and complexity was worth it, for such openness squared with their perception that historical reality was composed of situations that had been actualized out of an almost infinite number of possibilities. In addition, their quest for openness in historical explanation transformed the historians' sense of their own enterprise. Whether, like historians of the Revolution, they sought to narrate events in which they participated, or, like Edward Gibbon, the history of the Roman Empire, historians, as Gibbon observed, were always "surrounded with imperfect fragments, always concise, often obscure, and sometimes contradictory," so that they are "reduced to collect, to compare, and to conjecture."[8] Historians always faced such difficulties because history was filled with what the English theorist John Bigland called "innumerable . . . instances of historical uncertainty . . . with which it is almost morally impossible that the historian should be perfectly acquainted." Bigland thus cautioned the reader of history "against too easy a credulity when we find historians pretending to tell us what it is evident that they cannot possibly know." History was too intrinsically complex to be reduced to simple explanations: "the imperious circumstances [which] fix the destiny of nations and individuals" conspire with "various combinations of physical and moral causes, incalculably numerous, and extremely complex, [to] determine the political, religious, intellectual, and social condition of mankind."[9]

Despite this sensitivity to history's immense complexity, of course, neither American nor European historians despaired of writing useful and accurate causal narrative. Indeed, Gibbon's and Bigland's observations reveal a mock despair, calculated not only to point to history's intricacies, but to call attention to their own awesome achievements in the face of such enormous difficulties. Through their plaints resonates excitement over the possibilities open to the insightful and creative historian. To trace and make meaningful "all the different combinations of circumstances" that constitute "a train of moral causes, forming themselves, into an infinity of combinations, and operating with an infinite variety of influences," was both to appreciate the marvelous richness of history itself and to glory in the crucial imaginative role of the historian in giving voice and shape to history's interior processes.[10]

Unlike some of the philosophes, who joined David Hume in challenging conventional historical epistemology, none of the revolutionary historians expressed a doubt that causation was intrinsic to the historical process. When they challenged the providential interpretation and shifted the locus of causation from the transmundane to history itself, they did not expand that challenge into an epistemological skepticism which questioned whether causation resided in history (or in nature) at all. But they did challenge the notion that any event could be explained simply and they implied that no event could be explained completely. If history was too complex fully to yield its twistings, moreover, and if events were as "neutral" as John Marshall suggested, then they required the narrative voice of the historian to give them meaning and shape.

No longer the "Lord's Remembrancers," who recorded the track of God's will, the revolutionary historians not only recorded facts and chronicled events but helped to shape history precisely by giving order and continuity to the veritable chaos of complex coincidences. Indeed, Jonathan Boucher, a Tory minister, implied that the historians invented history as they narrated it.[11] Boucher missed the philosophical import of his accusation, phrasing it in strictly ideological terms. But, although the historians disputed the charge that they made history conform to their ideological predispositions, it was an appropriate and telling one. For philosophically considered it squared with the historians' growing awareness of their participation in history as the continuous narrative voice that gave it shape and interpreted its significance. Facts, David Ramsay observed, properly governed historical narrative: "It is the province of an historian to relate what has happened, and not to indulge in fancied conjectures about probable contingencies." This echoed Edward Gibbon's assertion that the historian "ought never to place his conjectures in the rank of facts." But Gibbon qualified his statement, as Ramsay did in practice, by observing that in the face of the uncertainty and inconclusive evidence that historians always confronted, the historian's "knowledge of human nature, and of the sure operations of its fierce and unrestrained passions, might, on some occasions, supply the want of historical materials."[12] Thus, while they were the very stuff of history, facts were brute and unmeaning. By bringing to their study a knowledge of human nature, of politics, religion, and society, the historians made coherent and articulate the facts, and the relationships among them, that were in themselves mute. Even if the historians would dispute the proposition that their own narratives conveyed—even constituted—causation in history, their histories suggest that causation was at least as important as a mode of explanation as it was a feature of history itself.

Causes, Necessity, and the Chain of Circumstances

The historians' belief that history was contingent and complex, frequently yielding no more than the vague sense that intricately combined circumstances generate a succession of events, prevented their developing a satisfactory theory of historical causation. It also prompted their many cautious statements that "no one can tell" why some events transpired, and the cavalier listing of causes, often bearing little systematic relevance to the event at issue, that Peter Gay found among the European historians. History revealed no "laws" (save two, as we will see in greater detail later—that human nature was fundamentally the same in all times and places, and that the same causes always produced the same effects—both of which were so heavily qualified that neither can be seen as "legal"). The revolutionary historians, like Enlightenment historians generally, were indebted to Montesquieu's incipient philosophy of history which based analysis on political institutions and on geographical conditions.[13] But they were likely to see geography, politics, economics, culture, and personal idiosyncrasy as equally causal depending upon the situation they were trying to explain.

Thus, in explaining the "various causes" that prompted the Separatists to emigrate from Holland to America in the seventeenth century, Abiel Holmes listed the following with no concern for priorities: "the unhealthiness of the low country," their "hard labours," "the dissipated manners of the Hollanders," their apprehension of a war between Holland and Spain, their fear of absorption into a foreign nation, their desire to establish their own church, "and a commendable zeal to propagate the gospel in the regions of the new world." And William Gordon had great difficulty in deciding precisely what triggered the attack on Governor Thomas Hutchinson's house during the Stamp Act crisis—so he listed what he thought to be all the "various causes," beginning with Hutchinson's unpopular support of a bill abolishing the currency two decades earlier, and concluding with the assessment that these circumstances, "cooperating with the general disposition in the people to tumult, produced by a prevailing persuasion, that they were deprived of the liberties of Englishmen, will account for the excessive outrages on him in particular."[14]

There is nothing particularly "wrong" in such accounts. In

these and hundreds of descriptions like them the historians discovered and listed a variety of causes to explain a variety of phenomena. What is missing, however, is a hierarchy of causal values, a sense that some causes are more efficacious than others. In addition, by merely enumerating such causes without supplying a means of determining whether the actors themselves experienced anything like them, the historians imply that the list is *their* list and that alternative lists could be almost endlessly created. One is left with the sense that the historians had no agreed-upon set of conventions that explained causations.[15] At the same time, precisely how causes and circumstances "cooperate" with one another to produce consequences remains as much a mystery as if Holmes and Gordon had ascribed the events to a "providential coincidence of circumstances."

Yet what is important about these causal accounts is not that they are imprecise or unsystematic, or even that they reveal the absence of an adequate theory of causation. It is that they are manifestly causal explanations at all. For if the historians were willing to confess their ignorance on many occasions (and by doing so to affirm their sense of chance and openness), they were also concerned with making the history of the Revolution meaningful by presenting it in an orderly fashion. Impressionistic as they frequently were, the narratives reveal a pattern of causal continuity that testifies to this concern. And although the historians clearly were aware of their own participation in history by giving it coherence, they wrote as if history were *intrinsically* orderly and that their participation was limited essentially to uncovering the "secret causes and springs" of events and to voicing history's processes.

It is also arguable that the revolutionary historians developed a somewhat more systematic (even if implicit) notion of causation than their European counterparts, because, as partisans of the movement which they narrated, they were devoted to justifying the Revolution to posterity.[16] History was fundamentally a political process. Its central theme was the struggle between liberty and arbitrary power, a struggle which revealed that politics and ethics were thoroughly intertwined.[17] Thus, although they used a wide variety of explanations to account for most events, when they reflected on the causes of the Revolution they relied most frequently upon political and constitutional arguments and a sense of the American "national character." Timothy Pitkin wrote most explicitly about the way in which the historians discussed causation, and he did so in the context of political and constitutional events. "The stamp act and the insignificant duty on tea, precipitated, but did not alone produce, the American Revolution." The patriots' *cause célèbre* of the 1760s and, in retrospect, one of the pivotal events on which the Revolution turned, was a "precipitating" cause. To identify it and to explore its ramifications was to make history coherent in causal terms. But the historian could not be content with reducing history's significance to a series of catalytic causes when lying behind them was a world of conditions and circumstances that gave them force: "This great event must be traced to *powerful and efficient causes* in existence, and in operation, long before the adoption of these particular measures; causes which, brought at length into more active operation by these measures, produced such wonderful effects."[18]

Pitkin's formulation points simultaneously to the way in which causation operated and to the historians' methods of investigation and narration. Causes and consequences are inseparable, for powerful and efficient causes not only produce effects which, by bearing consequences, themselves become precipitating causes, but those precipitating causes operate retrospectively as well to constitute the long-term efficacy of the earlier powerful and efficient causes. The historian's task was to read back from consequences to causes, particularly from precipitating to powerful and efficient ones, and thus to establish causal sequentiality in the narrative.

To write of powerful and efficient causes was to present an immanent theory of history, a theory which held that history is a self-generating succession of events. Causes may be baffling, accidental, trivial, opaque, coincidental, or entwined in such complexity that they defied complete analysis. But that they operated *effectually* was beyond question. Events occurred *because* antecedent conditions and circumstances made them possible, and *because* precipitating causes made them actual. As John Marshall succinctly put it, events "unfolded themselves."[19]

John Lendrum echoed Pitkin's distinction between powerful and efficient and precipitating causes by using the older language of "primary" and "secondary" causes. He referred to the actions of the colonists, the blunders of some British statesmen, and the assistance of foreign nations as "secondary causes which effected the revolution—as circumstances which forwarded its birth somewhat sooner than it would have happened in the common course of nature." But if these were merely secondary or precipitating causes which hastened a virtually inevitable conclusion, what would primary or powerful and efficient causes look like in the common course of nature? Lendrum continued:

> When the manners and the habits of the Americans are considered—the equality of rank which subsisted among them—their independent principles—their jealous and watchful care of their constitutional rights—the knowledge of their own strength, which they acquired in the war with France—the removal of hostile neighbours—their knowledge of the strong factions in the parent state—What might not have been expected from such a people, in such a country, and in such a situation, when their liberties were attacked?—Could it have been imagined, that an united body of three millions of people would tamely surrender up their natural and chartered rights?—No! Nothing but the height of infatuation could have fostered so vain a hope.

To appreciate the factors he enumerated was to recognize that American resistance was "not only natural and just, but it entirely corresponds with the American character." Lendrum thus identified primary causes with the American character itself.[20]

And he was hardly alone. When he wrote of powerful and efficient causes, Timothy Pitkin argued that American opposition to the Stamp Act "was not the work of a day or a year." To the contrary, "the opinions then simultaneously and universally expressed by the Americans, on the subject of their rights, were the opinions of their fathers, which they brought into this country, and here cherished and handed down to their posterity." Similarly, while he conceded that parliament's policies in the 1760s "were the *direct causes*" of American opposition, Noah Webster argued that "the open rupture . . . between Great Britain and the colonies, was not the sudden effect of a tumultuous opposition to a particular act of parliament, but the effect of hostile principles and habits which had grown up out of a long series of events, and which a few measures of the British government ripened into action."[21]

To discuss the basic historical conditions and circumstances which actuated a sequence was to adopt a long view of colonial history. It presupposed that the historian properly began with the Revolution itself and in effect deduced its causes over a century and a half of colonial development, reconstituting the events prospectively in narrative. This was "whig history," as Herbert Butterfield has described it: historical writing which imposes on events a single-minded linearity that attempts to account for its end-point.[22] Precisely how such a succession of events operated in the narratives is unclear, for the historians never addressed themselves to the relationship between powerful and efficient and precipitating causes as Puritan theologians, for example, had addressed the relationship between primary and secondary causes. But if the operation is unclear, the historians widely employed the metaphor of a chain to convey the sense of linear causal connectedness. The American victory at Bennington, Vermont, for example, a prelude to the momentous victory at Saratoga, "was the first link in a grand chain of causes, which finally drew down ruin on the whole royal army."[23]

This "chain-of-causes" metaphor was central to the purpose of locating in a series of self-generating events the causal connectedness of all later events. As Ramsay observed: "The repeal of the Stamp act, in a relative connection with all its circumstances and consequences, was the first direct step to American independency. The claims of the two countries were not only left undecided, but a foundation was laid for their extending at a future period, to the impossibility of a compromise."[24] Ramsay's exaggeration of the importance of the skirmish at Bennington echoed the historians' insistence upon the significance of the consequences of events. According to Mercy Warren: "The action at Lexington, detached from its consequences, was but a trivial *manoeuvre* when compared with the records of war and slaughter, that have disgraced the page of history through all generations of men: but a circumstantial detail of lesser events, when antecedent to the convulsions of empire, and national revolution, are not only excusable, but necessary."[25] Yet despite the fact that the historian could portray virtually any event, no matter how trivial, as the first link in a long series of consequences, the chain-of-causes metaphor represented a serious effort to describe a kind of historical necessity—a moral necessity that operated through a succession of events, guaranteeing the succession's continuity and pointing to its conclusion as virtually inevitable. Powerful and efficient causes were powerful and efficient because the consequences they generated issued like "the common course of nature."

In one of those long "natural causal" statements that over-explain the situation at issue, John Lendrum pointed to the kind of necessity that the historians built into their narratives. Seeking to account for the fading of Britain's early successes in 1776, he enumerated seven reasons that more appropriately answered the question why Britain could not have won the war at all. Among the causes

the principal may be supposed to arise from the vast extent of the American continent, with its uncommon divisions into large tracts of territory, some cultivated, and others in a state of nature; the great length of the sea coast in its front, and the immense wastes at the back of the inhabited countries, affording shelter to the provincials in all possible circumstances; the numberless impregnable posts, and natural barriers, formed by the various combinations of woods, mountains, lakes, and marshes. Added to these, the British found, to their cost, the unanimity of the colonies, and the judicious application of their strength, by suiting the defence of the country, to the nature, genius and ability of the people, as well as to the natural advantages of the country itself. . . . Add to this also, that the people were unfettered by strong cities; so that the reduction of the capital of a province had little or no effect upon the rest; and the army could retain no more territory than that which it immediately occupied, which was again lost as soon as it departed to another quarter.

These causes, cooperating together by a kind of process of addition, constituted a virtual necessity, for they "still continued to operate, and to militate effectually against the royal army, and, indeed, to appearance, *must have been* too powerful for any number of men which Britain could be supposed to bring into the field."[26]

Even though such factors generate "a train of moral causes" that in complex combination appear to create a virtual necessity, because of the infinite number of possible effects and the ever-present possibility of the chance occurrence, history yielded only probabilities, never certainties. The historians were not interested in replacing a providential determinism with a natural or political one. Thus, despite the fact that they frequently cited one of the basic maxims of experimental science—that like causes always produce like effects—even the leading proponents of that idea qualified its applicability to historical analysis. David Hume, for example, argued that "the same cause always produces the same effect, and the same effect never arises but from the same cause. This principle we derive from experience."[27] Yet in his famous discussion of "Liberty and Necessity" he showed that it represented no more than a tendency or probability in history: "We must not . . . expect that this uniformity of human actions should be carried to such a length as that all men, in the same circumstances, will always act precisely in the same manner." To the contrary, since "all effects follow not with like certainty from their supposed causes . . . a wise man . . . proportions his belief to the evidence . . . and when at last he fixes his judgment, the evidence exceeds not what we properly call 'probability.' "²⁸ Lord Bolingbroke specifically addressed the historian when he argued that historical causation was too complex to be reduced to the oversimplified like causes/like effects. The historian, he wrote, must examine "the strange combinations of causes, different, remote, and seemingly opposite, that often concur in producing one effect; and the surprising fertility of one single and uniform cause in the producing of a multitude of effects [which] are as different, as remote, and seemingly as opposite."²⁹

No more than Hume and Bolingbroke did the revolutionary historians write of a historical necessity that was an irreversible determination of events. Even when they seemed to affirm the principle of like causes/like effects they meant to convey no more than a tendency—a powerful, overwhelming probability, it is true, but a tendency nevertheless. Thus Mercy Warren wrote in universal terms of the debilitating effects that standing armies have on society: "The experience of all ages, and the observations both of the historian and the philosopher agree, that a standing army is the most ready engine in the hand of despotism, to debase the powers of the human mind, and eradicate the manly spirit of freedom. . . . *Wherever* an army is established, it introduces a revolution in manners, corrupts the morals, propagates every species of vice, and degrades the human character."³⁰ What could be clearer: standing armies always produce the same insidious effects. There is an immediate, apparently irreducible and necessary relationship between the presence of a standing army and the degradation of the morals and manners of the people: "experience" demonstrated this truth. Yet despite her resounding affirmation of traditional Radical Whig views of a standing army, Warren dated the Revolution from the moment British troops arrived in Boston in 1768. For the Bostonians' morals and manners were not corrupted or debased by their presence; to the contrary, the people manifested the virtue to resist.

The historians' use of the idea of moral necessity (which distantly resembled Jonathan Edwards's theological formulation) was an important narrative device for conveying the sense of prospective continuity. It also had ideological value, for it helped to establish the claim that the movement for independence was justifiable because events had made it necessary. In David Ramsay's view, the consequences of the Declaration of Independence made it clear that its passage "was an event which necessity had rendered not only justifiable, but absolutely unavoidable."[31] Like the chain of circumstances, the suggestion of necessity bound together causes and consequences that constantly seemed on the verge of splitting apart. The physical geography of America, unimportant in itself, made unimaginable the victory of an invading foe; the traditional unanimity of the colonists' political opinions made inevitable their resistance to unconstitutional policies; the American character made impossible the people's submission to Britain's efforts to enslave them.

Yet despite these apparent assertions of certitude, the historians refused to abandon the principle of uncertainty. Indeed, because their approach to causation was so unsystematic, their expressions of certitude amount to uncertainty. Of Britain's eventual recognition of American independence David Ramsay wrote: "Various auxiliary causes might be called in to account for this great change of the public mind of Great Britain, but the sum of the whole must be resolved into this simple proposition, 'That it was unavoidable.'"[32] This is simultaneously to say that Britain's recognition of independence was "inevitable" and that it was "inexplicable." And in a crucial sense it was precisely at the juncture of the inevitable and the inexplicable that the historians frequently turned to chance or to providence. To say that Britain's recognition was unavoidable was to say little if anything more than "no one can tell" why Britain changed its mind. It was to point vaguely to the "exigence of circumstances."[33]

The Shape of History

As the foregoing discussion should indicate, it is something of a contradiction to speak of a "shape" of history in the writings of the revolutionary historians, for the history they reveal appears to have little if any discernible shape at all. It is clear that the historians, like Enlightenment historians generally, wrote of causes in history without reference to the transmundane or to a hypothetical first cause that empowered the process as a whole. It is also clear that they believed that events were "event-full," that causes arising in history efficiently generated future consequences, and that a study of the relative connection of causes and consequences yielded a chain of circumstances or a long series of events. This indicates that the historians presented history as an immanent process capable of sustaining its own causal continuity. And this, I have been suggesting, was the key to their achievement. For even if they failed to make clear how causation operated, and even if the failed to develop a hierarchy of causal values, they had liberated American history (as Europeans had liberated European history more than a century before) from the providential interpretation and thus had reaffirmed history's complexity. Henceforth "enlightened" historians would view history in human historical rather than in theological terms.

But even as they freed themselves from unicausal explanation the historians were unable to find an alternative to an impressionistic, multicausal approach. Skeptical of theological-historical categories, they seemed to be doubtful of any systematic mode of explanation that threatened their sense of contingency and complexity. By insisting upon chance and variety, by presenting history as a "spectacle" or, as Hayden White has suggested, as a "richly textured arras web which on first glance appears to lack coherence and any discernible fundamental structure," they prompt one to doubt that history had for them any recognizable shape.[34] As I will show in Part II, history was for the historians purposive even if it was not teleological; events contained their own moral, ethical, and ideological imperatives and left tracks in time and space that were observable to the insightful and committed historian. But it bore no interior principles which explained its own processes.

The historians' mode of causal explanation, to use White's

terminology, was "Contextualist," the informing presupposition of which is "that events can be explained by being set within the 'context' of their occurrence." Interested both in the uniqueness of historical phenomena and in their intricate interrelationships, the Contextualist begins by identifying some event of concern—the American Revolution, for example—and then picks out the threads that bind the event to different areas of the context, tracing the threads outward "into the circumambient natural and social space within which the event occurred," and backward and forward in time in order to determine its origins, impact, and influence.

What is gained from a Contextualist mode of explanation ideally is a rich and complex portrait of an event, a narrative, like the revolutionary histories at their best, that is often exciting (despite the fact that its conclusion is generally known in advance) because the historian traces a myraid combination of circumstances and emphasizes their possibilities as well as their actualities. On the other hand, what is lost is a sense of wholeness or pattern, for "the impulse is not to integrate all the events and trends that might be identified in the whole historical field, but rather to link them together in a chain of provisional and restricted characterizations of finite provinces of manifestly 'significant' occurrence." Thus, despite his concern for discovering the interrelationships among events, the Contextualist historian tends to disperse or decompose structure by stressing the unique and contingent even as he attempts to link events into a meaningful continuity.[35]

To discern a shape of history in the historians' writings, then, is to impose an order upon them which they do not reveal, to effect closure where they sought openness. It is also arguable, as I suggested earlier, that whatever pattern we do discern in the histories may be the product of the narratives shaping events rather than a compelling sense that events shaped the narratives. This hypothesis is unprovable, of course, because as readers we have only the texts themselves, and they represent the indistinguishable confluence of historical event and historical narrative.

But the historians' dispersive impulse, their emphasis upon contingency and complexity, and their tendencies both to over-explain and to avoid explanation, lead one to believe that they relied on their own narrative voices to sustain continuity because events failed to do so. This interpretation helps to account for several of the historians' narrative techniques: for John Marshall's and Mercy Otis Warren's interrupting a linear flow of events to spend several chapters on decidedly secondary issues before returning to the narrative, which (while it may also imply an aesthetic failure on their parts) testifies to their confidence that their own narrative voices supplied the continuity.

More important, this interpretation also supports the idea that in the eighteenth century historical writing was a branch of literary art, an idea amply borne out by William Gordon's borrowing techniques from fiction and painting. Gordon's use of the epistolary form, the present tense, and shifting narrative perspectives evidences his concern to write history that both pleased literarily and gave the impression that he was creating "a well-executed historical painting."[36] Indeed, his ideas paralleled Sir Joshua Reynolds's views about historical painting and several of Samuel Richardson's and Henry Fielding's concepts concerning narrative. Reynolds suggested in 1786 that excellent historical painting played upon the viewer's "imagination and sensibility," rather than "upon any principles falsely called rational." Although art was surely not irrational, since it possessed "a sagacity which is far from being contradictory to right reason," nevertheless the meaning of a work of art was intuited rather than deduced; one "feels and acknowledges" its "truth" even though "it is not always in [one's] power, perhaps, to give a reason for it." When one viewed Poussin's best historical paintings, wrote Reynolds in 1772, "the mind is thrown back into antiquity, and nothing ought to be introduced that may tend to awaken it from the illusion."[37]

This is the impression that Gordon sought to create when he narrated events at the battle of Bunker (Breed's) Hill, June 17, 1775. Writing in the past tense that characterizes conventional narrative, Gordon recounted in detail how the Americans erected fortifications on Breed's Hill under a constant barrage from British men-of-war lying in Boston Harbor. The main part of the battle commencing, however, he shifts tense in order to close the distance between the reader and the action:

> Between twelve and one o'clock, and the day exceeding hot, a number of boats and barges, filled with regular troops from Boston, approach Charlestown. The men are landed at Moreton's point.... Major general Howe and brigadier general Pigot, have the command. The troops form, and remain in that position, till joined by a second detachment of light infantry and grenadier companies.... Generals Clinton and Burgoyne take their stand upon Cop's hill to observe and contemplate the bloody and destructive operations that are now commencing. The regulars form in two lines, and advance deliberately, frequently halting to give time for the artillery to fire.[38]

Gordon is painting a word picture, using language in the form of letters because, as Samuel Richardson wrote in the preface to *Clarissa* (1747-48), letters "abound, not only with critical situations, but with what may be called *instantaneous* descriptions and reflections"; they help to achieve, he wrote in the preface to *Pamela* (1740), "an immediate impression of every circumstance."[39]

Gordon quickens his images as the battle actually begins, enhancing the feeling of immediacy by making his account more impressionistic. As the Americans await the full fury of the British onslought, he positions himself, general-like, in a commanding position, as on the top of a nearby hill:

> What scenes now offer to our view! *Here* [as if pointing below him], a large and noble town, consisting of about 300 dwelling houses, and near upon 200 other buildings, in one great blaze, burning with amazing fury.... *There,* in Boston, the steeples, houses, and heights, are covered with the inhabitants.... *Yonder,* the hills around the country, and the fields, that afford a safe and distinct view of the momentous contest, are occupied by Americans of all ages and orders.

Having carried our attention from Here to There to Yonder, away from the scene of carnage, Gordon plunges back into the events—"The British move on steadily...."—shifting perspective in a way that suggests the participation of a wartime correspondent.

Gordon's techniques here and elsewhere evidence explicitly and dramatically the historians' view that facts alone are not history. His image of "a well-executed historical painting" and White's of an "arras web" are apt, for they suggest that narrative conveys a set of pictorial images that are woven together into a single tapestry and that the significance of the whole derives from the association of all the separate images. In linear (or narrative) terms, these images are historical *situations,* which are the basic unit of the revolutionary histories—situations which are significant in themselves and in conjunction with one another, but which require the voice of the narrator (or the hand of the artist) to effect for them a discernible pattern or shape. If this hypothesis is valid, then the shape of history owes more to the historians' mode of storytelling (which, as I will show, is intimately tied to their ideological aims) than to any philosophical notions they may have had concerning history's intrinsic causal unity.[40]

4

The Hinge of the Revolution:
The Efficacy of Man

In a speech to the House of Representatives in 1796 supporting the adoption of Jay's Treaty, Fisher Ames outlined the notion of historical responsibility to which the revolutionary historians subscribed. Irritated by what he saw as a failure of nerve on the part of his colleagues, Ames said: "It is vain to offer as an excuse, that public men, are not to be reproached for the evils that may happen to ensue from their measures." It was perfectly true, he declared, that no one could properly be held accountable when the consequences of one's actions were unforeseen or inevitable. But that clearly was not the case now, for "Those I have depicted, are not unforeseen, they are so far from inevitable, [that] we are going to bring them into being by our vote. *We choose the consequences, and become as justly answerable for them, as for the measures we know will produce them.*"[1] Ames was speaking about historical, not legal, responsibility—a kind of ethical accountability based upon society's reasonable expectation that public persons ought to consider the probable consequences of their actions before they acted.

One could not simply condemn actions in retrospect, John Marshall asserted. "It is much easier to look back, and condemn an unsuccessful system, than to select with discriminating judgment, before events shall have decided on their value, those measures which, under existing circumstances, are best adapted to the end proposed."[2] People's actions were limited and so, therefore, was the sphere of their responsibility. In Ames's formulation action and responsibility were bounded by two basic limits: by chance or the unforeseen and by circumstances which constituted necessity or inevitability. As I have argued in Chapters 2 and 3, the historians agreed with Ames's view. They insisted that history was both contingent and complex: on the one hand, events were frequently fortuitous and accidental, unexpectedly thwarting people's best-laid plans through no apparent fault of their own; on the other, events were sometimes the products of such powerful and efficient causes or such complex coincidences of circumstances that they were virtually inevitable, and no one could reasonably be held responsible for actions that were caught up in the flow of historical necessity. It is equally clear, however, that within the limits described by the contingent and the inevitable people were responsible for what they did.

I am less concerned with Ames's notion of historical responsibility for its own sake than I am with the two related assumptions that lie behind it and give it force. First and most important throughout this chapter is the assumption that human action is historically efficacious; that it is based on choice, that it generates a train of consequences, and that therefore people are responsible both for their immediate choices and actions and for the consequences "that may happen to ensue" from them. Second, implicit in Ames's idea is the assumption that the future is undefined and open-ended, that people make choices prospectively in the face of indeterminacy. These two peculiarly modern assumptions operate together in the histories, and they complete the movement from the providential interpretation to an immanent theory, which the historians began by rejecting providence as a mode of causal explanation. They are also crucial in providing a philosophical foundation for the historians' ethical approach to history, which will be explored in detail in Part II.

Causes, Consequences, and the Efficacy of Man

Although, as Ames pointed out, historical responsibility was limited because human action was limited, the historians described such a large area in which man *was* responsible that to say that chance and the inevitable were limits on action is somewhat misleading. For the historians constantly depicted chance, apparently inevitable, and even providential events as the products of human action. When John Lendrum wrote of the "unfortunate engagement" at Long Island (August 1776) in which George Washington's troops found themselves backed up against the East River, able to effect a retreat only providentially or fortuitously, he attributed the American defeat to the negligent action of General Israel Putnam. Speaking of Putnam's failure to defend the vulnerable point through which the British eventually passed, Lendrum wrote: "Through this piece of negligence, [the Americans'] defeat became inevitable." Presupposed in this judgment is that Putnam was responsible for his actions and for their consequences because his actions were historically efficacious. Thus, the "fortune" of war and the "inevitability" of the defeat were the products of his actions in a specific situation.[3]

The same assumption operates in Lendrum's account of the American army's situation at Trenton and in Mercy Warren's narrative of events immediately preceding Trenton. After defeating the surprised Hessians on Christmas night, 1776, Washington set up camp opposite the main British detachment. "This was, indeed, the crisis of the American revolution," Lendrum wrote, "and had his lordship [i.e. Cornwallis] made an immediate attack ... general Washington's defeat seems to have been inevitable; but a night's delay turned the fate of the war, and produced an enterprise, the magnitude and glory of which, can only be equalled by its success."[4] This is a typical description, as we have seen: it was a crucial moment in which a conclusion was virtually inevitable; but the apparently certain conclusion was, for reasons unexpected by the Americans, foiled, and the consequences of the unexpected were enormous.

What had happened? What was the "secret spring" of this event upon which turned the very fate of the war? The British delayed their attack for one night. Lendrum was not concerned with the question why the British delayed—had he been he might have concluded, as Mercy Warren had in an earlier instance, that it "remains involved among the fortuitous events, which often decide the fate of armies, or of nations, as it were by accident." But even if one could not decide why the British hesitated, one *could* tell what happened: the apparently inevitable event, the unexpected and perhaps inexplicable event, was the direct consequence of specific actions in a specific historical situation.[5]

The histories abound with accounts of blunders, neglects, errors of commission and omission, and mistakes of judgment (as well as heroic actions and well-planned and well-executed schemes). And while they sometimes appear in the context of accidental, fortuitous, or providential events, they represent quite simply the actions of people in precarious situations which resulted in failure *because* (the crucial word) the actors lacked sufficient prudence, insight, courage, or any number of other human virtues. Above all, they represent the final word on the issue of historical causation, for although chance did operate and although conditions sometimes overwhelmed human exertion, such actions were always consequential. Some mistakes were almost beneath the historians' notice as when, "by some unaccountable error, the [American] detachment [at Bunker Hill], which had been working for hours, was neither relieved, nor supplied with refreshments, but were left to engage [the enemy] under these disadvantages"; or when, "by some mistake," Breed's Hill was marked out for defense at all, instead of Bunker Hill as originally planned.[6] Perhaps because such mistakes were relatively trivial they evidence more strongly the historians' assumption that human action was the pre-eminent cause in history. Hence the hundreds of examples of capital military errors, neglected orders, the remissness of soldiers and statesmen, and the people's neglect or want of judgment that make the revolutionary histories narratives of human drama.[7]

In all such statements the historians necessarily presupposed that human action is historically efficacious—indeed, that it is the principal cause of events. This assumption makes possible the historians' willingness to assign responsibility in retrospect, for the entire ethical import of their narratives required the assumption of human efficacy. Although retrospective moral judgments might be suspect, nevertheless accountability had to be rendered. Thus David Ramsay attributed the failure of the Franco-American investment of Savannah (October 1779)— "considered as infallibly certain"—to the premature lifting of the siege. In consequence of raising the siege too soon a major southern seaport remained in British hands and brought on evils that otherwise would have been avoided. For if the allies had stayed, "the war would have terminated without the reduction of Charleston, the over-running of the southern states, and that loss of honour and property which resulted from the breach of publick faith." William Gordon made the same assessment as he recounted the Americans' failure to capture Staten Island (August 1777). The defeat, according to Gordon, resulted from General John Sullivan's blunders and lack of proper leadership: instead of following the proposed plan, Sullivan marched his troops out of the way, which lost time and tired the soldiers, so that "the misfortune of the day was increased." As Gordon saw it, "the grand design of the expedition failed by the general's varying from the plan concerted.[8]

The language of chance, fortune, and providence that pervades these accounts enhances the narrative import of human action, the central causal principle. People's actions caused misfortunes, unhappy events, and unexpected occurrences; they caused necessary or inevitable conclusions, even deliverances in the nick of time—witness Gordon's deserter at Saratoga and Holmes's energetic troops at Cowpens—and apparently trivial maneuvers the consequences of which resounded into the future. Historical conditions and circumstances were conditional and circumstantial only because they were brought into operation by people acting in specific situations. That human action effected historical events, in short, was the irreducible datum of historical causation and explanation. Indeed, without the assumption of human efficacy the historians' explanations of the Revolution make no sense. The arguments, for example, that Britain conspired to enslave the colonies, that the Revolution was the fulfillment of Britain's misdirected policies, that it had its roots in seventeenth-century political and economic conflicts (all of which are tied to the historians' ideological convictions) necessarily presuppose that the actions of Britons and colonists *could* produce such consequences.

The history of the Revolution was not, of course, the history of blunders alone. At the same time that the historians willingly assigned blame, they joyfully praised America's heroes for securing independence, and in doing so they underscored their assumption of human efficacy. No historian made the point more strongly than Mercy Warren: "The United States have procured their own emancipation from foreign thraldom, by the sacrifice of their heroes and their friends." It was "the wise and patriotic" who had "by inconceivable labor and exertion obtained the prize." Even as late as 1782, she observed with scorn, "It was difficult . . . to convince many of the most intelligent gentlemen in England, that *independence* was a gift that America did not now ask; the boon was their own; obtained by their own prowess and magnanimity, in conjunction with the armies of their brave allies."[9]

When we read, as we do here, that the Americans won their own independence through their courage, wisdom, and virtue, or that independence was the result of "the germ of discipline unfolding," we hear the voices of participant-historians surveying what the people had wrought and proclaiming it good.[10] To say this—that man is the author of his own history—is to rejoin the theological debate. It is thus worth noting that to presuppose human historical efficacy was a central assumption of Enlightenment history born of the encounter between secular and Christian historians. As Peter Gay has observed: "It is true that Christian historians were coming to visualize God as acting not directly, by intermittent personal appearances, but indirectly, through human instruments," a shift in theory that we observed even among Puritan historians at the beginning of the eighteenth century. "But inevitably," Gay continues, "in their histories, the most significant human shapers of history were mere marionettes; they fulfilled God's designs without wishing to, or knowing it." The result of such views was that Christian historians like Bossuet were "compelled to give religious—which is to say, incomplete, incorrect, inadequate, and often irrelevant—answers to questions men were beginning to ask about historical causation."[11]

The revolutionary historians did not engage such theological issues on their own terms. Nowhere did they write that man was not an instrument of divine will or that God was not the cause of all historical events. Nevertheless, it remains clear that they wrote as if people directed their own destinies and as if they were responsible for their actions and for the consequences of their actions. The assumption that pervades their histories (as we will see in a slightly different context in the ensuing discussion) is that human will and human action had to be free and efficacious or history would be a grisly jest on mankind, demanding human responsibility for what humanity was powerless to effect.

History as the Future, the Future as History

Implicit in Fisher Ames's notion of historical responsibility was a corollary of man's historical efficacy, that the future is indeterminate. Timothy Pitkin, the historian who cited Ames's letter, also quoted a letter of John Jay's addressed to George Washington in June 1786. The letter, filled with anxiety and melancholy, illuminates the relationship between human efficacy (and responsibility) and the indeterminacy of the future. And once again the issues strike at the heart of the providential interpretation as a theological-historical mode of explanation. "Our affairs seem to lead to some crisis, some revolution, something that I cannot foresee or conjecture," wrote Jay. "I am uneasy and apprehensive, more so than during the war. Then we had a fixed object, and though the means and time of obtaining it, were often problematical, yet I did firmly believe, that justice was with us. The case is now altered. We are going and doing wrong, and, therefore, I look forward to evils and calamities, but without being able to guess at the instrument, nature or measure of them."

Jay was anxious about the future, but his anxiety, unlike during the war, had no focus to which it could become attached and perhaps relieved. He believed, he said, that "we shall again recover," though when and how remained problematic. He and "the better kind" of citizen could probably stand firm amid the uncertainty, but he feared that others could not and that they might wish for "almost any change that may promise them quiet and security." The thrust of Washington's response to Jay is contained in a single sentence: "To anticipate and prevent disastrous contingencies, would be the part of wisdom and patriotism."[12]

Giving force to Jay's anxiety and lending it an almost tragic quality is the resounding "therefore" that causally links our "going and doing wrong" with his apprehension of future "evils and calamities"; "therefore" affirms his sense of responsibility for what happens between the present and the future. In addition, Jay's letter and Washington's response testify to their sense that the future is up for grabs and that only proper action can avoid disastrous contingencies. The dialogue thus vividly depicts the existential portrait of man confronting an indeterminate future the meaning and shape of which will be inscribed by what he does now. It also adds the final connotation to the concept of contingency: the future is contingent upon what people do.

As I will show in Part II, the historians wrote their histories *for* the future. Envisioning a future filled with possibilities, many of which appeared ominous if present signs were an indication, they presented their histories as revolutionary exhortations which echoed in impassioned terms Washington's more restrained advice to Jay. But they also wrote of the past with *its* future in mind, emphasizing moments pregnant with risk, turning points on which the Revolution literally "revolved." At the heart of such moments were people making choices and acting in the face of an indeterminate future.

Thus, referring to the meeting of the Massachusetts House of Representatives, forced to convene in Salem instead of in Boston in 1774, Mercy Warren wrote, "The leading characters in the house of representatives contemplated the present moment, replete with consequences of the utmost magnitude; they judged it a crisis that required measures bold and decisive, though hazardous, and that the extrication of their country from the designs of their enemies, depended much on the conduct of the present assembly." Upon such meetings, like the convention at Charleston, South Carolina (July 6, 1774), called in response to the closing of the Boston port, depended "all subsequent proceedings, which ultimately terminated in a revolution."[13] In hazardous times the people had to rely on the "exertions of their own valour" to make the future conform to their wishes. As Josiah Quincy, Jr., warned the Boston town meeting in December 1773, the month in which the Boston Tea Party was held, "The exertions of this day will *call forth events* which will make a very different spirit necessary for our salvation. Look to the end. Whoever supposes, that shouts and hosannas will terminate the trials of the day, entertains a childish fancy."[14]

Such statements did not deny traditional religious rites like prayer, but they did serve to emphasize the notion that man was the author of his own destiny. John Lendrum was surely aware of this implication when he observed that "in Virginia, the first of June [1774], the day on which the port of Boston was to be shut up, was held as a day of humiliation, and a public intercession in favour of America was enjoined. The style of the prayer enjoined at this time was, that 'God would give the people one heart and one mind, firmly to oppose every invasion of the

American rights.'" This is reminiscent of the long American tradition of calling days of humiliation, fasting, and prayer which Perry Miller rightly saw as a "wonderful fusion of political doctrine with the traditional rite of self-abasement." But Lendrum, in concluding his point, left no room to doubt where he located the final responsibility for dealing with future contingencies: *The Virginians, however, did not content themselves with acts of religion.* Instead, "They recommended in the strongest manner a general congress of all the colonies, as fully persuaded that an attempt to tax any colony in an arbitrary manner was in reality an attack upon them all, and must ultimately end in the ruin of them all."[15]

These statements reveal the historians' assumption that the future is a *cause* of history, an idea that brings us close to the juncture of their philosophical assumptions and their ideological convictions. The future is a cause of history because it is the constant motive for present action. At stake in these accounts, then, is hegemony over the future, the principle for which the Revolution was contested and, at the same time, the principle which motivated the historians to write history. "The prize," David Ramsay implied, was the future itself, "nothing less than the sovereignty of three millions of people, and five hundred millions of acres of land."[16] Throughout their narratives the historians kept alive the feeling that the struggle for independence was joined in the names of future sovereignty, self-determination, and freedom, the very principles which the historians presupposed about the historical efficacy of man. Thus when they wrote of the crucial decade of the 1760s, instead of emphasizing tyranny inflicted, they wrote of tyranny anticipated, for the danger of British policies was that they were seen as precedents and therefore as threats to the future.

During the French and Indian War, for example, the British ministry "laid hold of the alarming situation of the colonies . . . to constrain them into an acknowledgement of their right, or to the adoption of measures that might afterwards be drawn into precedent."[17] The same was true of the Stamp Act (1765), which

Timothy Pitkin saw as a major precipitating cause of the Revolution. Jared Ingersoll captured the contemporary sense of what such a tax would mean, saying that "if the Parliament once interpose and Lay a tax, tho' it may be a very moderate one . . . what Consequences may, or rather may not, follow?"[18] The consequences for the future were potentially awesome. Timothy Pitkin discussed the events at the Boston town meeting of May 1764, at which the Bostonians considered the implications of the impending Stamp Act. Sam Adams, Pitkin observed, pointed to the greatest apprehension about the tax: "that these proceedings may be preparatory to new taxes; for if our trade may be *taxed*, why not our *lands*? Why not the product of our lands and every thing we possess or use."[19] Adams's words expressed Pitkin's own concern: "No act of the parent country ever excited such universal alarm in the colonies, as this," he noted. "The colonists saw, and felt, that the act was not only a violation of their rights, but a fatal blow, aimed at the future peace and prosperity of their country." Not only was the Stamp Act an unprecedented revenue bill, it was also, as the historians depicted it, Britain's first manifest attempt to control the colonists' future.[20]

Mercy Warren wrote of the Townshend Duties (1767) in the same terms Pitkin used. They would, she observed, "establish a precedent, and strengthen the claim parliament had assumed, to tax [the colonies] at pleasure." John Lendrum noted the colonists' fears that the duty on tea might be "an inlet to others." Citing the argument of the Massachusetts House of Representatives against the Townshend Duties, Pitkin reasserted the point he made about the Stamp Act: "Such a power, under a corrupt administration, it is feared, would introduce an absolute government in America; at least, it would leave the people in a state of uncertainty of their security, which is far from being a state of civil liberty."[21]

Self-government, sovereignty, a state of security, control over the future—all these issues were intimately associated for the historians, and all rested upon the assumption of human efficacy; indeed, they were political expressions of precisely that assumption. "The meeting of this august assembly," wrote Timothy Pitkin of the Constitutional Convention of 1787, "marks a new era in the political annals of the United States. Men most eminent for talents and wisdom, had been selected and were met to form a system of government for a vast empire. Such an assemblage for such an object, the world had never before witnessed. The result of their deliberations, on which the happiness of so many millions depended, was looked for with extreme solicitude."[22] War and the overturning of the established order unsettled a people and the principles which united them. The Constitutional Convention met precisely to overcome the disorders attendant upon the unhinging of the political order, lest chance and accident intrude upon the nation's future. David Ramsey wrote that

> by this establishment the rising generation will have an opportunity of observing the result of an experiment in politics, which before has never been fairly made. The experience of former ages has given many melancholy proofs, that the popular governments have seldom answered in practice to the theories and warm wishes of their admirers. The present inhabitants of independent America now have an opportunity to wipe off this aspersion, to assert the dignity of human nature, and the capacity of mankind for self-government.

A page later he reminded his readers of the point presupposed throughout: "Citizens of the United States! you have a well-balanced constitution established by general consent. . . . *If you are not happy it will be your own fault.*"[23]

These statements echo Fisher Ames's speech and the letters of John Jay and George Washington. The Constitutional Convention, like the various meetings called in response to the Intolerable Acts, met to anticipate and prevent disastrous future contingencies. Indeed, its purpose was to institutionalize the American future and thus to diminish the possibility of accident to the extent that was humanly possible. Ramsay's emphasis upon self-government, like Pitkin's upon sovereignty, contains the crucial issue, for in the histories the political principle of self-government is to the philosophical principle of self-determination as civil freedom is to human freedom. Without the assumption that the human will is free to enact its own future, political freedom is an empty concept. This was Pitkin's point when he wrote that the people's uncertainty about their control over the reins of the future was "far from being a state of civil liberty," for civil liberty presupposed the liberty of self-determination. This was also the point that Samuel Williams made most eloquently when he wrote that the Constitution was only a symptom, not the cause, of self-government. Only the original cause of America's freedom—that is, the people themselves—"will prove sufficient to support and preserve it." Constitutions "derive their whole authority and force from the public sentiment," he admonished, "and are of no further avail to secure the liberties of the people, than as they tend to express, to form, and to preserve the public opinion." "Upon what then can the people depend, for the support and preservation of their rights and freedom?" he asked; and he answered, "Upon no beings or precautions under heaven, but themselves. The spirit of liberty is a living principle. It lives in the minds, principles, and sentiments of the people. It lives in their industry, virtue, and public sentiment: Or rather it is produced, preserved, and kept alive, by the state of society."[24]

These statements reveal more than the zealous rhetoric of people who not only narrated but participated in the Revolution (though they reveal that too). They manifest the sense of urgency, anxiety, and challenge presented by an indeterminate future and by the feeling that people are responsible for the future's shape. It is worth nothing, then, that the historians' new appreciation of the future as an undefined "out-there" was as radical a re-vision of history as was their appreciation of chance. For in the providential theory the future, while an unknown from man's standpoint, was understood to be a *fait accompli* preconcerted by God from the beginning of time. Puritan historical theory denied both human efficacy and the notion of an indeterminate future.

But these are principles that the historians had to assume if the history of the Revolution was to make sense. And it would be difficult to overstate their appreciation of the anxieties inherent in facing an undefined future in the knowledge that its actuality was being molded by people's present deeds. By locating contingency in the future—in human time, not in the transmundane—the historians recognized that people lost the cosmic consolation which resulted from believing that the future already had meaning and form. But if they saw that such consolation was lost, they also recognized that finite human freedom was gained in the trade and that the bargain was a good one. For people were thus also rid of the sense of impending doom that worked according to its own transcendent logic, bearing no reasonable relationship to what people did. Better, they implied, to live with the "therefore" that linked people's actions irrevocably to their future consequences, even if the future held "evils and calamities."

But anxiety and urgency were only part of the picture—opportunity was another part. At the same time that they created a sense of urgency by emphasizing the need for decisive action in the face of a hazardous future, the historians also recognized in the future's openness the possibility for creating a new social and political order. Mercy Warren thus portrayed the future as fertile ground to be cultivated. "A new constitution, and an extensive government . . . open a new field of observation," she wrote. America "may with propriety be styled a land of promise." It was, she continued, using another metaphor that characterizes her work, "a theatre just erected, where the drama was but begun." It was "now a fair field for a transcript of all the virtues and vices that have illumined or darkened, disgraced and reigned triumphant in their turn over all the other quarters of the habitable globe."[25]

Striking in Warren's statements, as it was in Pitkin's and Ramsay's observations on the new Constitution, is the sense of "newness," the feeling that America was and could continue to be a unique nation in the history of the world. And this sense of freshness rested upon the assumption that the future was man's to work upon. America was a "new-born" nation, wrote Warren, "emancipated by the uncommon vigor, valor, fortitude, and patriotism of her soldiers and statesmen"—a newborn nation conceived by people in human historical time.[26] Or, as David Ramsay told the American people near the end of his *History of the American Revolution*, "It is now your turn to figure on the face of the earth, and in the annals of the world. You possess a country which in less than a century will probably contain fifty millions of inhabitants." And to what do we owe this bountiful future, this source of opportunity and challenge? "You have, with a great expence of blood and treasure, rescued yourselves and your posterity from the domination of Europe. Perfect the good work you have begun, by forming such arrangements and institutions as bid fair for ensuring to the present and future generations the blessings for which you have successfully contended."[27] This new event in human history was brought about *by people* acting in light of future possibilities. What remained to them was perfecting their work.

Human Nature and Environment: Conclusion and Transition

It was a commonplace of Enlightenment historical theory that human nature was fundamentally the same in all times and places. David Hume believed that "Mankind are so much the same, in all times and places, that history informs us of nothing new or strange in this particular. Its chief use is only to discover the constant and universal principles of human nature."[28] This assumption was important, Peter Gay suggests, because "history was usable as sociology, and understandable as history, only insofar as the past was in some significant sense like the present."[29] But this "law" of history was no more legal in practice than was the equally common and parallel concept that the same causes will always produce the same effects. For, as Hume also observed, one could not expect people always to act in the same manner even in the same circumstances "without making [an] allowance for the diversity of characters, prejudices, and opinions." Although history appeared to be more regular and orderly when one assumed the uniformity of human nature, still "such a uniformity in every particular, is found in no part of nature. On the contrary, from observing the variety of conduct in different men we are enabled to form a greater variety of maxims which still suppose *a degree* of uniformity and regularity." That degree of uniformity and regularity was owing to the universality of "the fundamental passions" only, wrote Gay; but "customs, religions, institutions, forms of social organization, and styles of life were susceptible to almost infinite, almost unimaginable variety."[30] Thus, even as they paid lip service to the idea that human nature was everywhere the same, Enlightenment historians were finally more interested in cultural variation.

The revolutionary historians also mouthed the rhetoric of human nature. "Human nature is always the same," wrote John Marshall, "and consequently man will in every situation furnish useful lessons."[31] To the extent that they saw human nature as invariable, they were less than optimistic about what history taught of its potentialities. Experience showed man to be "an absurd and ferocious, instead of a rational and humane being," according to Mercy Warren, who also confided to John Adams, "I am more and more convinced, of the propensity in human nature to tyrannize over their fellow men." William Gordon thought that "the loss of public spirit, virtue and common honesty" demonstrated just "what mankind is, and how little dependance is to be had upon human nature."[32]

As Arthur H. Shaffer has shown, however, the historians, like so many intellectuals of their generation, were environmentalists; they were much less concerned with human nature as a determinant of character and conduct than they were with the environment—particularly the natural environment—as the sphere in which human character and conduct developed. So much has been written about naturalistic environmentalism in late-eighteenth-century American thought that it is unnecessary to recount those discussions here.[33] Suffice to say that the historians (again like many of their generation) believed that American character and institutions were intimately tied to the new world as a geographical and physical space. Although regional variations in climate, soil, topography, and so forth tended to produce differences in the temperaments of New Englanders and Southerners, for example, those differences were much less important than the fact that the natural environment throughout America exerted crucial influences on Americans' manners and habits, so that nature in America formed the foundation for political freedom.[34] Moreover, in the fashionable "stage theory" to which the historians subscribed, social and political organization were associated with nature, so that republican government and habits of mind were thought to arise and persist in the stage of natural development between wilderness, at one extreme, and overrefined civilization, at the other.[35]

Yet important as nature was in American theories of man and society, the historians seem to have been more concerned with the political and social environment than with the natural. "The result of human action," Mercy Warren contended," is owing *more* to the existing state or stage of *society*, than to any deviations in the nature or general disposition of mankind."[36] Similarly, acknowledging that human nature was "radically the same" in England and America, David Ramsay nevertheless argued for the priority of environment, and on this score "the state of society has an influence not less than climate. . . . Europeans affect to under value Americans. I acknowledge an inferiority but this is chargeable on the state of society."[37] In short, Ramsay wrote, "the difference between nations is not so much owing to nature, as to education and circumstances," the products of social and political practices.[38]

Several reasons help to explain why the historians should have emphasized the formative influence of the social and political environment more strongly than the natural. One, which will be of greater significance in Chapter 7, is that the relationship between nature and human society and character was a precarious one. If, as the historians believed, human virtue was the genius of republican government, and if Americans' virtue was principally related to the stages of nature, then American virtue would inevitably degenerate, precisely as the character, morals, and manners of all earlier republicans had degenerated. If, on the other hand, these characteristics of human conduct were tied to the institutions and practices of government and society—to "republicanism" construed as a constellation of cultural values and practices—then American history could be liberated from the endlessly repetitive cycle of birth, growth, decay, and death.

A second explanation involves the historians' use of political environmentalism to argue that human nature itself could be altered in America. Instead of seeing human nature as a closed system of passions and appetites that irrevocably determined people's conduct in all times and places, the historians began to depict human nature, like the American future, as open-ended. "I have always been sensible of the difficulty and delicacy of drawing living characters," wrote Mercy Warren, who was probably less sanguine about human nature than any of her colleagues. "It is my opinion that the character of man is never finished until the last act of the drama is closed."[39] The drama to be enacted in America was, for David Ramsay, a romance: "I am confident that the cause of America is the cause of Human Nature," he said, such were "the glorious consequences of Independence." American nature would play a significant role in the alteration of human nature, for the great expanse of fertile lands would prevent urban stagnation and provide millions with the chance to cultivate freedom and self-discipline in the very process of cultivating the earth. But Ramsay wrote of the flowering of human nature primarily in a social and political context. "Is it not to be hoped, that Human Nature will here receive her most finished touches?" he asked rhetorically. "That the Arts and Sciences will be extended and improved? That Religion, Learning, and Liberty will be diffused over this continent? And, in short, that the American editions of the human mind will be more perfect than any that have yet appeared?"[40] The newborn nation was to be inhabited by a new man.

What is important about these observations is less the rhetoric of optimism (which is, on the whole, a guarded optimism in the histories) than the crucial association between the historians' vision of the possibility of a new human nature and their insistence upon human efficacy. For if the natural environment was to some important degree *independent* of man's ability to control it, the political and social environment was man's own creation. Thus, the political and social environment which would exert such a significant influence upon human conduct, character, and manners—to the point, in fact, of altering human nature itself—would be the product of man's own choices and actions. Man, in short, was capable of perfecting his own basic nature by establishing a political and social environment which would reflect his own best inclinations.

These views bring us to the juncture of philosophy and ideology in the revolutionary histories. At this point the distinction between philosophical assumptions and ideological convictions loses its heuristic value, for it becomes impossible to dissociate the historians' assumptions about human nature from the possibilities they saw inherent in republicanism, about the future as a category of historical causation from the future as the dwelling place of virtuous Americans. It is no longer desirable or useful to preserve the distinction between philosophy and ideology because they operate together to make the histories simultaneously revelations of historical meaning and exhortations to complete the Revolution. It is worth pausing briefly to summarize a few points.

The historians of the revolution were revolutionary historians philosophically speaking[41] because they developed an immanent theory of history to replace the providential theory they only half-consciously discarded. Their rejection of providence and their development of an immanent theory seem not to have been a calculated process. Only rarely were they aware of theological

issues lurking on the fringes of their historical explanations—
when William Gordon posed his question about chance and
providence, for example, or when Abiel Holmes explicitly rejected the providential interpretation of Antonio de Solis, when
Mercy Warren insisted that she was not writing of miracles, or
when John Lendrum contrasted prayer with more vigorous
practical action. Still more rarely, indeed, did they indicate any
concern that theological issues might be involved at all. Yet at the
same time that they depicted America's revolutionaries emanci-
pating the nation from British tyranny, they wrote in a way that
emancipated American historical writing from the providential
interpretation. Had there been something manifestly "wrong"
with the providential interpretation, the historians might self-
consciously and explicitly have formulated their objections to it;
or, conversely, they might explicitly have adopted it had it suited
their purposes. Their writings indicate that providence was simply inappropriate for explaining the history of the Revolution,
largely because providential history was transcendent rather
than immanent, because it was God's history rather than man's,
and because it wrested authority over history's processes out of
man's hands rather than lodging responsibility with him. Revolutionary history, in short, was manifestly concerned with
human freedom in risky, precarious situations. By banishing
both human efficacy and the very concept of contingency from
the universe of historical discourse, the providential interpretation was lost to revolutionary historical explanation.

For all practical purposes, the historians achieved an immanent theory in two ways, one in a sense negative and the other
positive: by admitting chance into historical discourse they removed causation from the transmundane; and by arguing that
historical conditions and circumstances were efficient in themselves to cause later events they relocated causation in the historical process itself. These two ideas guaranteed that whatever
happened in human history happened *in* human history from
causes that arose in human time. They also went two steps further, making the break from the traditional American theory of

providence irrevocable: they emphasized the complexity of historical causation and explanation, rendering unicausal explanation hopelessly simplistic; and they wrote of human action as free, efficacious, and responsible, relegating to the domain of ancient dogma the notion that man was an instrument of divine will.

The historians' "re-visioning" of the future, a corollary of their insistence upon human efficacy and responsibility, was but an extension of their immanent theory. In a certain sense, in fact, their notion that the future was indeterminate—a perpetually undefined out-there that constantly confronted people with choices to make against the backdrop of the past and present—was a *precondition* for their immanent theory. For, as the Puritans had also recognized, one senses the contingency of finite existence in the first place when one faces the gap between the present and the future, the space, so to speak, in which contingency resides. In this sense, the *beginning* of the historians' quest for historical meaning was the future from the historians' own standpoint. They wrote their works at the edge of history, to use William Irwin Thompson's phrase, a moment decisively new, as they saw it, in the history of the world—a pivotal moment on the verge of indeterminacy from which they could "recollect" the past and use it (or their version of it) to control the future. With this, though there remain important philosophical issues to explore, one returns to the intersection of philosophy and ideology. And since the historians' vision of the future was so intimately tied to the ideology of republicanism, one must pursue their treatment of the Revolution in its ideological context.

PART II

THE CULTIVATION OF VIRTUE:

IDEOLOGY, LANGUAGE, AND FORM

I draw courage from the remembrance that history is never, in any rich sense, the immediate crudity of what "happens," but the much finer complexity of what we read into it and think of in connection with it.

—Henry James, *The American Scene*

5

Justifying the Revolution:
Natural Law and American Independence

The authors of the Declaration of Independence were not
interested in stating a *fait accompli.* They sought to justify the
American separation from Britain on grounds of historical
necessity. They attempted, therefore, to outline not only the
reasons that validated America's separation from Britain, but
also a set of general rules for determining whether or not any
revolution was properly begun. Affirming the proposition that a
people ought not to revolt for "light and transient causes," the
document argues that a revolution is justifiable only when the
course of human events makes it necessary—only when conditions become intolerable and "a long train of abuses and usurpations, pursuing invariably the same object, evinces a design to
reduce them under absolute despotism." Under such conditions
a people has not only the right but the obligation to revolt, and
therefore its revolution is justified.

According to the Declaration and to commonly received
maxims of eighteenth-century political theory, government is in
itself merely a convenience. It operates on the basis of positive
law which is created by people for the administration of the
state. When government is properly constituted, however, deriving its authority from popular consent, its aim is to secure the

happiness of the people and the people's inalienable rights, rights which are rooted in the Laws of Nature and of Nature's God. A properly constituted government thus makes positive law an organic outgrowth of Natural Law.

The argument of the Declaration is elegantly constructed to demonstrate the truth of its claims. It articulates a set of conditions under which any people might justifiably revolt, thereby establishing the universality of its argument and, at the same time, preempting the anticipated counterclaim that it was merely an expedient way of rationalizing actions already taken. Similarly, to avoid the suggestion that it was designed solely for expediency, the Declaration rests the morality of revolution on its historical necessity: because British policies subverted the British constitution, leading inexorably toward the creation of an "absolute despotism," the Revolution was necessary; and because it was necessary, it was morally justifiable.

More important, the argument of the Declaration is a subtle, if ambiguous, blending of empirical historical analysis and the metaphysics of Natural Law. To prove its central contention—that the Revolution was made necessary by British policies—the document enumerates twenty-seven specific events in recent history which reveal precisely how Britain acted to establish a despotism. These twenty-seven events, listed as grievances, constituted a strong case for the advantage of a revolution, for this people's rebelling at this time; and the reader of the document who would be satisfied with arguments of expediency alone could accept the enumerated grievances as sufficient reason for strenuous action, even action of a revolutionary nature.

But the revolutionaries meant to transcend such arguments, which were always subject to the vicissitudes of opinion; opinion might lead one to conclude that a revolution was in fact unnecessary and therefore unjustifiable. To remove their claims from the arena of opinion and to ground them with certainty, the revolutionaries felt constrained to found the argument for justification on the principles of Natural Right which were rooted in the theory of Natural Law as applied to politics and society.

Thus the grievances enumerated in the Declaration, weighty in themselves for some readers, were for others concrete examples of how one nation attempted to subordinate another to an absolute despotism. The grievances, taken together, demonstrated that British policies had violated the fundamental principles of the Natural Law itself.

By thus attempting to join universal rules with specific historical conditions, moral truths with historical necessity, and metaphysical principles with empirical historical facts, the Declaration sought to justify as well as to account for the American separation from Britain. But "justification" meant more than the creation of a useful myth or a politic rationale for the revolutionaries' actions. It entailed the articulation or, at the very least, the presupposition of an immutable standard of value against which the necessity and the propriety of revolution could be measured. That standard was Natural Law, a standard which assured epistemological certitude because it was transcendent, universal, and immutable, and thus beyond the ravages of historical exigency.

At the heart of the Declaration, then, was an unstated epistemological assumption about the universal truth of Natural Law and about how people could in practice know that truth. Because the Declaration was not only a statement about a series of practical political events, but was itself a crucial event in that series, this unstated epistemological assumption could remain unstated. Precisely by juxtaposing, without resolving, the empirical and the theoretical, the immanent and the transcendent, the Declaration left to its readers or auditors the problem of making clear the relationship between specific historical events and the truths of Natural Law. Attempting to justify the Revolution in retrospect, however, proved a more difficult task. For in retrospect the ambiguity that persisted through the Declaration— the equivocal relationship between the historical and the transcendent—became glaring. To justify the Revolution in retrospect on the basis of principle required a new mode of interpretation, and that new mode, practiced by the historians of the Revolution, involved the transformation of Natural Law into a historical process.[1]

The Transformation of Natural Law

The revolutionary historians sought to accomplish what the authors of the Declaration seemed to have achieved so elegantly and easily: to justify the separation from England on the ground that historical conditions had made a revolution necessary. Like the authors of the Declaration, the historians, as Mercy Otis Warren put it, meant "to justify the *principles* of the defection and final separation from the parent state." The purpose was educational, even didactic. John Lendrum said that he wrote history in order to provide future generations of Americans with the means "to form just ideas of the liberties and privileges to which the colonies were entitled by their charters." No argument for expediency would suffice to justify the Revolution. Justification required statements of fundamental principle.[2]

Indeed, the historians, even more than the authors of the Declaration, were careful to make clear the distinction between arguments for expediency or utility and arguments for necessity which could be founded only on fundamental principle. Jedidiah Morse, for example, sharply distinguished between what he called "a mere question of EXPEDIENCY," and "metaphysical disquisitions about abstract rights," each of which was a valid form of argumentation as long as each was confined to its proper sphere.[3] Mercy Warren emphasized the same distinction, stating her disgust with some members of parliament who would "shamelessly . . . avow the necessity of leaping over the boundaries of equity, and [wink] out of sight the immutable laws of justice." Accusing parliament of giving in to arguments of expediency, she observed that the greatest evils lay in the idea, espoused by Lord Mansfield, " 'that the original question of *right* ought no longer to be considered; that the justice of the cause must give way to the present situation.' " Warren railed at this sacrifice of principle to a relativistic, situational ethic, reaffirming the idea that, when questions of truth and right were concerned, one properly appealed to the immutable laws of justice and to "the principles of rectitude."[4]

Justification depended upon arguments of principle, and only such arguments could constitute the necessity of a movement for independence. Timothy Pitkin found the emphasis upon necessity in the colonies' instructions to their delegates to the Continental Congress. New Jersey, for example, instructed its delegates to support a motion for independence "'in case they judged it necessary and expedient for supporting the just rights of America.'" Similarly, Pennsylvania stated that it would support independence, but "at the same time, asserted, that this measure did not originate in ambition or in an impatience of lawful authority, but that they were driven to it, in obedience to the first principles of nature, by the oppressions and cruelties of the king and parliament, as the only measure left to preserve and establish their liberties, and transmit them inviolate to posterity." Maryland, according to Pitkin, affirmed the same notion that independence was a proper action only if it were deemed a necessary action, and only if it were taken as a last resort to preserve fundamental rights and liberties.[5]

The historians' concern for demonstrating the necessity of the separation from Britain was nowhere clearer than in David Ramsay's simple assertion that "necessity, not choice, forced [the Americans] on the decision" to revolt. Following the argument of the Declaration itself, he added that the historical conditions then prevailing "made a declaration of independence as necessary in 1776, as was the non-importation agreement of 1774, or the assumption of arms in 1775." The logic of necessity was inexorable: the declaration "naturally resulted" from these earlier events, just as they had been compelled by still earlier ones.[6]

Writing in 1788, William Gordon presented a similar case. By the time British and American forces engaged at Lexington and Concord, the contest would have to "issue in independence, or slavery" for the colonies. The decision to declare independence "may be deemed by some presumptuous," he continued. "But," he added rhetorically, "how could it have been avoided?"[7]

Jedidiah Morse coupled his claim for the necessity of independence with the notion that the stakes of the contest involved nothing less than Americans' "natural and indisputable rights," the parameters of which were "certain and thoroughly-understood."[8] Mercy Warren presented perhaps the clearest case for the relationship between historical necessity and the Natural Rights–Natural Law thesis when she observed that the American people "considered [Britain's] measures as a breach of a solemn covenant, which at the same time that it subjected them to the authority of the king of England, stipulated to them the equal enjoyment of all the rights and privileges of free and natural born subjects." When such a solemn covenant is broken, when the king demands subjection but at the same time refuses to acknowledge the people's rights, then the obligation to obey is annulled and, as Warren stated it, the people must "hazard the consequences of returning back to a state of nature, rather than quietly submit to unjust and arbitrary measures continually accumulating." It was precisely when a people is returned to a state of nature that Natural Law and its concomitant Natural Rights begin to operate directly and immediately.[9]

The historians sound confident that the separation from Britain was justified because historical conditions had made a revolution necessary. The Crown's policies constituted a threat not merely to positive law but to the Law of Nature itself. But the historians were writing in retrospect and certain difficulties arose as a result. The easiest argument to make, after all, was that what had happened in fact happened by necessity. The historians had no difficulty *asserting* the necessity of the Revolution, but the ground upon which they raised their assertions was eroding under their feet. They discovered that necessity and justification could exist independently of one another, and that even if they could demonstrate that the Revolution was necessary they still might not be able to make an absolute case for its justification.

In fact, the historians found themselves leaning heavily on arguments of expediency, and yet it was exactly such arguments which they felt constrained to transcend. David Ramsay noted that "Several [people] on both sides of the Atlantic, have called the declaration of independence, 'a bold, and accidentally, a lucky speculation,' but subsequent events proved, that it was a wise measure."[10] John Marshall also resorted to a retrospective analysis based on expediency when he observed that, despite the opposition of a formidable minority, "it cannot, however, be questioned, that the declaration of independence was wise and well timed."[11] The problem, of course, was that it *could* be questioned. Relying on subsequent events seemed to prove nothing.

Similarly, when William Gordon claimed that the separation from England was unavoidable, he attempted to demonstrate the truth of his claim by asserting, "The people were ripe for it. Prudence dictated a compliance with their expectations and wishes. A disappointment might have disgusted [them], and produced disorder." By the same token, declaring independence might result in many advantages to the Americans; it might make the French less "timid" and "animate" them to exertions on behalf of the new nation. The people, moreover, "have nothing worse to apprehend from the declaration than before. . . . Beside, the quarrel is in such a stage, that it cannot be ended with safety to the inhabitants, but by their separating from Great Britain, and becoming independent."[12]

What more utilitarian argument for expediency could Gordon have presented? He not only made no reference to the transcendent, immutable Laws of Nature, nor to "the principles of rectitude," but he depicted the Declaration of Independence as a cunning subterfuge, a ploy to gain material and political advantages for the American cause. Indeed, Gordon's argument represented the same cynical sacrifice of principle to expediency for which Mercy Warren had excoriated parliament.

Even Jedidiah Morse, the historian who had so scrupulously distinguished between questions of mere expediency and metaphysical principles of Natural Law, resorted in his own writings to the argument for utility. With the events of 1775, he wrote, "the question of the expediency of independence" was decided. "While the *legality* of this measure was thus argued," he continued, "its immediate necessity was proved."[13] Here the final twist of logic was turned, confusing altogether the usual terms of the debate. For Morse was willing to see the necessity of independence as a function of its expediency; and the obvious implication of his statement is that, even if debate were to conclude that independence was illegal it was, nevertheless, necessary, and because it was necessary it was justifiable.

The problem of reconciling arguments of expediency with arguments of principle which would justify the Revolution was nowhere clearer than in the historians' attempts to discuss a sympathetic figure who had opposed independence. Tories were one thing, John Dickinson was another. Almost all the historians made it a point to observe that some "worthy men," among whom they numbered Dickinson, had given serious thought to the implications of a decisive break with Britain. When the Continental Congress was debating the issue of independence, such people as Dickinson had doubts that a separation was even desirable, much less necessary. David Ramsay referred to these doubters as misguided but honest men, "respectable individuals whose principles were pure, but whose souls were not of that firm texture which revolutions require." William Gordon added that when Dickinson opposed independence he did so "openly, and upon principle."[14]

But how could one say with such certainty that John Dickinson, a man who had been in the forefront of the struggle against British policies since the 1760s, was misguided? And if he were an honest man whose principles were pure, did that imply Dickinson was appealing to some standard or set of principles other than the Laws of Nature, or "the immutable laws of justice," or "the principles of rectitude" to have arrived at his erroneous opinions? Insight into Natural Law required intuition, according to John Locke. Whose intuition into the Laws of Nature was brighter, more immediate, more certain: Ramsay's or Dickinson's? Any answer would be as absurd as the question.[15]

Something clearly was wrong, and the problem seemed to lie in the traditional theory of Natural Law or with its retrospective application to concrete historical events. Indeed, the traditional theory seemed to be flying back in the face of the historians, for its greatest virtue—the fact that it offered epistemological certitude because it was transcendent—now seemed to be its greatest liability. For the gap between the transcendent and the historical seemed to have widened beyond people's ability to bridge it philosophically. Peter Gay has observed that, by the end of the eighteenth century, European thinkers had given up the Natural Law thesis and become confirmed proponents of the principle of utility. Leo Strauss has also suggested that the seeds of the crisis of Natural Rights theory which were being harvested in the late eighteenth century had been sown as early as the mid-seventeenth century, when Thomas Hobbes had written *De Cive* and *Leviathan*.[16] America's revolutionary historians, however, tried to face the difficulties which others had either avoided or overcome to their own satisfaction. But in the face of such troubling logic, Mercy Warren, for one, resigned herself to the idea that, try as man might to understand and to live by transcendent imperatives, he "yet discovers a deficiency of capacity to satisfy his researches, or to announce that he has already found an unerring standard on which he may rest."[17]

If the logic of transcendent, immutable Natural Law seemed no longer to work in practice, why, then, did the historians persist in using the rhetoric? It is tempting to conclude with good twentieth-century "political realism" that Natural Law had become a fiction, providing no more than a rhetorically strategic language which was enormously useful for disguising the real, less than divine, reasons for separating from Britain. It is also tempting to view the revolutionary historians' use of Natural Law theory in light of how nineteenth-century idealistic philosophers transformed it, or in light of the Utilitarians' rejection of the theory altogether. The historians, however, did not articulate an incipient theory of dialectical idealism, nor were they prepared to abandon the theory of Natural Law and to replace it with the principle of utility. For they feared that to eliminate a transcendent standard of truth and value meant to plunge man into a chaos of relativism, leaving him to sink or swim in an ethical and historical whirlpool which was devoid of certitude or even meaning.

There was, however, already present in the histories an alternative to both relativism and transcendent absolutism, although the modern reader will almost doubtless agree with Daniel W. Howe's judgment that it was at best "a brave front," which for a time "helped stave off intellectual chaos."[18] The alternative involved the perpetuation of the theory of Natural Law, but it was a Natural Law no longer conceived as a static body of immutable principles. Rather, Natural Law was historicized; it was seen as a process by which fundamental principles were made concrete in the course of history itself. Natural Law was thus conceived to require historical action or practice for it to be "legal."

James Wilson, America's most important legal philosopher of the period, came closest to stating this processive theory of Natural Law *as* a theory. By doing so he pointed to the problem and to the possibility of its solution in practice. In his essay "Of the Law of Nature," Wilson wrote unequivocally that "the law of nature is immutable" and "the law of nature is universal." But he also observed that "it is the glorious destiny of man to be always progressive," and that man's progress was directed by immutable principles.[19] Perhaps contrary to one's expectations, Wilson did not resolve this apparent ambiguity by suggesting that man's progress was itself a law of nature. Rather, he argued that "the law of nature, though immutable in its *principles,* will be progressive in its operations and effects. Indeed, the same immutable principles will direct this progression."[20]

Because Wilson continued to affirm the transcendence of Natural Law, his thesis failed to overcome the difficulties inherent in the traditional theory, difficulties which the historians encountered when they attempted to justify the Revolution in retrospect on the ground of necessity. But Wilson had opened another dimension of Natural Law theory by seeing it as a process in which the Natural Law "will not only be fitted, to the cotemporary [sic] degree, but will be calculated to produce, in future, a still higher degree of perfection."[21] Natural Law, then, while immutable in its principles, required history for its fulfillment.

If Wilson and, to some extent, Thomas Jefferson pointed the way to a processive theory of Natural Law, it remained for the historians to realize the theory and to make it work in practice.[22] In the writings of the historians the theory was, in the first place, shorn of its transcendence. The Natural Rights of man, which are rooted in the Law of Nature, wrote Mercy Warren, "are improved in society, and strengthened by civil compacts: these have been established in the United States by a race of independent spirits, who have freed their posterity from the feudal vassalage of hereditary lords."[23] The significance of Warren's formulation is twofold: In it she implies that Natural Rights are abstract rights; they become actual rights only in historical situations, only when they are put into practice. Second, to demonstrate the legality of Natural Rights and to know, therefore, when they have been violated, the historian must establish that those rights have a tradition, that they have been exercised, for generations.

In his historical survey of the *Canon and Feudal Law*, John Adams exhorted, "Be it remembered, that liberty must, at all hazards, be supported! We have a right to it, derived from our maker! *but if we had not,* our fathers have earned it and bought it for us, at the expense of their ease, their estates, their pleasure and their blood."[24] Liberty is an absolute right, derived from God, according to Adams; it is in *principle* eternal and immutable. But what gives Adams's point its power is his reliance on tradition, for experience has shown that principle is frequently trampled under the boot of expediency. Therefore, even if liberty were not a right derived from God, Americans still had an absolute claim to it because of what the fathers had done to earn it. Liberty is, in short, a fundamental dimension of the American constitution.

As a practical form of historical analysis the processive theory of Natural Law resembled Edmund Burke's theory of tradition. Burke identified concrete historical practice with Natural Law, arguing that the natural constitution is identical to the constitution which a society had developed in the course of generations.[25] It was with this conception of Natural Law, incidentally, that Burke found the means of supporting the American Revolution but not the French. Consistent with Burke's view, Jedidiah Morse wrote that Americans' rights had not only been "stipulated and confirmed by royal charters, [and] acknowledged by the people of Great Britain"; in addition, they had been practiced by Americans, "enjoyed by the colonies for more than a century." Any violation of such rights "would be inconsistent with the British constitution, and an infringement on [Americans'] natural and essential rights."[26] Morse thus blurred any distinction between Natural Rights and traditional rights, precisely as he blurred the distinction between a people's "natural charter" and their "constitutional rights" elsewhere.[27]

The historians applied the same reasoning to the great issue of taxation and representation. Lord Camden, quoted by practically every historian, said in 1766 that "taxation and representation are inseparable. This position is founded on the laws of nature. It is more, it is itself an eternal law of nature."[28] The historians, of course, agreed with Camden in principle. But they recognized that it was no longer sufficient to invoke the self-evidence of Natural Law, however satisfying self-evidence was epistemologically. One had to show that the rights at issue were rights in practice. Thus Timothy Pitkin wrote that taxation and representation were indeed inseparable, but it was because "the colonists, from their first settlement considered themselves entitled to the rights of Englishmen, as secured by magna charta, and confirmed by the bill of rights. The most important of these rights, were those of *representation* and *taxation*."[29] Similarly, referring to the seventeenth century, David Ramsay noted, "Long before the declaration of independence, several of the colonies on different occasions declared, that they ought not to be taxed but by their own provincial assemblies, and that they considered subjection to acts of a British Parliament, in which they had no representation, as a grievance."[30] And Mercy Warren, believing that Natural Rights were "improved in society," thought that "old opinions, founded in reason" had become so firmly intrenched in the American mind since the settlement that they had become no less than a "part of the religious creed of a nation."[31]

The processive theory of Natural Law, involving as it did the reliance upon traditional practice, prompted the historians to treat their ancestors as incipient revolutionaries themselves. To show that the Natural Rights of which they spoke were not mere abstractions, the historians argued that the principles of the Revolution were those brought by the forebears "to the dark wilds of America." Indeed, even before the settlement, "these were the rights of men, the privileges of Englishmen, and the claim of Americans: these were the principles of the Saxon ancestry of the British empire, and of all the free nations of Europe, previous to the corrupt systems introduced by intriguing and ambitious individuals."[32] These long-standing, traditional principles were supported, even institutionalized, by the settlers of America who "were all of one rank; and were impressed with the opinion that all men are born entitled to equal rights." Those "sober, industrious, and persevering people" established "the same spirit among their descendents, finally [leading] them to liberty, independence, and peace." David Ramsay stated the point clearly and emphatically: "The English Colonists were from their first settlement in America, devoted to liberty, on English ideas, and English principles. They not only conceived themselves to inherit the privileges of Englishmen, but though in a colonial situation, actually possessed them."[33]

Such idealized portraits of the ancestors are more befitting hagiography than biography. But one must appreciate the historians' intent in idealizing their forebears. By creating a usable past the historians meant to demonstrate that Natural Law and Natural Right had been established in the constitution of American society. But by "constitution," the historians, like Edmund

Burke, did not mean a compact which symbolized the transition from the state of nature to civil society; they meant the order of things, how principles were lived in practice—in short, the way in which society was "constituted."

By understanding Natural Law as a historical process rather than as a static body of transcendent principles, one can return with an altered perspective to the historians' efforts to justify the Revolution on the ground of its necessity. The Revolution was justified because the British had violated rights which traditionally had been believed and practiced by the American people. They were "Natural Rights" precisely because they had grown up *in* historical experience, modified by the demands of the environment, and organically transmitted, generation by generation, from the settlers to the revolutionaries.[34] They were "Natural Rights" because they were taken for granted; they were assumed in the very process of living in the colonies. British policies, then, threatened not merely abstract rights—models of what rights would be like if they were ideal—nor merely positive laws which were practiced by convenience. What the British threatened were "constitutional rights," rights practiced for so long that they constituted the very structure of society. The British threatened, therefore, American existence itself.

With this view of Natural Law, the tension between necessity and expediency was overcome, for by seeing both Natural Law and specific historical events as immanent in the historical-societal order of things, the historians no longer had to create a bridge between the transcendent and the mundane. Thus an appeal to traditional practice—to concrete historical usage and custom—was itself an appeal to Natural Law. It was, of course, conceivable that some revolution might not be justified because it was merely expedient, because it was not demonstrated that traditional, practical rights had been abridged. This was the ground of Edmund Burke's hostility to the French Revolution.[35] Necessity was still established by appealing to Natural Law, but an appeal to Natural Law had become an appeal to history itself.

The effect of historicizing Natural Law theory was double-edged. At the same time that the historical theory resolved certain problems and ambiguities it tended to generate others. While, for example, it overcame the epistemological separation between the transcendent and the immanent, it also required the historians to repudiate in practice what had amounted to a religious faith in the transcendent as an immutable standard against which historical action could be measured with certainty. Equally important, while the historical theory freed the historians to make moral judgments about events without being required to point to any standard outside the events themselves, Tory commentators could argue that historical morality thereby became situational—not only relativistic philosophically, but suspiciously subject to the vagaries of ideology.

Similarly, the historical theory of Natural Law made problematic the idea of "historical necessity." As long as necessity was understood in the context of the divinely ordained providential, it was taken to be an absolute imperative of the transcendent. Once historicized, however, necessity was seen to arise *in* history rather than from without, and as a uniquely historical principle, necessity raised problems of interpretation. For, as I argued in Chapter 3, in the revolutionary histories, historical necessity meant something more like the manifest tendency of events rather than absolute determination. But in presenting an argument for the general tendency of events, the historians, who were as much participants as they were the narrators of those events, opened themselves to the charge of bias. Their claim that the Revolution was historically necessary was easily construed as the product of political blindness or, less charitably, ideological motive.

These difficulties with the historical or processive theory of Natural Law underscore the point that there was still room to debate the justifiability of the American Revolution. The patriot historians were not going to convince the Tories that the Revolution was justified because Natural Rights had been violated. Jonathan Boucher, the Tory exile, would still write with bitterness that historical writings were too often "entirely exculpatory—compiled on purpose to vindicate [the historians'] own characters and conduct."[36] But precisely by denying that the Revolution had been necessary, precisely by arguing that Natural Law had not been transgressed because traditional American rights and practices had not been abridged, Boucher and the Tories affirmed the revolutionary historians' new mode of analysis. For by quarreling with the patriot historians' interpretation of the past, the Tories had to quarrel in a new context. They could no longer question whether abstract, transcendent principles had been violated and, in the absence of revelation or intuition, disagree as a matter of opinion. Henceforth the debate would have to be conducted in the arena of historical fact and historical experience.

Conspiracy Theory and Prior Independence

Boucher and the other Tories were, of course, correct: the revolutionary histories *were* designed—as was the Declaration itself—"to justify, in the sight of mankind, the renunciation of [the Americans'] former allegiance."[37] The historians' immediate ideological intention was to vindicate the revolutionaries and to validate their Revolution. But the historians would fail to justify the Revolution on both philosophical and ideological grounds unless their histories could persuade readers that conditions had in fact become "intolerable" and that Britain had indeed designed to "reduce them under absolute despotism." The processive theory of Natural Law required no less, and the historians' ideological aims would rise or fall on their historical arguments. Consistent with the view that Natural Law was traditional practice, the historians used two related strategies to demonstrate that Britain had abridged the colonists' rights and meant to enslave them. One was to show that the British had in fact *conspired* to destroy their rights, and the second was to argue that the Americans had been free and independent people from the very beginning of new world settlement.

In the decade before 1776, Bernard Bailyn writes, the colonists "saw about them, with increasing clarity, not merely mistaken, or even evil, policies violating the principles upon which freedom rested, but what appeared to be evidence of nothing less than a deliberate assault launched surreptitiously by plotters against liberty both in England and in America." They perceived signs of this conspiracy everywhere and evidence of it mounted almost yearly: the efforts to establish an American Episcopate in dissenting New England; the Stamp Act and the Townshend Duties, which threatened the colonists' right, as they saw it, to initiate legislation and taxation, and which led to the strengthening of the customs administration and the placement in the colonies of corrupt and avaricious administrators; Britain's assault on local judicial authority and the corresponding expansion of Vice Admiralty jurisdiction; the establishment of a standing army in Boston—in all these actions the colonists read with increasing clarity a concerted plot to deprive them of their rights and, ultimately, to enslave them. And their conviction "that they were faced with conspirators against liberty determined at all costs to gain ends which their words dissembled" was finally what "propelled them into Revolution."[38]

As revolutionaries themselves, the historians affirmed the conspiracy theory prior to 1776. As historians, they used the conspiracy theory retrospectively to justify the Revolution. "What fatal infatuation has seized the parent state," Mercy Warren asked Catharine Macaulay in 1773, "that she is thus making illegal encroachments on her loyal subjects, and by every despotic measure urging these populous, brave, and extensive colonies to a vigorous union in defense of their invaded rights."[39] A year and a half later she answered her own rhetorical question: the agents of the British court "have been long forming a system of despotism that should reach beyond the Atlantic; that should involve this growing Continent in the same thraldom that awaits the miserable Asiatic." Warren's grievances read like a list from Bailyn's analysis. The British have blockaded the port of Boston and abridged the people's charter privileges by altering the Massachusetts government. Acting "like an unnatural Parent," Britain is "ready to plunge her dagger into the bosom of her affectionate offspring." And "there is little reason to expect [conciliation]," for "such is the prevailing luxury and dissipation of the times: such the undue influence of the Crown, from the tribes of placemen, pensioners, and dependants, backed by a large standing army, that nursery of slavery and vice, that bane of every free state that America has much to apprehend."[40]

At the same time that Warren indicated her belief in a conspiracy she prefigured its importance as a historical strategy, for she wrote of Britain's concerted plot to enslave the colonists in the context of the historians' proper role. "How absurd will the plans of modern policy appear to posterity," she wrote in the same letter to Macaulay, "when the faithful Historian shall transmit to them the late maneuvres of a British administration.... Astonishment will be enhanced when our Children are told" this evil story.[41]

John Lendrum recognized that the conspiracy theory as a strategy of historical presentation derived its value not from its being true but from its being believed. Realizing that both Americans and Britons employed the conspiracy theory, he observed, "Unfortunately for the peace of both countries, the parliament of Great Britain believed that the claims of the colonists amounted to absolute independence, under the specious show of a redress of grievances. On the other hand, the colonists were confident that Britain harboured designs not only hostile to their interests, but that it was resolved to introduce arbitrary government." Politically speaking, when a conspiracy theory arises, polarization has become manifest and possibly irremediable. Thus, although "probably neither of these opinions were true in their utmost extent ... matters had now proceeded so far, that every idea of reconciliation or friendship with Britain was lost."[42] Nevertheless, even if no conspiracy existed in its utmost extent, Lendrum was as perceptive as the others in seeing its ideological value and he used it in his historical analysis. Referring to the dangerous period of the French and Indian

War, he wrote that "it is obvious that the British ministry laid hold of the alarming situation of the colonies . . . to constrain them into an acknowledgement of their right, or to the adoption of measures that might afterwards be drawn into precedent." Thus, about the administration's call for revenues in the 1760s he would conclude, "The hostile policy which led the colonies to examine scrupulously the nature of their dependence on Great Britain, followed, but did not precede, her attempts upon the rights and liberties of America."[43]

Whether or not the conspiracy theory correctly identified a British plan to enslave the colonies, it became for the historians a narrative strategy for holding together and making meaningful the events between 1763 and 1776. Beginning in 1763 there were, according to David Ramsay, "suspicions in the minds of the jealous colonists, that the mother-country harboured designs unfriendly to their liberties." By then, in fact, Britain already had it in mind not only to tax the colonists but to alter their governments in order to make them increasingly dependent on the crown. And this, argued Timothy Pitkin, was consistent with the basic development of Britain's policies since the Restoration: to bring the colonies increasingly into the orbit of the crown and parliament, essentially because the colonies were becoming more prosperous.[44] Already mildly apprehensive, by 1765 the colonists were prepared to view the Stamp Act as "the sad preface to a system of American revenue, which would . . . enslave . . . themselves and their posterity," according to Jedidiah Morse. And from this point forward, wrote Mercy Warren, "the watchful guardians of American freedom never lost sight of the intrigues of their enemies, or the mischievous designs of such as were under the influence of the crown, on either side [of] the Atlantic." On top of these, the Quartering Act was obviously designed so that regular British troops would mix with the citizens of Boston, so "it might become more easy to awe the people into submission, and compel them by military terrors to the basest compliances."[45]

By June 1768, when a standing army took residence in Boston, Britain's plot was absolutely clear, and Warren dated the war to the moment the troops arrived. After that everything else fell into place. The Americans refused to accept East India Company tea in 1773 because "letters from Britain insinuated into the minds of the colonists, that a plan was laid to bring them into a snare; that a noble resistance on this occasion would free them from the slavery intended for them; that if this opportunity was lost they never would have another; and that if they suffered the ships to land the tea and the duty to be paid, they would rivet their own chains."[46] Thus by 1775, although the southern colonies were not immediately threatened by the Intolerable Acts, wrote David Ramsay, "yet they were sensible that a foundation was laid for every species of future oppression." And the events at Lexington and Concord could bear no other interpretation in light of a decade of plans and schemes: "Great Britain, instead of redressing American grievances, was determined to dragoon the colonists into submission."[47]

The conspiracy theory served the historians' efforts to justify the Revolution. To show that for a decade the British government had systematically threatened the colonists' rights was to satisfy the historians' claim that British policies represented a threat to colonial practices. No further evidence was needed to demonstrate that a separation from Britain was expedient. But to show that a revolution was *necessary*—the requirement of the Natural Law argument—the historians needed to establish a *long train* of abuses and usurpations. To this end they wrote the conspiracy back into the seventeenth century.

The historians were ambivalent about the history of pre-Revolutionary British-colonial relations, and their ambivalence seems to have been owing entirely to their sense of the ideological possibilities of their histories. They sometimes depicted colonial history as a century and a half of peaceful relations with the mother country, a portrait that heightened the enormity of Britain's "crimes" after 1763. At other times they argued that the colonial era presented an unremitting series of British threats and colonial resistances, an argument that comparatively diminished the heinousness of Britain's policies in the 1760s but which heightened the sense of a long train of unconstitutional practices. Whichever portrait they painted, their vision of the past—conflict or harmony—was a function of ideology. Generally speaking they wrote of turbulent times filled with instances of British threats to colonial rights, a picture that served their overarching view that British-colonial history was one of the extension of British prerogative and the drive for colonial self-government. Such a view, they believed, would fulfill the requirements of an argument justifying the Revolution on the ground of its necessity.

As the historians generally described it, then, American independence grew out of conflict. The colonists lived peaceably as English subjects until their rights as Englishmen, as guaranteed by their charters, were threatened—and threats were presented every step of the way. Disputes over colonial charter rights "commenced in Massachusetts, as early as 1635," asserted Timothy Pitkin, "nor did they end, till the American revolution." Indeed, added John Lendrum, "from the year 1629, to 1639, [the Virginians] were ruled rather as the vassals of an eastern despot, than as subjects entitled to English liberties; but it is to their credit that they opposed with a firm spirit, during the reign of Charles [I], all attempts upon their liberties."[48]

Emphasizing New England's history, Noah Webster argued that "during the reign of Charles the First, the colonies were frequently alarmed with the report of some act of the English government, to abridge their freedom." When the colonists resisted such encroachments on their rights, "their enemies represented the people as aiming at an entire independence, and a plan was devised and nearly matured, to deprive the colonies of their charters, and place over them a general governor." Later, the plan *was* matured, demonstrating that a concerted plot to enslave the colonies was never far from the administration's mind, and there arrived in Massachusetts the despotic Edmund Andros as agent for the tyrant James II. As expected, Andros "overacted his part; and his tyrannical proceedings only served to alienate the people's affections from the parent state, and prepare the way for that independence which the king dreaded."[49] Resisting Andros's unconstitutional actions, the people of Ipswich, led by their pastor, John Wise, rebelled and were brought to trial before "star chamber judges... and a packed jury." But Wise and the others refused to submit and, wrote Timothy Pitkin, they "may justly claim a distinguished rank among the patriots of America." For Mercy Warren the lesson was clear: "the intelligent yeomanry of the country, as well as those educated in the higher walks, became convinced that nothing less than a systematical plan of slavery was designed against them."[50]

Writing the conspiracy theory back into the seventeenth century, the historians concluded that "the *germ* of the Revolution, which issued in the establishment of the Independence of the British American Colonies, appeared at the very *origin* of their settlements." Or, as John McCulloch put it, creatively misreading the significance of Bacon's Rebellion (1676), in Nathaniel Bacon's day "the doctrine of Independence was first advanced; and it was probably never lost sight of by some bold characters, till it was actually declared an hundred years afterwards."[51] In a variety of seventeenth-century episodes—ranging from the attacks on colonial charters to the attempts to establish military governors, from the dissolution of the Virginia Company to the institution of the Navigation Acts—the historians portrayed a series of conflicts begun by England's desires to aggrandize herself at the expense of the colonists' cherished rights.

The conspiracy theory was an obvious strategy for assigning blame for the Revolution on the British; British administrators were portrayed as demons bent on the destruction of American liberties and, in consequence, the agents of England's own constitutional decline. Indeed, the Revolution was a self-fulfilling prophecy as the historians saw it, for the ministry sought to achieve certain ends and brought about their opposite. "By repeatedly charging the Americans with aiming at the erection of a new government, and by proceeding on that idea to subdue them," wrote David Ramsay, "predictions which were originally false, eventually became true." And then, in retrospect, when independence was a *fait accompli,* the ministers "inverted the natural order of things, without reflecting that their own policy had forced a revolution contrary to the original design of the Colonists, the declaration of independence was held out to the people of Great Britain as a justification of those previous violences, which were its efficient cause."[52]

Despite Ramsay's evident assurance here, there is a ring of anxiety in his statement. He seems to be aware that conspiracy arguments can be treacherous when used retrospectively, as if *he* might be accused of "inverting the natural order of things." And, in fact, the Maryland Loyalist Joseph Galloway turned the revolutionaries' arguments back upon them. An opposition to legal government has been common in every society throughout human history, Galloway observed. And, he conceded, "in almost every instance . . . it has arisen from a continued series of extreme injustice and oppression in the rulers. But," he continued, "the American Rebellion in this respect stands distinguished from all others. It can appeal neither to antecedent injustice nor oppression for an excuse. At the time it broke out, the people in the Colonies were more free, unincumbered and happy than any others on earth." Adding insult to injury, Galloway played upon the revolutionaries' own sense that until 1763 British-colonial relations had been peaceful and mutually advantageous. "The Congress themselves," he observed, "confess, that the Colonies have no grievances to complain of before that period."[53]

How then, according to Galloway, did the Revolution come about? Obviously, it resulted from an *American* conspiracy to establish the independence of the colonies. The colonists' words belied their actions: "while they professed themselves subjects, they spoke in the language of allies, and were openly acting the part of enemies; and while in their petition they declared their subordination, by their actions they proved their design to be that of independence." In fact, Galloway argued, this American conspiracy was not of recent vintage; to the contrary, "the American republicans had the same design from the beginning constantly in their view."[54]

Galloway used to his own advantage the revolutionaries' emphasis upon the colonial settlers' commitment to liberty. He agreed that the settlers loved freedom, loved it to the point that any subordination to constituted authority was anathema to them. Thus, he located the origins of the American scheme for independence precisely in the period of colonization. The Puritans, after all, held "principles of ecclesiastical polity [that] were as directly repugnant to those of the established Church, as their ideas of civil government were to those of a mixed monarchy." And a people who insisted upon "popular independence" in both civil and ecclesiastical affairs, "could [never] make good and faithful subjects to a state, where the licentiousness of popular power was checked and restrained by that of monarchy and aristocracy." Galloway argued, precisely as the historians did later, that the Puritans' intention was to create "an independent Church, and a republican society . . . resting the powers of direction and punishment, in all cases whatsoever, in the people at large." By their very charter, in fact, "the grantees were constituted a body politic, with all the rights necessary to form a complete independent civil society."[55] The historians, writing a few years later, could hardly have made a better case, though what for them was a laudable exercise in freedom was for Galloway a clear sign of political licentiousness.

Galloway's logic was inexorable. There was no chance that the early American settlers, particularly the Puritans, "governed by these [democratic] principles, and possessed of the unlimited powers of this charter, would ever adopt the laws of England, or even found their own laws upon the same principles; much less that they would retain an attachment to, or even a favourable opinion of, the principles of the English Government." By the middle of the eighteenth century a people with such a habitual belief in its own sovereign independence was ready to resist any British policy that did not square with its own prejudices. Thus, these "republican sectaries were prepared to oppose the Stamp Act, before the time of its commencement." The people were led by "a dangerous combination of men" whose views remained fundamentally opposed to the established church and the British government: "It was these men who excited the mobs, and led them to destroy the stamped paper; who compelled the collectors of the duties to resign their offices ... ; and it was these men who promoted, and for a time enforced, the non-importation agreements; and by their personal applications, threats, insults, and inflammatory publications and petitions, led the assemblies to deny the authority of Parliament to tax the Colonies, in their several remonstrances."[56]

Writing a few years before the historians, Galloway seems to have anticipated and tried to preempt their strategies for justifying the Revolution. But the historians had the last word and the more sympathetic audience. They merely ascribed *his* notions to so much inverting the truth of history in an effort to exculpate *Britain* from blame. Yet Galloway's views were rich with implications for the historians and they used ideas like his to support an interpretation that was congenial to them in any case. They argued that the colonists *were* independent—in a sense at least—from the beginning of settlement. And they used their argument for prior independence to justify the Revolution by demonstrating that the colonists' subordination to England was *voluntary* and therefore obligatory on them only as long as the arrangement was mutually advantageous. By arguing that the colonies' relationship to Britain was essentially contractual—a voluntary association implying rights and obligations on both sides—the historians implied that Britain's invasion of the colonists' rights was akin to its invasion of a foreign and independent nation.

David Ramsay made the most impressive and complete statement of prior independence and his views are worth considering in some detail:

The circumstances under which New-England was planted, would a few centuries ago have entitled them, from their first settlement, to the privileges of independence. They were virtually exiled from their native country by being denied the rights of men—they set out on their own expence, and after purchasing the consent of the native proprietors, improved an uncultivated country, to which, in the eye of reason and philosophy, the King of England had no title.

In the eye of Lockean reason and philosophy, he might have added. For every historian would follow Ramsay's lead in insisting upon the colonies being founded at the settlers' own financial expense and the expense of their labor. In good Lockean fashion the argument assumed that property (in a state of nature, at any rate) was based upon labor or, more precisely, on cultivation. In addition,

> the settlers of New-England were always so far independent, as to owe no obedience to their Parent State, but such as resulted from their voluntary assent. . . . Though the prevailing ecclesiastical and political creeds tended to degrade the condition of the new settlers in England, yet there was always a party there which believed in their natural right to independence. They recurred to first principles, and argued, that as they received from government nothing more than a charter, founded on ideal claims of sovereignty, they owed it no other obedience than what was derived from express or implied compact.[57]

To the fact that the settlers colonized the new country at their own expense, then, Ramsay added that their relation to the mother country was purely contractual. The colonists, as the historians never tired of repeating, retained all their rights as Englishmen (to which the historians added the Natural Rights of man).

Neither Ramsay nor the other historians went so far as to argue that the colonists were absolutely independent from the beginning, because to argue that would be to fall into Galloway's trap. Besides, to portray the colonists voluntarily entering into a contract only to see it repeatedly violated for a century and a half was to portray a long-suffering people patiently waiting for the government to come to its senses. The Americans were thus reluctant revolutionaries who, by December 1775, when Britain cast them out of parental protection once for all, considered themselves "discharged from their allegiance, and that to declare themselves independent was no more, than to announce to the world the real political state in which Great Britain had placed them."[58]

Central to the notion of prior independence were two ideas: first, that the colonists had settled America on English principles and had adopted English practices, implying that England had acted for a century and a half contrary to its own constitution, and that America was already becoming the fulfillment of the great English vision which the mother country betrayed; and second, that the colonies had grown up largely in isolation, a notion which contradicted the view that conflict had characterized pre-Revolutionary relations, but which had the virtue of enhancing the idea of colonial autonomy. "The English Colonists," argued Ramsay, "were from their first settlement in America, devoted to liberty, on English ideas, and English principles. They not only conceived themselves to inherit the privileges of Englishmen, but though in a colonial situation, actually possessed them." Thus, from the beginning of settlement the colonists took for granted the following principles of the English constitution: that one held and alienated one's property by voluntary consent; that taxes were the free gift of the people; that sovereign authority was legitimate only insofar as it was used for the welfare and happiness of the people; that the people were free to assemble and petition the government; and that ultimately, all proximate means failing, the people had the right to revolt against tyrannical government. These were no more than the principles guaranteed to all Englishmen, and they were confirmed once for all in 1688.[59]

But the colonists were Americans as well as Englishmen, and "that attachment to their sovereign, which was diminished in the first emigrants to America, by being removed to a great distance from his influence, was still further diminished in their descendants." Time and distance tended to isolate the colonies from Britain, and in isolation the fundamental principles of the English constitution tended to evolve according to a new-world logic, parallel though not in opposition to their development in England. Thus

> When the American revolution commenced, the inhabitants of the Colonies were for the most part, the third and fourth, and sometimes the fifth or sixth generation, from the original emigrants. In the same degree as they were removed from the parent stock, they were weaned from that partial attachment, which bound their forefathers to the place of their nativity. The affection for the Mother Country, as far as it was a natural passion, wore away in successive generations, till at last it had scarcely any existence.

Trade, of course, operated to sustain intercourse between the colonies and Britain, but trade was relatively unimportant during the first few decades of the seventeenth century. Distance, again, was an enormous factor: "The bulk of the people in New-England knew little of the Mother Country, having only heard of her as a distant kingdom, the rulers of which had, in the preceding century, persecuted and banished their ancestors to the woods of America."[60] In short:

> The distance of America from Great-Britain generated ideas in the minds of the Colonists favourable to liberty. . . . Colonists, growing up to maturity, at such an immense distance from the seat of government, perceived the obligation of dependence much more feebly, than the inhabitants of the parent isle, who not only saw, but daily felt, the fangs of power. The wide extent and nature of the country contributed to the same effect. The natural seat of freedom is among high mountains and pathless deserts, such as abound in the wilds of America.[61]

Although the notions of prior independence[62] and parallel development contained their own difficulties—most notably that they could be construed as confirming Galloway's view that the colonists harbored designs of independence from the outset of settlement—they strengthened the impact (if not the accuracy) of the conspiracy theory. For the only thing more abominable than Britain conspiring to deprive its own people of their rights was its conspiring to reduce an independent people to slavery. And the notion of prior independence implied no less than that the colonies constituted independent entities which in time generated closer cultural and political ties to one another than they did collectively to the mother country.

The historians wanted it both ways: on the one hand they wanted to portray a pre-Revolutionary past that was politically calm and beneficial to both the colonies and the mother country, in order to show that Britain subverted its constitutional responsibilities from 1763 onward; and, on the other, they wanted to identify a long train of abuses and usurpations beginning in the seventeenth century, in order to demonstrate that Britain had persistently violated traditional rights and therefore the natural rights of the colonists. At the same time, the argument for a long history of repeated injuries provided the historians with an opportunity to create the settlers in the image of the revolutionaries, thus establishing for themselves a revolutionary past. The first argument rested on the notion of a broken compact or covenant; the second, on a notion of separate and parallel cultural and political development. The two arguments were by no means mutually exclusive except in the abstract; the historians easily argued that the conflict manifest for 150 years was intensified after 1763, when Britain fell deeply into debt at the close of the French and Indian War, and when the colonies had grown sufficiently in population and wealth to be considered a mature fruit ripe for the picking. On balance, however, the historians would argue more strongly for traditional grievances, describing a past filled with the conflict of threats and resistances, for that argument had two significant advantages: it fulfilled the requirements of the new Natural Law theory, and it provided the historians with ammunition for their argument that Britain had declined politically and culturally over the last two centuries. The latter point had crucial implications for the writing of narrative history, for the historians would point to Britain's decline as a prime reason for developing a distinctively *American* history.

6

An American History:
Ideology, Language, and Style

At the same time that they avowed their intention to justify the Revolution, the historians also wrote that their aim was historical truth impartially and objectively narrated. In his *History of the Revolution of South-Carolina* (1785), David Ramsay established a virtual formula for preface writing from which few later historians deviated. Writing in the third person, a tactic suggesting that the first-person singular had no place in an objective narrative, he observed, "During the whole time of his writing he has carefully watched the workings of his mind, lest passion, prejudice or a party-spirit, should warp his judgment." The historian risked both his credibility and his reputation. Thus, "he has endeavored to impress on himself how much more honourable it was to write impartially, for the good of mankind, than to condescend to be the apologist for a party."[1]

Ramsay later appealed "to the actors in the great scenes which I have described for the substantial truth of my narrative." William Gordon and Mercy Warren appealed to no lower a standard than God, avowing that they were "conscious of . . . being answerable to a more awful tribunal than that of the public."[2]

One might well expect a Jonathan Boucher to look cynically upon such pronouncements of impartiality, but no less a patriot than John Adams was also unconvinced. In 1789 Adams wrote to Jeremy Belknap, "My experience has very much diminished my faith in the veracity of History." By 1813 the exasperated Adams exclaimed to Thomas Jefferson that he wished for "a Tory History" of the Revolution, for "I should expect to find more Truth in a History written by Hutchinson, Oliver or Sewell" than in those written by Marshall, Gordon, or Ramsay.[3]

Adams's criticisms of the revolutionary histories arose from complex motives, not the least of which were personal pique and party prejudice. But in his blast of Mercy Warren's history he pointed to a crucial dimension of what for him constituted true history. "Mrs. Warren," he addressed her in 1807, conspicuously avoiding the friendly salutations that had characterized their correspondence for more than thirty years, "it is my opinion . . . that your History has been written to the taste of the nineteenth century. . . . The characters are not such as you esteemed them in the times when they acted, but such as will please the present fashion."[4] Warren must have felt pained by her old friend's insinuation that she wrote to the taste and fashion of the nineteenth century, for she explicitly identified the virtues of the revolutionaries with "the notions of the *last century.*" And she wrote of the "patience, probity, industry, and self denial" of the patriots in a letter to Adams himself. Indeed, she also lamented the neglect of the older patriots and wished for Adams's speedy return from Paris because the rising generation required his firm example. "We need the steady influence of all the old republicans," she added, "to keep the principles of the revolution in view."[5]

Warren agreed with Adams's aversion to contemporary fashion, remarking to her son Charles that "we live in an age when we much oftener meet with men of taste than of genius; true genius is bold and enterprizing . . . whereas taste attends to the minutiae of objects—sorts the ideas which genius has handed down, and arranges every thing in such order, beauty, and precision as strikes the moment it is beheld. . . . But the productions of real genius command the respect of future generations and immortalize the human character." Warren was concerned here with truth, which she saw as the aim of genius, and prayed that genius would guide the pens of historians and philosophers.[6]

Adams's doubts about historical truth (to which I shall return) arose essentially in the context of ideology. His overriding point was simply that political bias and party prejudice could only obstruct the quest for truth. With this all the historians agreed. But his notion that taste and fashion had become the polestars of historical discourse pointed to a dimension of historical writing that the historians would have to face. And, judging from the vehemence with which they defended their professions of objectivity and truth, the historians and contemporary critics betrayed an anxiety about challenges like his. Their defense led them to question the criteria of "good history" and to concentrate on such issues as impartiality, style, and language.

The Impartial Historian

Despite John Adams's doubts about their actual performances, the historians were very much aware of the role of ideology in historical writing. If they neglected certain epistemological problems concerning the possibility of knowing and narrating "historical truth," they nevertheless recognized that partisan zeal was transparent to readers and that they risked hurting their cause by failing to write according to accepted conventions of impartiality. The historians thus adopted the prevailing English view that historical truth was realizable if the historian wrote impartially, carefully scrutinized the historical record, and used a plain narrative style that allowed the truth to reveal itself.[7] The first two criteria presented little difficulty (at least in theory).

As the historians saw it, one wrote impartially by refusing to take sides in partisan disputes, by recording all relevant facts, and by portraying characters rather than caricatures. "I write not for a party but for posterity," remarked David Ramsay to Jedidiah Morse, and Mercy Warren explained to John Adams, "I aimed to make [my history] a concise and just narrative of facts, and to give a correct...detail of character." Jeremy Belknap observed in 1792 that "a regard to truth" was little enough to expect of a historian, for "to have disguised or misrepresented facts would have been abusing the reader." By 1805, apparently feeling constrained by the conventions of preface writing, Abiel Holmes dared to expose their conventionality by noting that "professions of impartiality are of little significance." But he hastened to add, "Although not conscious of having recorded one fact, without such evidence, as was satisfactory to my own mind, or having suppressed one, which appeared to come within the limits of my design; yet I do not flatter myself with the hope of exemption from error." In short, publicly and privately the historians claimed that their "object has been to give a plain and connected, but faithful and impartial account" of events during "a most interesting period" of American history.[8]

The historians' professions of unbiased perspective were equalled only by their concern for what today would be called scholarship. Henceforth, the impartial historian would have to search the public record as never before in pursuit of the materials to be objectively narrated. David Ramsay wrote letters to friends and acquaintances posing to each a series of questions about persons and events about which they might have special knowledge.[9] In addition, as a member of the South Carolina Assembly, the Continental Congress, and the South Carolina Ratifying Convention, Ramsay had particularly easy access to a wealth of public papers. He wrote to Benjamin Rush that he steeped himself in the material, for months spending from five to eight hours every day at his work. And, once having the facts collected, said he figured to "write the general history of the revolution with more ease than I have wrote a part of it."[10] Mercy Warren also relied upon her many friendships and political connections for firsthand information. She once chided John Adams, then minister to the Netherlands, that if he did not provide her with a particular detail of his diplomatic activities, as she had several times requested, "a *blank* shall be left in *certain annals* for your Dutch negotiations"—a jest that would return to haunt her.[11]

William Gordon not only gained access to the papers of the Continental Congress but, after much flattering and importuning, persuaded George Washington to allow him to use the commander-in-chief's wartime papers. Gordon—like Ramsay, Holmes, and Pitkin, all of whom made special reference in their prefaces to their scholarly enterprise—was convinced that the intensive examination of documents was the only means to history's truth. "You have been so obliging as to promise me your assistance in my designed history," he reminded Washington. "Truth and impartiality are what I aim at; and therefore am for getting the best information possible, which must be by having a recourse to original papers in the possession of those who have borne a distinguished and active part in the transactions of the day."[12] Gordon again reminded Washington of his promise two years later, saying that Washington's papers were invaluable "for I am in search of genuine truth and not a fairy tale."[13] Gordon also asked his friend, General Horatio Gates, for Gates's papers. Modestly asserting, "I shall not have the best pen," he remarked that he would nevertheless have "the best materials"; and that, of course, was the crucial asset, for "in history truth is the diamond."[14]

Such pious professions of truth, impartiality, and objectivity were characteristic of eighteenth-century historians; and, indeed, emerging ideas of historical criticism *were* challenging traditional assumptions about proper methodological procedures. Gibbon, Bolingbroke, Voltaire, Robertson, Hume—all acknowledged that the first requirement of good history was its quest for truthful knowledge impartially related, and wrote extensively about how that aim was to be achieved.[15] But if professions of impartiality presented no difficulties, performance did. History, after all, had to be narrated—it required a proper "dress" or style. The new demands that critical historiography imposed on eighteenth-century historians affected "content alone," argues Lionel Gossman; but they "did not alter the fundamental fact that [the historian's] task was to *write,* to compose a coherent work of literature with data provided by history."[16]

Thus, when William Gordon, wrote to Horatio Gates that "in history truth is the diamond," he added in sexually typified language characteristic of his day that "fine composition is but the polish—laboured elegance and extravagant colouring only brings her into suspicion, hides her beauty, and makes the cautious reader afraid lest he is in company with a painted harlot." Yet though too much adornment made history suspect, the artful historian did not merely render the "naked" truth, but "proportioned" and "wrought" its lines in order to make it attractive. Since history was "designed to appear in public," it "must be decently and neatly appareled so as not to offend the eye." Thus narrative style was of the utmost importance. Gordon thought that he could strike the perfect balance by clothing the truth "in a colour that shall suit her complexion—in a taste that shall please the present and future generations—and in a dress that shall improve instead of concealing her beauties."[17] Such a notion may have failed to suit John Adams, who professed a disdain for pleasing tastes and fashions, but it typified the historians' ideas about the characteristics of proper narrative.

The historians were very much aware that when they raised such issues as style, taste, and language, they invaded the domain of ideology as much as literary consciousness. Apparently having in mind to return to his native England as early as October 1782, William Gordon remarked that if England reformed its politics "an Historian may use the impartial pen there with less danger than here." He felt that too many prominent Americans had so high a stake in the kind of history that was written, that America "will be most horribly affected by an *impartial* history." In England, on the other hand, he could write "not only the *truth* but the truth *truly* represented, for you may tell the truth so as to make a lie of it in the apprehensions of him who reads or hears the tale."[18]

Gordon's last statement points to the issue that John Adams raised in his criticism of Mercy Warren's history. For if one had

to distinguish between "the truth" and "the truth truly represented," then clearly the modes in which the truth was represented were crucial to a narrative's veracity. Indeed, Gordon's
observations reveal a contradiction in the historians' standard of
truth, and they suggest that the historians were caught between
competing ideals of historical writing: on the one hand, they
believed that their proper role was impartially to narrate the
events of the Revolution in a plain style, an ideal that presupposed that historical facts spoke for themselves; on the other,
however, they believed that their task was to use their histories to
justify the Revolution—to employ history as an instrument of
ideology—an ideal that presupposed that historical facts had to
be given voice and shape in order to be meaningful and instructive.

As the historians saw it, these competing ideals were not
mutually exclusive; true history, they believed, would vindicate
the revolutionaries and justify the American separation from
Britain. But to make a case for this belief they had to do more
than merely assert it; they had to perform it as well, and that
required them to enter the realm of literature. What emerges
from an examination of their literary views are two related
points: that their interest in language and style was tied to their
ideological commitment to the principles of the Revolution, and
that their ideology motivated them to attempt to develop what
they saw as an American historical language, a language appropriate to the history of a republican revolution.

Toward an American Historical Language

The revolutionary historians' search for an American historical language and style began with a literary and cultural
critique of eighteenth-century English historical writings. A
month after New York's *American Magazine* carried a paean to
the greatness of Edward Gibbon's *Decline and Fall* and compared
Gibbon to the finest historians of classical antiquity, another
anonymous essayist wrote that Gibbon was not only "liable to

exceptions" on certain matters of fact, but "his stile [sic] is uniformly the *worst* model of the historical style, that has appeared in the language." Gibbon's style "is indeed smooth and harmonious," the critic continued; "the regularity of the periods charms the ear—but let a person read aloud one hour, in Gibbon's history, then in the best writings of Bolingbroke, Swift, or Addison, and the difference of fatigue will soon convince him that such a labored and uniform structure of periods, is the greatest fault a writer can commit."[19]

At the heart of this criticism was the distinction between content and form. A person "reads such a style without improvement," the critic observed. "The ears are gratified at the expence of the understanding. The music of the language charms the mind from the *matter* to the *manner;* from the *subject* to the *dress* it appears in; and after reading a chapter, [one] cannot recollect the facts related."[20] A year later in another essay on Gibbon's history for the *Massachusetts Magazine,* Noah Webster, lexicographer, historian, and commentator on culture, concentrated on the same issue: "The general fault of this author is, he takes more pains to form his sentences, than to collect, arrange and express the facts in an easy and perspicuous manner. In consequence of attending to ornament, he seems to forget that he is writing for the *information* of his reader, and when he ought to *instruct* the *mind,* he is only *pleasing* the *ear.*"[21]

Webster's observations echoed those of William Gordon. For Webster, "history is capable of very little embellishment; *tropes* and *figures* are the proper instruments of *eloquence* and *declamation*; *facts* only are the subjects of *history*." Webster, like Gordon, thus acknowledged the importance of style in historical narrative. But while Gordon thought that he could "improve" the truth by writing in such a way that its beauties would best be revealed, Webster thought it essential to strip historical writing of all literary embellishment, leaving only "plain narrative." Indeed, as Webster saw it, for the historian to engage in literary performance was to turn history into fiction. Gibbon's history "is not properly a 'History' of the decline and fall of the Roman empire;' but a 'Poetico Historical description of certain persons and events, embellished with suitable imagery and episodes, designed to show the author's talent in selecting words, as well as to delight the ears of his readers.' In short, his history should be entitled, 'A display of words.'"[22]

Gibbon had forgotten what genuine history was and what it was supposed to accomplish. He had forgotten that history was "the most instructive branch" of practical philosophy and that it was, when written properly, socially and politically useful. On the issue whether a history or a novel best cultivated the mind, all clear thinkers had to accept that "the majority of sensible people prefer plain truth expressed in clear and comprehensive language." As one critic summarized the relative importance of content and form: "Truth, not mere probability, is the first law enjoined [by history]; without the observance of which, all other merit is lost. To instruct, is the principal view of the historian; to entertain, is only a secondary prospect. Unless they go hand in hand, he only performs part of his work, it is true; but we much sooner forgive him for being faulty in the second point than in the first."[23]

But if historians and critics generally accepted the superiority of history to fiction and content to form, why did so many English critics praise Gibbon's work, when it was clear to the Americans that the *Decline and Fall,* because of its style, was little better than a novel? Noah Webster's answer, indicates that ideology, not epistemology, lay at the heart of historical taste. In language strikingly similar to Mercy Warren's and John Adams's he argued that "The encomiums of his countrymen proceed from false taste; a taste for superfluous ornament" characteristic of contemporary English intellectuals. Those who sought levels deeper than the superficial—the "minute springs of action; the remote and collateral, as well as the direct causes and consequences of events; and the nice shades of character [that provide] rules from living examples"—such people must avoid ornament and tap the works of original writers and collections of authentic documents.[24] Webster's criticism of Gibbon—

motivated by a desire to eradicate false taste in America and to call his countrymen "back to nature and truth"—was reminiscent of his concerns in his *Dissertations on the English Language* (1789), in which he asked rhetorically, "The question now occurs; ought the Americans to retain these faults [in English orthography] which produce innumerable inconveniencies in the acquisition and use of the language, or ought they at once to reform these abuses, and introduce order and regularity into the orthography of the AMERICAN TONGUE?"[25] This is no longer only a linguistic concern—it is ideological. To call for the reform of the language and the introduction of order and regularity into it was to echo the words of the revolutionaries when they spoke of English politics and the need for revolution. It reveals Webster's desire to declare independence even from the mother tongue.[26] Webster characterized his project as the quest for an American national language, for "a *national language* is a band of *national union*. Every engine should be employed to render the people of this country, *national*; to call their attachments home to their own country; and to inspire them with the pride of national character."[27]

Thus, at the same time that he called for a return to a proper standard of historical taste, he exhorted the American people to "seize the present moment," and establish their own language, as well as their own government, thereby tying his attitudes toward history to his theories on the social and political functions of language.[28] The clear implication of his idea for a national language is that, within its framework, an American *historical* language was necessary to narrate the American Revolution. This explains Webster's criticism of Gibbon's work, for the problem with Gibbon's history—its emphasis on form over content, rhetoric over substance, sensuality over enlightenment, entertainment over instruction—was that it was written in *English*, a language suffering from decline and corruption and thus long past the time when it could adequately be used to write true history.

Webster, like other cultural nationalists in the Revolutionary era, saw a dialectic between culture and politics, such that a corruption in language (or literature) was not only symptomatic of political decline but might actually cause it. "I assume it as a fact, conceded by all philosophers and historians," he wrote, "that there has been, in every civilized nation, a particular period of time, peculiarly favorable to literary researches; and that in this period, language and taste arrive to purity; the best authors flourish, and genius is exerted to benefit mankind." In Greece, according to Webster, the great age of literature was the era of Themistocles, after the invasion of Xerxes. In Rome, it was the age of Augustus Caesar; in France, of Louis XVI; in England, of the mid-sixteenth century to the end of the reign of George II. Scotland's literature and language were now at their zenith, or perhaps just past it. Clearly, American culture was in the ascendancy, an obvious corollary of the republican revolution. There is, then, in the evolution of culture a point at which improvement ends and corruption commences. "This has been the case in all nations, and is now true of England," Webster asserted. "The candid among the nation acknowledge and lament the decline of taste and science. Very few valuable writings appear in the present age; plays, novels, farces, and compilations fill the catalogue of new publications; and the library of a man of fashion consists of Chesterfield's Letters, Tristram Shandy, and a few comedies."[29] Thus, because England's politics and language were degenerating, English historians were tempted by the blandishments of ornament and rhetoric instead of accurate reporting. The only language capable of narrating the American Revolution, *republican* history and, by implication, true history at all, was an American historical language.

Noah Webster was the most articulate exponent of a theory of language that tied literature to culture and ideology. But Webster was by no means alone. The historians of the Revolution operated within the linguistic and ideological framework that Webster outlined in calling for an American historical language. And the historians were motivated by the same concerns. Mercy Warren, as already noted, was concerned by the age's overemphasis on taste. She had "no quarrel with the graces, I love the *Douceurs* of civility, the placid manners, *La Amiable,* and all the innocent arts of engaging the esteem and alluring the affections of mankind," she wrote to her son Winslow, who had mentioned his infatuation with Lord Chesterfield's *Letters.* But, conceding all this, she added that Chesterfield's *Letters* were "dangerous." "I tremble least the honeyed poison that lurks beneath the fairest flowers of fancy and rhetorick should leave a deeper tincture on the mind than even his documents for external decency and the outward semblance of morality." For Chesterfield "sacrifices truth to convenience, probity to pleasure, virtue to the graces, generosity, gratitude, and all the moral feelings to a momentary gratification." It was obvious to Warren that Chesterfield's love of ornament and grace at the expense of genius and enlightenment was symptomatic of England's cultural decline and the product of the nation's political degeneration.[30]

It is no accident that Gibbon and Chesterfield, as well as Samuel Johnson and David Hume, who also came in for abuse, were considered "Tories" by American patriot standards. One critic argued in 1792 that, although a few English writers were still concerned with communicating ideas, "by far the greater number are absorbed in the structure of sentences. We may call them the style builders of the age. Their manner is loose, florid and pompous, to the last degree." Among them, Dr. Johnson was the worst offender, the man who corrupted the language by uniting the "florid and bombastick" styles, creating the current rage, "the frothy manner." Echoing Warren's language and Webster's critique of Gibbon, the critic attributed such pretentious writing to "corrupt taste."[31]

English writers whose political reputations remained high in Revolutionary America were praised for their style. "Dean Swift may be placed at the head of those that have employed the plain style," wrote Hugh Blair, the admired Scottish rhetorician and divine. Swift knew "the purity, the extent, the precision of the English language." Indeed, as if to praise with faint damning, he added that "we must not look for much ornament and grace in his language." Blair need hardly have added the obvious: that precisely such a style is the style of truth. Mercy Warren wrote much the same about Addison, "who did more to improve the English language and correct the style of the age than any other man." Addison, she pointed out, provided an exemplary counterpoint to Chesterfield, particularly to the youthful explorer. And Benjamin Rush avowed his admiration for certain English writers, among them Swift and Bolingbroke, for they led him "to prefer *Simplicity* to every thing in composition."[32]

The American historians and critics also discussed one another's writings, and their statements indicate that the categories of criticism remained consistent. Contrary to the writings of effete and decadent English authors, in Jeremy Belknap's works, remarked one reviewer, "depth of erudition, energy of thought, profound reflection, and purity of style, are happily united together."[33] Belknap, wrote another, "founds his sentiments upon facts and rational principles, with a view of giving his readers just and useful information."[34] David Ramsay, referred to as "the Tacitus of America" and as "the Polybius of America," wrote "in a clear, elegant, and nervous style, and with a degree of impartiality, worthy the philosopher who determines never to sacrifice truth at the shrine of bias, party or prejudice."[35] George Richards Minot's style was "of the pure, elegant, narrative kind," without "affectation" or "pompous diction," and without being overloaded with "facts with an exuberance of ornament." "In avoiding these faults, so common in modern histories, and so much relished by the false taste of the present age," wrote a reviewer, Minot "has shown a just taste himself, and rendered his work entertaining to every class of readers." What another critic wrote about Belknap's *History of New Hampshire* succinctly summarizes the general attitude toward the style of the revolutionary histories: "No language could be better chosen for history."[36]

This rhetoric of condemnation and praise constitutes a kind of code indicating that literary consciousness was a function of ideology. For at the same time that an American historical style had to be plain, factual, enlightening, and unadorned, it also had to be *American*. The Reverend James Madison, for example, explained that David Ramsay's particular merit was "that his Dress is altogether American, of which he makes no small Boast." And, in fact, Ramsay wrote to his fellow historian Jeremy Belknap applauding Belknap's *History of New Hampshire* and Samuel Williams's *Natural and Civil History of Vermont* (1794) as instruments of national unity. A reviewer of Ramsay's own *History of the American Revolution* could not have been more explicit, writing that it was a "necessity that the history of the American revolution should be written in our own country, by a person of suitable abilities, who witnessed the incidents attendant on that great event."[37] It seems quite clear, then, that attitudes toward style were ideologically motivated—that the language of purity, the plain style, enlightenment, rationality, genius, and the like were applied to the patriot histories, whereas affectation, froth, bombast, florid, and so forth were epithets reserved for the works of "Tories" like Gibbon, Chesterfield, Johnson, and Hume.

What, precisely, these code words meant is difficult to determine, for when they claimed to write impartial, objective narrative in a plain style, unadorned with rhetorical flourishes, the historians were affirming the aims of English historians throughout the eighteenth century. And examination of the revolutionary histories as literary performances hardly reveals any manifest stylistic improvements over English works. Clearly, then, what the critics lauded in the histories was their "Americanness" rather than their technical literary merit.

Yet it is arguable that Americanness for the historians and critics had come to mean something more than a narrow political identification, something more like a cultural identity. An American historian would not write so much in a different style—construed as a technical literary term—as with a different style of mind. The Americans would concern themselves with issues that, as they saw it, English historians, overly involved with formal matters, were neglecting. As many of the critics' statements suggest, what was missing in English historical writing, though present in the revolutionary histories, was an *ethical* content revealing an ethical style of mind. History had to be made "subservient to the cause of virtue & human happiness," wrote David Ramsay in a statement typical of the historians' participation in the "exemplary" tradition of historical writing.[38]

Whether or not the Americans were correct in believing that English historians had abandoned their proper ethical roles, their pursuit of an "exemplary history" helps us to see the connection between their ideological and ethical concerns. English historical writing, like the nation's politics, was corrupt because it no longer concerned itself with instructing the people (particularly young people) in history's ethical lessons. The American historian, on the other hand, was always to keep in mind that virtue and republican values were inseparable, and that the historian's proper task was to guard both the ethics and the ideology of the republic, exposing corruption wherever it appeared and calling the people back to the standards of republicanism whenever they strayed. Thus, insofar as the historians served what they saw as an ethical theory of history, and insofar as they coupled their ethical and ideological interpretations, they did indeed develop an American historical language, a language of virtue, simplicity, and freedom and their antitheses, corruption, degeneracy, and servility.[39]

But this pursuit of an American historical language underscores the contradiction in the historians' and critics' standard of judgment. For at the same time that they criticized Gibbon and other "Tories" for participating too artfully and self-consciously in their histories, making themselves too much the subjects at the expense of the intrinsic value of the facts, they also affirmed the notion that language and style were crucial instruments of persuasion which, used effectively, could be ideologically valuable. Or, to state a different dimension of the issue, at the same time that they criticized the English writers for using a corrupt language and style to conceal the truth, they called for an American historical language which, suffused as it was with republican values, would reveal the truth in its purity.

Thus, while the criticism and praise seem to reveal clear

examples of partisan politics masquerading as literary taste, what was at stake in the observations on language and style was ideology in the deeper sense of a constellation of political and cultural values that served as lenses through which principles were filtered. Two deeply planted values lay beneath the partisanship giving it enormous power: first, Noah Webster's idea (already touched upon) that culture and politics were dialectically related so that English historical writing *had* to be corrupt, making an American history necessary in order to account for republican principles; and second, the notion that an American history was a "democratic" history, a notion that involved a shift in the perception of history's proper audience from an elite group of gentlemen politicians to the people at large.

The Style of Virtue

Noah Webster was certain that politics, language, and literature affected one another, and, since habits, manners, and principles were "the springs of government," a servile imitation of English manners and style could become habitual, at first tainting and finally corrupting politics as well as culture.[40] Hence his plea for a national language as a bulwark against the subtle and insidious influences of English taste:

> However they may boast of Independence, and the freedom of their government, yet their *opinions* are not sufficiently independent; an astonishing respect for the arts and literature of their parent country, and a blind imitation of its manners, are still prevalent among the Americans. Thus an habitual respect for another country, deserved indeed and once laudable, turns their attention from their own interests, and prevents their respecting themselves.[41]

The effects of such a dependence on English authorities transcended politics, wrote Webster to Joel Barlow; it also impeded development. Naively viewing English books as the measure of truth, Americans stood to lose that "spirit of investigation" that characterizes vital cultures.[42] Mercy Warren agreed, revealing to Catharine Macaulay her fear that America "may renounce her dignity if not her independence by too servilely copying either the fashionable vices or the political errors of those countrys where the inhabitants are become unfit for any character but that of master and slave."[43]

This kind of thinking was associated with the emergence of a broader cultural nationalism in literature, education, and the arts. Arthur H. Shaffer has argued that the revolutionary histories served the purposes of cultural nationalism by attempting to consolidate a common past and define an American national character which would generate a sense of pride in American society.[44] The movement was broader still. Phillip Freneau, for example, lamented the fact that by 1788 Americans remained backward in literature. He observed that "a political and a literary independence" were "two very different things," and that while political independence was accomplished in only seven years, the literary "will not be completely effected, perhaps, in as many centuries." Freneau was distressed that "polite" writings should be considered a "nuisance" in America, and he implied that Americans' failure to support a native literature was a sign of the country's provinciality.[45]

Royall Tyler insisted upon the ethical dimension of literature. He applauded New Englanders for their literacy and for their love of contemporary fiction. But he deplored their turning to English novels rather than American because, "Novels being the picture of the times, the New England reader is insensibly taught to admire the levity and often the vices of the parent country. While the fancy is enchanted, the heart it corrupted." The English novel might not inculcate vice directly, but it does leave the young mind with false impressions of the world. "It paints the manners, customs, and habits of a strange country; excites a fondness for false splendour; and renders the homespun habits of [America] disgusting."[46]

Thomas Jefferson, Benjamin Rush, and others expressed the

same concerns for the education of America's youth, and their attitudes toward education reveal an insularity born of a nativist anxiety, as well as a deep conviction that the children of the Revolution needed to be taught in a republican environment. Jefferson wrote to John Bannister, Jr., that, except for learning foreign languages, every field useful for an American education "can as well be acquired at William and Mary College as at any place in Europe." Jefferson's attitudes were formed largely by negative impressions of European education which was filled with so many disadvantages that "to enumerate them all would require a volume." The American youth who studies in Europe

> acquires a fondness for European luxury and dissipation and a contempt for the simplicity of his own country: he is fascinated with the privileges of the European aristocrats, and sees with abhorrence the lovely equality which the poor enjoys with the rich in his own country: he contracts a partiality for aristocracy or monarchy; he forms foreign friendships which will never be useful to him, and loses the season of life for forming in his own country those friendships which of all others are the most faithful and permanent ... he recollects the voluptuary dress and arts of the European women and pities and despises the chaste affections and simplicity of those of his own country ... he returns to his own country, a foreigner, unacquainted with the practices of domestic economy necessary to preserve him from ruin; speaking and writing his native tongue as a foreigner, and therefore unqualified to obtain those distinctions which eloquence of the pen and tongue ensures in a free country.

In short, "the consequences of foreign education are alarming to me as an American. I sin therefore through zeal whenever I enter on the subject."[47]

Benjamin Rush made explicit the Lockean environmentalist epistemology that undergirds these observations. Like Ramsay, Jefferson, and Webster, Rush saw the principal aim of American education to be the creation of homogeneity, for "a uniform system of education" will "fit them more easily for uniform and peaceable government." Rush saw the young mind as a "perfect blank," and what was inscribed on it ought to be republican impressions, for "our business is to make them men, citizens, and christians." Indeed, "I consider it possible to convert men into republican machines. This must be done if we expect them to perform their parts in the great machine of the government of the state." To mold American children into republican machines required a solid grounding in American history (or, more precisely, *American* history). "As soon as he opens his lips," wrote Noah Webster, an American youth "should rehearse the history of his country; he should lisp the praise of Liberty and of those illustrious heroes and statesmen who have wrought a revolution in his favor."[48]

All these views presupposed that politics and culture mutually influenced one another, and they fed upon the historians' argument that England was in political decline. As I will show more clearly in Chapter 7, the cause of this decline, as the historians saw it, was avarice, the lust for wealth and power at the expense of virtue. And just as avarice corrupts the constitution, manifesting itself in luxury, dissipation, and conspiracies to deprive the people of their rights, it is manifested as well in language, literature, taste, and style. Thus, when the historians and critics wrote of affectation, florid, "bombastick," and frothy styles, the placing of form before content, even the wild idea, subscribed to by some Englishmen, that fiction was somehow superior to history, they were using ideological categories, for these were clear signs of England's political degeneration. America, in contrast, as David Ramsay hardly needed to add, had "glorious prospects." "It is now our turn to figure on the face of the earth, and in the annals of the world." The reason was obvious: because American politics and culture were pure. "The arts and sciences are planted among us, and, fostered by the auspicious influence of equal governments, are growing up to maturity."[49]

A sure sign that American history was being written properly, and therefore that America was politically healthy, was its "democratic" premise: that republican history was to be written for the people. One of the criticisms of Samuel Johnson was that his style was obscure, overly Latinized, and multisyllabic, demonstrating that he practiced a "willful exclusion of the unlearned readers."[50] Noah Webster criticized Gibbon for the same reasons, as well as for making references to people and places, real and mythological, that only the erudite could possibly understand.[51] What better way to keep the people uninformed about their past and therefore ignorant of history's lessons than to make their history inaccessible to them! George Richards Minot, on the other hand, "rendered his work entertaining to *every class* of readers." And David Ramsay's style was so "simple and elegant," "the leading events are so ably traced to their causes; and the manner in which those causes produced their effects, are stated in so masterly a manner, that the whole form . . . a well connected history, calculated to inform the judgment, and, at the same time, to captivate the attention of the reader."[52]

Webster thought it essential that the government concern itself with the language of the people, since in the long run a republican literature was the chief bulwark against encroachments on liberty. Echoing the criticisms of Gibbon and Johnson, Webster noted in his first *Dictionary* (1806) that "the *learned* have changed the *written* language—the *people* have retained the original *oral* language." And it was precisely such class distinctions, stemming from society and politics, that made the written language inaccessible to the lower orders. Thus, "the ease of speaking, the beauties of the language, its established analogies, must be sacrificed to artificial refinements and a fashionable aversion to every thing common!" Making strikingly clear the relationship between politics and language, Webster concluded, "It is a curious fact . . . that the principal corruptions of our language, within the last five hundred years, are the work, not of the vulgar, as is commonly supposed, but of authors and writers, pretending to purify and refine the language."[53]

Although in England the notion of history's proper audience expanded throughout the eighteenth century, English theorists from Locke to Priestley presupposed that historical writings were of pre-eminent importance to gentlemen because they might be called into public service.[54] Dorothy A. Koch has argued, moreover, that history was generally used as a conservative force even among those who thought that it should be taught to the middle class as well as to the aristocracy. Peter Shaw argued in 1750 that history is useful because it showed "that we must beware of sudden political change, which usually, instead of reforming the state, brings new evils." Some critics, notably Jonathan Swift, Daniel Defoe, James Burgh, and Joseph Priestley, sought to transcend the aristocratic bias of historical teaching, but, Koch argued, even their criticisms were motivated by conservative attitudes.[55]

Joseph Priestley lamented the fact that for too long only the clergy were thought to need education, thus excluding, to society's immense disadvantage, potential leaders from the bourgeoisie. This exclusion of public-minded citizens from the educational process meant that social and political change was left to occur "by an accidental concurrence of circumstances" instead of by designed policy. But the situation had become socially dangerous, Priestley argued, for "the objects of human attention are prodigiously multiplied; the connexions of states are extended . . . and . . . without superior degrees of wisdom and vigour in political measures, every thing we have hitherto gained will infallibly be lost." Education, in short, and particularly historical education, had become essential "both to ministers of state, and to all persons who have any influence in schemes of public and national advantage."[56] Priestley's concern here was typical of English reformers in the eighteenth century, a time when many believed that the nation was declining precipitately. But, argues Dorothy A. Koch, the task of braking the decline and setting culture back on course was understood to be "the political role of the *aristocracy*."[57]

Although liberal English theorists sought to expand historical education to include members of the middle class, such education remained restricted by American standards. As long as sovereignty was understood to reside in government (albeit in the House of Commons) it was sufficient to educate those who served the government and an expanding economy. But with the theoretical shift in the location of sovereignty from the government to the people, an American history would have to be written for the *people* of the republic precisely so that they could be an effective check on the government's potential for tyranny.[58] That is why the critics condemned histories that appealed only to a learned and politically powerful elite. Such histories were the tools of monarchy and aristocracy, for by excluding the mass of people from their audience, they hid public policy from those it affected and lulled the people into a stupor of unconcern. But because the revolutionary historians had adopted the role of protectors of the people's civil rights and the public virtue, they dwelled incessantly on the improper acts of public officials both in England and in America. And, they claimed at any rate, they performed this essential service more effectively by writing in a style that could be understood by all.

Mercy Warren addressed this issue pointedly, remarking that even the Americans, who were in general more politically aware than the "common classes" of other nations, had too little knowledge of humankind. "They were not generally sensible," and therefore had to be taught, "that most established modes of strong government are usually the consequences of fraud or violence, against the systems of democratic theorists. They were not sensible, that from age to age the people are flattered, deceived, or threatened, until the hood-winked multitude set their own seals to a renunciation of their privileges, and with their own hands rivet the chains of servitude on their posterity."[59] This was the way most republics had been subverted in the past, and it was clear to the historians that this was the way the English constitution had been undermined. Warren explicitly addressed the possibility of tyranny and corruption in America as well, and she called upon "some unborn historian" to remind the people of their responsibilities as republicans.[60]

The Impartial Partisan

"What are we to think of history," John Adams wrote with bitterness to Mercy Warren, "when, in less than forty years, such diversities appear in the memories of living persons, who were witnesses?"[61] Adams was persuaded that partisan politics stood perhaps irrevocably in the way of truthful and impartial history. As he complained to Benjamin Rush, even "300 years after the event it cannot be written without offending some powerful and popular individual[,] family[,] party, some statesman, some general, some prince, some priest or some philosopher. The world will go on always ignorant of itself, its past history, and future destiny."[62] Gordon's and Marshall's histories "were written to make money: and fashioned and finished, to sell high in the London Market." Marshall's *Life of Washington* was especially contemptible—it was "a Mausoleum, 100 feet square at the base, and 200 feet high. It will be as durable, as the monuments of the Washington benevolent Societies."[63]

Adams recognized that the claims of the historians—that they wished simultaneously to justify the Revolution and to write impartial history—were contradictory; he also recognized the contradiction between pronouncement and performance. Adams's cynicism was probably strengthened, moreover, when the impartial, objective William Gordon announced to him, "I am a Protestant in politics as well as in Divinity" and, "I mean not to publish the *whole* truth of what I know, tho' nothing but what I know or believe to be true."[64]

If Adams wished to see pure, true, objective history, he was to be sadly disappointed. Jeremy Belknap knew very well that "in tracing the progress of controversy it is impossible not to take a side, though we are ever so remote from any personal interest in it: Censure or applause will naturally follow the opinion we adopt."[65] The historians did want to write impartial, truthful history but, unlike Adams, they saw no contradiction between taking the American side and telling the truth. They clearly believed that the ideals of objectivity and impartiality subserved ethical imperatives. At the same time, they felt strongly that historical writings were, or ought to be, instruments of an American vision. They felt, in short, that for the truth to emerge the historian of the Revolution had to be a revolutionary historian.

7

The Historian of the Revolution as a Revolutionary Historian

The historians wanted it both ways. On the one hand, they aimed to write impartial history, dedicated to truth and the service of humanity and pure in language and style; while on the other, they meant to develop a distinctively *American* history, intended to justify the Revolution and to inculcate the principles of republicanism in future generations of Americans. They wanted, in short, to write both true history and propaganda, a common enough aim of enlightened historians.[1] In fact, however, the historians saw no contradiction between their efforts to be objective and their insisting upon the principles and values of the Revolution. Indeed, except for their pious disclaimers of bias and party prejudice, they made no effort to conceal their partisanship. For if their claims to truth and their ideological purposes clashed when directly opposed to one another, they did not conflict when both were made to serve a higher set of *ethical* values.

The historians wrote their works in a mood of anxiety. As early as 1777 William Gordon bemoaned the "horrid corruption" that he saw spreading rapidly through the new nation, and he was shocked that within a year of declaring independence "we should have adopted so many of the Old England vices." Two years later, David Ramsay mourned the "spirit of money-making

[that] has eaten up our patriotism. Our morals are more depreciated than our currency." By 1786 he feared that "we have neither honesty nor knowledge enough for republican governments."[2]

This apprehension of widespread corruption, which is especially pronounced in the historians' narrative of events from the late 1770s to the passage of the Constitution, is not surprising, for corruption had been a dominant patriot concern since the 1760s.[3] But the historians' persistent focus on corruption reveals more than patriotic zeal. The anxiety it reflects also prompted them to develop a theory of history which was designed to unite ideology and ethics into a single interpretive framework. The historians presupposed a dialectic between politics and ethics, such that republican principles and institutions and the ethical practices of the people affected one another. They assumed, moreover, that the dialectic was driven from its ethical side, that principles and institutions were founded upon the people's practice of republican virtue. The historians adopted what they saw as an ethical stance toward history—one which they found so sorely lacking in English historical writing—because it squared perfectly with their perception of themselves simultaneously as participants in the Revolution and as narrators of it. They stood, they believed, at the nexus of history-as-lived and history-as-written, a privileged location from which the very writing of history was a revolutionary act.

As participants in the Revolution, the historians were apprehensive about the future of American republicanism; as historians, they wrote their anxieties into their narratives. Believing that the ethical foundation of society was weakening, they portrayed the years after independence as a period rife with the possibility of decline. At precisely the time that republican institutions were being shaped, they were in danger of crumbling, and at precisely the time that republican principles were being voiced, they were in danger of dissipating. Political events were ethical events, signs of the people's moral condition. And events clearly indicated decline: the monetary crisis of the late 1770s, the fraudulent activities of the early eighties, the obvious weak-nesses in society and government under the Articles of Confed-eration, Shays's Rebellion (1786), and the debilitating spirit of faction which emerged in the nineties—all suggested the people's moral degeneration.

Mercy Otis Warren, the most articulate exponent of the ethi-cal interpretation (and the only Antifederalist among the major historians),[4] believed that the nation was deeply in trouble. In-stead of demonstrating that independence would cement Americans' attachment to republican values, events of the 1780s and nineties, when her *History* was taking shape, seemed to con-firm her worst apprehensions about human character and about the people's unwillingness to exercise political self-discipline. Her narrative was filled with her "cool reflections on the danger a young country was in, just relieved from a long war," she wrote to John Adams in 1807. Like Gordon and Ramsay, she was con-cerned about America's future because public virtue was yield-ing to private ambition, the rising generation "laying aside their simple habits, and ... hankering after the modes, distinctions, and ranks of the servants of European despots." She added rhetorically, "was it not obvious that dangers would thicken?"[5]

The historians' anxiety stemmed from the view, shared by many of their generation, that the Revolution was not yet com-pleted; it required for its fulfillment an assiduous attention to virtue modeled upon the seventeenth-century settlers and upon the revolutionaries themselves. Warren perceived herself as a writer "who wishes only to cultivate the sentiments of public and private virtue in whatsoever falls from her pen." It was her special obligation as a poet, playwright, and historian "to form the minds, to fix the principles [and] to correct the errors [of] the young members of society," and to encourage them to tread the path of true virtue "instead of the hackneyed vulgar walks crowded with swarms of useless votaries, who worship at the pedestal of pleasure or bow before the shrine of wealth." This ethical intention was suffused with political values. Concerned as early as 1780 that the spirit of the Revolution was already showing signs of erosion, she called for "the steady influence of all the old republicans, to keep the principles of the revolution in view." For the "giddy multitude" was sacrificing all the gains of independence, by failing to adhere to "the manners that would secure their freedom." With these ends in mind, she presented her *History* as a work of partisan ideology that would indeed justify the Revolution; but it would also be a work of moral suasion, a manual of republican ethics designed to exhort future generations of Americans to persist in the uncompleted struggle.[6]

For the historians, justificatory history meant more than merely partisan writing that glorified the revolutionaries and, at the expense of truth, exculpated them from wrongdoing. Because they viewed history in a way that fused ideological and ethical principles, they used the past to establish the centrality of ethical categories in historical and political interpretation, and to generate a vision of an American future that fulfilled the promise of the Revolution. Such a project required an ethical mode of historical explanation, and exhortation as its proper mode of argument.

History as a Looking Glass:
The Exemplary Theory of History

The historians' immediate aim was to justify the Revolution, but they saw that aim subserving a higher ethical good: "History is philosophy teaching by examples," wrote Bolingbroke; it trains people in "private and public virtue" by inculcating images of virtue and vice. This "exemplary theory" of history required history to instruct people in personal morality and public virtue, and, since it was assumed people learned more from example than from precept, enjoined the historians to serve the public good by suppressing their biases and by providing models of exemplary conduct, both virtuous and vicious.[7]

Consistent with the exemplary theory, David Ramsay thought that recording "past events, for the instruction of man, ought to be the object of history"; for William Gordon instruction was its very *"soul."*[8] Ramsay applauded John Eliot's *Biographical Dictionary* (1809) because it "rendered an essential service to the living by holding up so many excellent models for their imitation from the illustrious dead." The historian, according to Gordon, "should oblige all, who have performed any distinguished part on the theatre of the world, to appear before us in their proper character; and to render an account of their actions at the tribunal of posterity, as models which ought to be followed, or as examples to be censured and avoided."[9]

The historians thus participated in one of the oldest and strongest traditions in historiography, for the exemplary theory had its roots in classical antiquity, reaching its highest expression among the Romans.[10] Plutarch, whose *Lives*, according to George H. Nadel, was the most important work in perpetuating the theory, added a personal dimension to it, thereby affirming the historian's participation in his own theory: "It was for the sake of others that I first commenced writing biographies; but I find myself proceeding and attaching myself to it for my own; the virtues of these great men serving me as a sort of looking-glass, in which I may see how to adjust and adorn my own life."[11]

Despite assaults on it from several directions—from Christian providential theory to historical skepticism—the exemplary theory became the stock in trade of "Humanist" historians from ancient Rome to Enlightenment England. Didactic in purpose, it aimed at moral instruction and emphasized "the Roman ideal of public virtue and service to the state."[12] By the eighteenth century, theorists armed with Lockean epistemology would argue that, because "the human understanding is a blank, which may be filled up with various kinds of matter," historical writings operated environmentally to stimulate impressions of virtue and vice.[13] Mid-eighteenth-century commentators including David Fordyce and George Turnbull wrote that historical writings were particularly important in educating youth because they would encourage virtuous action. Indeed, Fordyce argued, "by seeing Virtue in such a Variety of engaging Attitudes, exemplified in living Patterns, a spirit of Patriotism, an invincible Love of Liberty, and undaunted Contempt of Danger and Death, will creep upon them, and insensibly rouze them to perform Actions great and beneficial to mankind." More important, if less heroic, was Turnbull's notion that from the study of history one could evolve not only "all the rules of justice and decency relative to civil states" and "the terrible effects of bad or ill-constituted government," but even "all the various springs and causes of changes and revolutions in governments of every sort. 'Tis therefore the best political as well as moral master."[14]

The exemplary theory presupposed, of course, that history *could* teach true values; and this presupposition in turn assumed that the truth could be known and, once known, articulated. For centuries proponents of the theory defended it against the challenges of skeptics, foremost among them "historical pyrrhonists," the most extreme of whom questioned whether historical truth—if it existed at all—was accessible to human reason. "There is no reason to believe that any one page in any one history extant, exhibits the unmixed truth," wrote William Godwin in 1797. "Human affairs are so entangled, motives are so subtle and variously compounded, that the truth cannot be told."[15] Skeptics questioned every facet of historiography: historians' selection of materials, their criteria for determining the relevance of facts and events, their notions of what constituted evidence, their own political, religious, and cultural biases (and whether they could suspend them in the interest of truth), even their use of language and literary techniques to narrate events—all these issues were seized on to question the possibility of developing an adequate historical epistemology.

Yet despite the challenges of skepticism, the exemplary theory flourished at least until the middle of the eighteenth century. Even Edward Gibbon, who had his own doubts about historical truth, was concerned lest eighteenth-century historians adopt "an historical scepticism, as dangerous as it may be useful." Perhaps surprisingly, Gibbon and David Hume, the most important philosophical skeptic of the age, argued for the possibility of historical truth on experiential grounds.[16] And although

Bolingbroke was ambivalent about historical truth and knowledge, revealing in his writings both a strong measure of skepticism and advocacy of the exemplary theory, he remained convinced, according to Dorothy A. Koch, that genuine knowledge led to virtuous action and that the student of history was excited to virtue through vivid examples.[17]

Still later and more powerfully did the exemplary theory prevail in America which had been insulated from the influence of radical skepticism for nearly two centuries. In addition, the theory had strong American roots, for it comported beautifully with Puritan didacticism. Cotton Mather, to cite only the most self-conscious exponent of the theory, addressed the same problem the revolutionary historians later did, announcing in his *Magnalia*: "Reader! I have done the part of an Impartial Historian.... I have endeavored, with all *good Conscience,* to decline ... writing meerly for a *Party.* ... Nor have I added unto the just Provocations for the Complaint . . . [t]hat the *greatest part of Histories* are but so many *Panegyricks* composed by *Interested Hands.*" Citing a vast array of ancient historians, emphasizing Tacitus and Polybius in particular, Mather noted, "I have not *Commended* any Person, but when I have really judg'd, not only *That* he *Deserved* it, but also that it would be a Benefit unto Posterity to know, Wherein he deserved it." Following Tacitus, Mather would not permit friendship to hinder his pursuit of truth; he would "mention many *Censurable* things, even in the Best of my Friends," although he preferred to "plead my *Polybius*" and stress positive examples, for "the Readers of History get more good by the Objects of their *Emulation than of their Indignation.*"[18]

The historians adopted the conventions of exemplary history both because they were convinced philosophically that people learned from historical example and because the theory provided an ideal framework for uniting their ethical and ideological convictions. The exemplary theory was not only right, it was useful. British cruelties during the war must be handed down "with redoubled infamy, when the tragic tale shall be faithfully transmitted to generations yet unborn," wrote Mercy Warren to Catharine Macaulay.[19] The historians thus joyfully embraced the principles of the exemplary theory because the theory required them to write what they longed to write: that the Revolution originated in British avarice against which the colonists responded with moral outrage and political and military resistance. The Revolution epitomized the exemplary theory itself, for it pitted the forces of virtue against those of avarice. As a result, the historians could feel satisfied that their works remained within the bounds of objectivity, for, as they saw it, they were partisans only of the ethical truth that the exemplary theory demanded. The exemplary theory also accomplished two further aims: it provided the historians' theory with its explanatory categories, and it laid the foundation for their use of historical writing as a mode of social and political criticism.

Explaining the Revolution: Virtue and Avarice

In the historians' version of the exemplary theory, "virtue" and "avarice" were the fundamental categories of historical analysis, the terms which historians properly used to interpret and shape events because they were the leading principles of human character. Believing that the study of history "requires a just knowledge of character," Mercy Warren outlined the characterological terms that constituted history's ethical dynamic:

> The study of the human character opens at once a beautiful and a deformed picture of the soul. We there find a noble principle implanted in the nature of man, that pants for distinction. This principle operates in every bosom, and when kept under the control of reason, and the influence of humanity, it produces the most benevolent effects. But when the checks of conscience are thrown aside, or the moral sense weakened by the sudden acquisition of wealth or power, humanity is obscured, and if a favorable coincidence of circumstances permits, this love of distinction often exhibits the most mortifying instances of profligacy, tyranny, and the wanton exercise of arbitrary sway.[20]

Warren tried here to unite traditional views of human nature with eighteenth-century environmentalism and the result is somewhat ambiguous. It is not clear whether she believed that human character is fundamentally virtuous and that evil is introduced environmentally, when various social conditions (notably the acquisition of wealth and power) operate against the "noble plant"; or whether she believed that virtue and avarice were equally basic to character, and that one or the other would be manifested to a greater degree under certain social conditions. In light of her preoccupation with avarice in history, it is surprising that she did not describe two "plants," one virtuous, the other avaricious; her failure to do so suggests that, while avarice is as fundamental in history as virtue, social conditions exert a preponderance of determining power.[21]

It is clear, however, that avarice was unavoidable in history because people are social beings who crave distinction from their fellows, notwithstanding their fundamental equality in nature. Equally clear, virtue and reason were inseparable, and both rested on the principle of self-discipline. Virtue is "the moderation and government" of the "appetites, desires, and passions, according to the rules of reason," wrote Bolingbroke; and therefore virtue was often in opposition to passion's "blind impulse." Warren wrote to her son James in virtually the same language, arguing that self-knowledge "teaches [us] to resist the impulse of appetite [and] to check the sallies of passion," leading us to happiness and rendering us "useful to society." Virtue was not for Warren or the other historians principally a religious concept, although they believed that true religion always counseled the cultivation of virtue.[22]

As historians, Warren and her colleagues were interested in virtue and avarice less as traits of individual character than as principles of society and history. Thus, while the exemplary theory traditionally lent itself most readily to biography, the historians elevated its basic terms into a historical dynamic. Unfortunately, history revealed that avarice usually got the better of virtue, for "ambition and avarice are *the leading springs* which

THE CULTIVATION OF VIRTUE

generally actuate the restless mind. From these *primary sources of corruption* have arisen all the rapine and confusion, the depredation and ruin, that have spread distress over the face of the earth from the days of Nimrod to Cesar, and from Cesar to an arbitrary prince of the house of Brunswick."[23] The historian had to recognize and applaud virtue when it appeared in history. But sadly, its appearances were infrequent because few people were guided by reason and concern for the public good. Thus history showed that when "private interest" is incompatible with "the ties of honor, or the principles of patriotism," ambition and avarice usually tipped the scales, and "it is not uncommon to see virtue, liberty, love of country, and regard to character, sacrificed at the shrine of wealth."[24]

Virtue and avarice were timeless and culturally universal because they were fundamental principles of human character. Unlike Good and Evil, however, they were not ideal or abstract concepts, for their observable manifestation in time constituted history's ethical dialectic. Thus they provided the historians an explanatory schema for analyzing not only the American Revolution but all of human history. The historians dwelled incessantly on the rise and fall of nations, particularly republics, and Mercy Warren saw in Geneva a striking example of how republics usually were undermined. Subversion there was accomplished not by a lone tyrant, but by "the pride of a few families, the ambition of individuals, and the supineness of the people." The few exercised such compelling authority over "the middling class of mankind" that "the mass of the people" was rendered "abject and servile."[25] The "middling-class," of course, should never become supine or inattentive of their political condition, and it was the responsibility of the republican historian to keep the people well informed, to point out the danger of tyranny, and to call the people back to virtue and reason whenever their rights were threatened. But the problem persisted in history: cowed by an avaricious minority, the people fall into a stupor of unconcern, and their voice "seldom breathes universal murmur, but when the insolence or the oppression of their rulers extorts the bitter complaint."[26]

As Warren indicated by her reference to "an arbitrary prince of the house of Brunswick," the historians' immediate concern was to explain the Revolution, and they did so in ethical terms. Upsetting the general harmony that had prevailed for most of a century and a half, George III and his ministers began in the 1760s to tie imperial policy to trade objectives, making the colonists virtual slaves of English merchants, the crown, and parliament. "During the infancy of their settlements, the poor colonists, were left to shift for themselves," wrote Timothy Pitkin, and Britain seemed "in a great measure, regardless of their fate." But as the colonies became more populous and wealthy, the mother country wanted a share, and no small one, of colonial profits. Like misers, "whose love of wealth increases with the means of acquiring it," English merchants and manufacturers viewed the colonists as easy prey to satisfy their avarice and became even more anxious to maintain a monopoly on American trade. As mercantile policy hardened, imperial measures also became more stringent. Instead of allowing the colonists to raise their own taxes by the voluntary consent of the people's representatives, George and his ministers, "grown giddy with the lustre of their own power," pursued "such weak, impolitic and unjust measures" that the colonists were compelled to resist. John Lendrum's conclusion seemed inescapable: the true cause of the Revolution was "the desire of power on the one hand, and the abhorrence of oppression on the other."[27]

The contrast between British avarice and American virtue grounded the theory that Britain (and Europe generally, until the French Revolution) was degenerating politically and culturally, whereas America was on the ascendancy. As early as 1774 Mercy Warren wrote to Hannah Lincoln: "You ask why did we urge on this sudden display of ministerial power? In return let me ask by whose avarice and ambition the people were precipitated to take some rash and unjustifiable steps?" The answer was obvious, she pointed out a year later: a nation that already was internally corrupt. It had long been her opinion that Britain's "venality and vice," its "corruption and wickedness" were "nearly compleat." In light of such corruption, the patriots' actions at Lexington and Concord could only be viewed as "the natural struggles which ensue when the genius of *liberty* arises to assert her rights in opposition to the ghost of Tyranny." In retrospect John Lendrum identified the signs of British degeneration even earlier, in 1763, when "the spirit of venality and corruption was remarkably prevalent." At that time, "licentiousness and riot were become general among the lower ranks; and tumults, and a spirit of disorder, affected most parts of the kingdom."[28]

Thus, precisely as earlier republics had fallen—Greece, the Achaean League, the Amphyctions, Rome, Venice, Geneva—so England's republicanism and freedom had waned since the accession of the first Stuart. England had become "an ungrateful, dissipated Nation," fallen into barbarism, her people in war "the ensigns of cruelty." In fact, Britain's degeneration was at no time more apparent than during the war. Hiring foreign mercenaries was only one clear sign. Another was British treatment of the colonial citizenry. The Bostonians, observed Warren in 1775, "are exposed to the daily insults of a foe, who seem not only to have lost that sense of honour, freedom, and valour once the characteristics of the British nation—but that generosity, and humanity, which has long been the boast of the most civilized parts of the world." The many atrocities attributed to British soldiers served to prove that pride, avarice, injustice, and ambition had become the emblems of British character.[29]

The question remained whether the Americans would, like the citizens of earlier republics, lie supine in the face of tyrany or whether they would discover the spirit of virtue and resist. "I tremble for the events of the present commotions," wrote Warren in 1774; "there must be a noble struggle to recover the existing liberties of our injured country; we must repurchase them at the expence of blood, or tamely acquiesce, and embrace the hand that holds out the chain to us and our children." The prospect was hazardous: it was uncertain "whether the Patriots of the present day will be able to effect their laudable designs in our time."[30]

In retrospect, however, the historians depicted the Americans manifesting the kind of virtue only rarely witnessed in history. Although a common maxim held that "a state of war has ever been deemed unfavourable to virtue," the Americans, at least until the late 1770s, displayed the virtues of patriotism, self-denial, industry, and prudence to an astonishing degree. It seemed to David Ramsay that "the war not only required, but created talents," and that British oppression "did more to re-establish the independence of [South Carolina] than could have been effected by the armies of Congress," for the citizens responded with resistance out of a native sense of liberty.[31] On the civil front virtue reigned supreme. The colonists answered British trade policies with boycotts and encouragements to domestic manufactures, wearing the products of their own looms as a badge of honor. In 1775, after England dissolved the government of Massachusetts, the people lived for more than a year "without any legal government, without law, and without any regular administration of justice, but what arose from the internal sense of moral obligation." With society "reduced nearly to a state of nature," it was "almost incredible, that the principles of rectitude and common justice should have been so generally influential." Yet virtue did prevail, and vice was "abashed" by the people's exemplary "moderation, disinterestedness, and generosity." For more than a decade, despite the threats to the very fabric of society and law, "it must be ascribed to the virtue of the people, however reluctant some may be to acknowledge this truth, that they did not feel the effects of anarchy in the extreme."[32]

Thus, the Revolution was properly to be explained in terms of virtue and avarice, terms which derived from the exemplary theory of history. But whereas the traditional theory tended to emphasize biographical studies in which particular persons were held up as *exempla* of virtue or vice, the historians expanded the theory by extracting its central principles and using them to build a view of history as a vast morality play in which the people's ideological commitments were inseparably wedded to their ethical conduct. The American Revolution was the most recent in a series of historical situations in which the lust for wealth and power attempted to subvert the principles of freedom. In this one, however, the oppressed resisted, manifesting almost unparalleled virtue in the face of a superior foe.

The historians easily explained the Revolution in terms of a simple moral opposition between American virtue and British avarice, an opposition that appears to subordinate ethical interpretation to ideological conviction. How else would zealous patriots rationalize the Revolution in retrospect? But that the ethical dimension of the histories was more than a convenient rationale is better understood by focusing on two crucial and related issues: first, the historians' anxiety that *America* was becoming avaricious, already manifesting the symptoms of decline; and second, the worrisome problem of distinguishing the American republic from all earlier ones, lest the logic of historical experience hold true and America decline precisely as they had. With respect to these issues the historians of the Revolution asserted themselves as revolutionary historians, writers who used historical narrative as an instrument of social and political criticism. For if the past was to be made comprehensible through the categories of virtue and avarice, the future still had to be lived in their terms—and the future was very much in doubt.

History as Exhortation

Thomas Jefferson expressed the same anxiety in concluding his discussion of religion in *Notes on Virginia* (1786) with a prophecy of America's future. Religious liberty was temporarily safe, he argued, because in the first flush of independence "the spirit of the times" would protect religion against pernicious legislation. But he predicted that the spirit of the times would alter: "Our rulers will become corrupt, our people careless. A single zealot may commence persecutor and better men be his victims." There seemed to be only one safe solution: "every essential right" of the people had to be fixed now, "while our rulers are honest, and ourselves united." Because, he warned, "from the conclusion of this war we shall be going down hill."[33]

The very metaphor "down hill" presaged an American decline precisely as Warren had outlined it. At the same time that the rulers become corrupt, the people "will forget themselves, but in the sole faculty of making money, and will never think of uniting to effect a due respect for their rights."[34] The historians' attitude toward the likelihood of American decline was even gloomier than Jefferson's, for they believed that the attempt to institutionalize the future by stabilizing rights constitutionally would prove fruitless without the precondition of a virtuous people. In three decades of correspondence and in their narratives, the historians revealed an insistent and impelling apprehension that American avarice was leading to corruption. Unlike the reviled Gibbon, who blindly refused to see the decline of Britain prefigured in the fall of Rome, the historians would learn through historical example; and it was clear to them that American degeneration was virtually inevitable, especially if decline were the natural phenomenon that many theorists assumed it was.

"Corruption," "decay," "degeneration," the terms most frequently used to describe the fall of republics, were borrowed from the language of nature and were laden with connotations of necessity. Like other eighteenth-century theorists who viewed history as a series of cycles, the anonymous author of "Thoughts on the Decline of States" argued in 1791 that all nations inevitably decline and die: "he must think little of the order of nature who sees not that all our efforts must be defeated at last, whether for the preservation of individuals, or the body politick." The logic of nature presented difficulties to the historians, for they sought to distinguish the American republic from all earlier ones. Thus, when they used naturalistic terms at all, they tended to agree with such writers as Joseph Galloway, who thought that, although the body politic is indeed "liable to disorders, which often terminate in death," *inevitable* decay could be avoided by performing "a radical cure."[35]

The historians also went a step further: they attempted to abandon the language of nature altogether by using an ethical and social language to account for decline. While traditional theory held that corruption acted like a cancer, metastasizing through the state, eating away at its vitals until the nation died, the historians centered their analysis in virtue and avarice—fundamentally societal, not natural, terms—in order to explain decline in a way that freed America's future from the teleology of nature. Since avarice was the cause of corruption, and since avarice manifested itself under certain social and political conditions, the historians' proper task was to exhort their compatriots to virtue, even as they pointed to the budding signs of corruption and decay.

The historians identified the symptoms of corruption in the decade following independence. The war, of course, played its insidious role, for war usually resulted in "a relaxation in virtue." "[B]ut such a total change of manners in so short a period, I believe was never known in the history of man," Warren wrote to John Adams in 1778. The people's indulgence in "rapacity and profusion, pride and servility, and almost every vice" evidenced their unwitting transformation into the avaricious and licentious Englishmen for whom they professed such abhorrence.[36]

The problem was that avarice, once introduced into society, led to corruption of a systemic nature, infecting not only the manners of individuals but society's ethical and political order as well. Burning with frustration, Warren wrote to John Adams in 1786: "Emancipated from a foreign yoke, the blessings of peace just restored upon honourable terms, with the liberty of forming our own governments, framing our own laws, choosing our own magistrates, and adopting manners the most favourable to freedom and happiness, yet sorry I am to say I fear we have not virtue sufficient to avail ourselves of these superior advantages." Republicanism and independence "are nearly dwindled into theory," she observed a few months later. Republicanism is "defaced by a spirit of anarchy," while independence is "almost annihilated" by "private ambition and a rage for the accumulation of wealth," which amounted to "a kind of public gambling." Democracy "would be a good form of government, could virtue be preserved immaculate, and property be always distributed equally," wrote Ébenezer Hazard to Jeremy Belknap in 1784; "but in our present circumstances it is *monstrum horrendum, informe, ingens.*"[37]

Heedless of the dialectic between private ambition and public calamity, Americans blithely ignored the symptoms of decline. But William Gordon saw them clearly and argued that *"the fraud, the peculation, and the profusion"* practiced by the people *"have done us more injury than the whole force of our foreign enemies."* All the signs of avarice pointed to one painful end, concluded David Ramsay: "Riches are not a blessing to a people"; they tend to corrupt the mind and degrade the morals, disqualifying a nation from "accomplishing any great undertakings."[38]

For a decade the historians perceived the signs of discord and degeneration. Clearly, something had to be done if disaster were to be averted. David Ramsay's suggestion went to the heart of the historians' project. He called upon the press, the pulpit, and "all the powers of Eloquence . . . to counter-act that ruinous propensity we have for foreign superfluities & to excite us to the long neglected virtues of Industry & frugality."[39] Historical writing was just such an instrument of eloquence, and it was precisely in this context that Warren wrote of her anxiety over the rising generation and called for the vigor of "all the old republicans." Indeed, it was precisely in this context of imminent decline that she wrote of the enormous social and political significance of the historian:

> It is an unpleasing part of history, when "corruption begins to prevail, when degeneracy marks the manners of the people, and weakens the sinews of the state." If this should ever become the deplorable situation of the United States, let some unborn histo-

rian, in a far distant day, detail the lapse, and hold up the contrast between a simple, virtuous, and free people, and a degenerate, servile race of beings, corrupted by wealth, effeminated by luxury, impoverished by licentiousness, and become the *automatons* of intoxicated ambition.[40]

That far distant day had obviously arrived, for it was clear to the historians that the generation who had suffered British oppression, declared independence, mobilized America's forces for war, and created new state constitutions was being superseded by a younger generation who were sacrificing liberty and virtue on the altar of private ambition. To this rising generation the historians addressed their histories in a mixture of condemnation and hope that moral suasion and the examples of the old republicans would turn attention back to the virtues of the revolutionaries. The histories were thus radically contemporary documents, less concerned with the past itself than with its bearing on the present and future.

Thus, the signs of decline the historians observed between 1777 and 1786 found their way into the histories, for if the past held out lessons they had to be made public. John Lendrum and David Ramsay seized on the period of the late 1770s when depreciation of the currency had transformed paper money into what Mercy Warren called "immense heaps of paper trash." It was a time, Lendrum contended, that "the morals of the people were corrupted beyond any thing that could have been believed prior to the event." Even as "the paper currency in Philadelphia was daily sinking . . . yet an assembly, a concert, a dinner, or supper, which cost two or three hundred pounds, did not only take men off from acting, but even from thinking of what ought to have been nearest their hearts."[41] Ramsay was saddened and frustrated that in those years of licentiousness the virtuous suffered most. With the reversal of "the commonly received maxims of prudence and economy," the virtuous man, concerned with his neighbors' welfare, refused to pay his debts in depreciated currency, preferring to risk his reputation as well as his fortune against a day when he would repay them in dearer money. But at the same time, "many bold adventurers made fortunes in a short time by running in debt beyond their abilities. Prudence ceased to be a virtue, and rashness usurped its place. The warm friends of America, who never despaired of their country, and who cheerfully risked their fortunes in its support, lost their property, while the timid, who looked forward to the re-establishment of British government, not only saved their former possessions, but often increased them." In a grisly echo of the popular song "The World Turned Upside Down," Ramsay observed: "In the American revolution for the first time the friends of the successful party were the losers."[42] Such financial problems were precisely ethical problems, for the evils produced by currency fluctuations struck at the principle of virtue, eradicated the people's commitment to honor and justice, and turned their attention "from the sober paths of industry to extravagant adventures and romantick projects."[43]

Motivating these statements about American decline is the zeal of the revolutionary-as-historian who believes that narrative history is an instrument of ideology and ethics. Revolutionary history would prove to be instructive only if it exhorted future generations not to forget, for the tendency of avarice was to engender a kind of collective amnesia. As a result, Warren argued, echoing her Puritan ancestors, "the inhabitants of America cease to look back with due gratitude and respect on the fortitude and virtue of their ancestors, who, through difficulties almost insurmountable, planted them in a happy soil."[44] Consistent with the exemplary theory, the historians fashioned the revolutionaries and the settlers as *exempla* of virtue, the standard against which the rising generation was to be measured. It was hardly a contest. One of the historians' most successful rhetorical strategies was to turn to the younger generation with a vengeance, detailing their lapses from the standard of the forebears while at the same time bespeaking their optimism that all was not yet lost, that American youth could still learn from the failures of others before it was too late.[45]

The historians compared the rising generation with the

settlers and the revolutionaries in order to establish hegemony over the future. They sought not merely to influence how future generations would interpret the Revolution, but, more important, to establish the very categories within which interpretation was properly to be conducted. It was bad enough that the rising generation already was acting avariciously; it would be worse yet if they were permitted to abandon altogether the ethical terms in which revolutionary history was to be understood. And they showed signs of doing just that, for in addition to adopting new manners they were adopting "new ideas" that, "from a rivalry of power and a thirst for wealth, had prepared the way to corruption, and the awakened passions were hurried to new images of happiness. The simpler paths which they had trodden in pursuit of competence and felicity, were left to follow the fantastic fopperies of foreign nations, and to sigh for the distinctions acquired by titles, instead of that real honor which is ever the result of virtue."[46] Even as the revolutionaries fought for human freedom and dignity, some Americans engaged in factitious politics, placing party over the public good. Others were corrupted by a European love of distinction and the splendor of courts, undermining republicanism itself. In short, "avarice without frugality, and profusion without taste, were indulged, and soon banished the simplicity and elegance which had formerly reigned."[47]

Future generations might dispute this grim picture of political, ethical, and social decline, but dispute would only confirm the historians' major point: that the Revolution was properly to be interpreted in the ethical categories of virtue and avarice, in the language of simplicity, elegance, competence, and felicity, as against rivalry, corruption, and passion. This was the language of exhortation, indeed of the jeremiad. To write the history of the Revolution was an imperative of the Revolution itself in much the way that Puritan historians saw the writing of history as an imperative enjoined by God. The Puritan analogy is further instructive for, insofar as they were exhortations, the histories challenged future generations to live up to the standard of the forebears. In addition, the historians' constant harping on wealth, luxury, artificial distinctions, and power echoed the Puritans' insistence that worldliness, particularly the pursuit of material gain, was the greatest threat to the holy commonwealth. The historians' use of the exemplary theory thus followed the tradition of didacticism in American historiography from the mid-seventeenth century to the Great Awakening and provided a thread of continuity between the Puritans and the revolutionaries.[48]

Progress and the Problem of Stasis

The historians' persistent emphasis on avarice in history strongly suggests that they refused to adopt the notions of historical progress emerging in Enlightenment Europe.[49] Progress required more optimism than they could muster and more than they thought was strategically sound. Their use of the exemplary theory, their view of the historian's ethical and prophetic roles, and their sense of the imminent possibility of catastrophe all militated against the notion of progress. Faith in historical progress was simply incompatible with their ethical and ideological commitments. J. B. Bury has set forth in his now classic formulation the idea of progress as a theory "which involves a synthesis of the past and a prophecy of the future," one "which regards man as slowly advancing . . . in a definite and desirable direction, and infers that this progress will continue indefinitely."[50]

Several aspects of the histories lead logically toward an idea of progress as Bury outlined it, particularly the depiction of an American past that revealed a steady growth of self-government. But the idea is effectively undermined by the historians' repudiation of any notion that mankind was destined to advance gradually in a definite and desirable direction. If anything, they believed that the reverse was true, that history contained no interior principle leading to human betterment, for all past republics had been eaten away from within by corruption caused by avarice, and no subsequent republic had been capable of founding itself on the failures of earlier ones. (Indeed, this was a principal factor in the historians' failure to discover a "shape" in history.) America, it appeared, would be no exception if the early signs of avarice were genuine presages of a trend.

Equally important, perhaps more so, the historians had no stake in showing abstractly that history was progressive. For it was precisely such comfortable ideas that lulled people into a false sense of security or, worse yet, provided them with a rationale for avarice, as if civilization would progress regardless of what they did. The historians repudiated any principle—call it Progress or Providence—that guaranteed the course of the future at the expense of wresting control and responsibility from people's hands.

Yet short of accepting a concept of historical progress, the historians generally wrote optimistically. To do so was part of the strategy of exhortation. Even a jeremiad could not be a story of unrelieved gloom lest it inculcate despair; exhortation demanded at least the possibility of a desirable future. Thus, at the same time that they depicted the rising generation declining from the ethical and ideological standard of the revolutionaries, they held out the hope of a resurgence of American virtue, painting the future as a realm of opportunity.

Consistent with their philosophical commitment to human efficacy, the historians wrote of the promise of the Revolution even as they condemned the younger generation for threatening to undermine it. They did this in order to point simultaneously to the people's responsibility for what was wrought and to their own sense of the value of their histories as exhortations. "[T]he rising generation will have an opportunity of observing the result of an experiment in politics, which before has never been fairly made," wrote David Ramsay. At the same time, however, he pointed with caution to the historical context out of which the Constitution emerged, a history of almost universal failure. "The experience of former ages has given many melancholy proofs, that the popular governments have seldom answered in practice to the theories and warm wishes of their admirers."[51] Challenge—indeed threat—was as conspicuous in Ramsay's statements as was promise. "Citizens of the United States!" he wrote in a hortatory aside designed to make more immediate his relationship with his audience:

> you have a well-balanced constitution established by general consent, which is an improvement on all republican forms of government heretofore established. It possesses the good qualities of monarchy, but without its vices. The wisdom and stability of an aristocracy, but without the insolence of hereditary masters. The freedom and independence of a popular assembly, . . . but without the capacity of doing those mischiefs which result from uncontrolled power in one assembly. The end and object of it is public good. *If you are not happy it will be your own fault.*[52]

Similarly, despite her many devastating pronouncements on American avarice, Mercy Warren realized that for her *History* to be viable as exhortation it had to speak to the future's positive possibilities. Clearly addressing the generation of 1800, she announced: "[A] new century has dawned upon us. . . . From the revolutionary spirit of the times, the vast improvements in science, arts, and agriculture, the boldness of genius that marks the age, the investigation of new theories, and the changes in the political, civil, and religious characters of men, succeeding generations have reason to expect still more astonishing exhibitions in the next."[53] Warren wrote this hopefulness back in time, attributing it to the revolutionaries throughout their efforts to secure independence. But at the same time she stressed a guarded optimism because the nation's virtue still required vigilant protection. Despite the advantages that may derive from the new Constitution, "yet it is necessary to guard at every point, against the intrigues of artful or ambitious men, who may subvert the system." The people had every reason to congratulate themselves on the success of their Revolution and on the spirit in which they achieved it. But they now had to solidify their gains "by a strict adherence to the principles of the revolution, and the practice of every public, social and domestic virtue."[54] These statements are written in the style of the secular jeremiad, at once a challenge and a hope.

The sense of threat, however, predominated. For even after hostilities had ended, it remained unclear whether a union could be consolidated under free modes of government. Indeed, it remained uncertain whether such government, if it could be established, "would be administered agreeable to laws founded on the beautiful theory of republicanism." For although we may have acquired the jewel of liberty today, Warren wrote, scarcely veiling the challenge to her readers, "perhaps to-morrow the world may be convinced, that mankind know not how to make a proper use of the prize, generally bartered in a short time, as a useless bauble, to the first officious master that will take the burden from the mind, by laying another on the shoulders of ten-fold weight." This, as Warren repeatedly pointed out, was what usually happened in history: "The game of deception is played over and over" to mislead people's judgments and tempt their enthusiasms "until by their own consent, hereditary crowns and distinctions are fixed, and some scion of royal descent is entailed upon them forever."[55]

The threat was clear enough as the historians outlined it. But what could be done to reverse the pernicious tendencies to which they pointed? Historians and political scientists have traditionally argued that America's revolutionaries attempted to avoid the failures of earlier republics by establishing a properly mixed mode of government. They tried to overcome what they saw as institutional failures by erecting more perfect institutions.[56] This, in fact, was the principal means of avoiding the logic of nature, for it substituted a political framework and language for the then-conventional natural ones. The traditional theory had much to recommend it. No less an optimist about man's educability than Thomas Jefferson, comparing people's potential for self-discipline and need for external political constraints, felt that the latter were imperative. To Edmund Pendleton he wrote: "The fantastical idea of virtue and the public good being a sufficient security to the state against the commission of crimes, which you say you have heard insisted on by some, I assure you was never mine."[57] Nor would it have been for the man who argued for the institutionalization of rights and obligations now, once and for all, "while our rulers are honest and ourselves united."

John Adams was, with James Madison, the most articulate exponent of mixed government and the political constraints that he thought inhered in it. In a letter to Mercy Warren he argued, as he did throughout his political writings, that the only way for America to avoid the decline of earlier republics was to establish such a balance. "My pictures of the confusions and dissolutions [of past republics] were of republics ill constituted, improperly mixed, or not mixed at all; and this with the single view of convincing my countrymen of the necessity and duty of constituting their republics with such balances as would protect them from tyranny in every form. . . . Republics well constituted have been the best governments in the world, but republics ill-constituted have been the worst."[58] Adams and Jefferson were hardly unconcerned with virtue. They believed that a well-ordered republic gained strength and vitality from the voluntary self-discipline of its citizens. Nevertheless, one could more securely depend upon external political controls than on the people's virtue.[59]

By the same token, as students of political philosophy, the historians were thoroughly imbued with enlightened social and political theories concerning the value of balanced government. Indeed, as Mercy Warren made clear to John Adams, a well-constituted republic, one "established on the genuine principles of equal liberty," did more than merely guard the people against their own excesses. It actually produced "many excellent qualities, and heroic virtues in human nature—which often lie dormant for want of opportunities for exertion." But Warren qualified her statement with an observation that reasserted the fundamental priority of ethicality to institutionalization, adding, "I have my *fears,* that American virtue has not yet reached that sublime pitch which is necessary to baffle the designs of the

artful, to counteract the weakness of the timid, or to resist the pe-
cuniary temptations and ambitious wishes that will arise in the
breast of many."[60] Adams, of course, had the same fears, which
was precisely why he turned to governmental form as a remedy.
But implicit in Warren's statement, as it is in all the criticisms
leveled by the historians, is the belief that, while the form of
government is of obvious importance, a republic is *impossible*
without a virtuous people. They took Montesquieu's injunction
seriously, emphasizing the word "necessary" in the last sentence:
"There is no great share of probity necessary to support a
monarchical or despotic government. The force of laws in one,
and the prince's arm in the other, are sufficient to direct and
maintain the whole. But in a popular state, one spring more is
necessary, namely virtue."[61]

The ideal government was a republic in which the people were
virtuous: the form would reflect and be strengthened by the
people's virtue, and the virtue of the people would be enhanced
and perpetuated by the form—thus the people and their institutions would reflect one another, as in parallel mirrors, to infinity. But experience taught that such static visions were doomed
to failure, and that there was no escape from the vicissitudes of
history. As the historians saw it, it was chimerical to believe that
America could avoid the failures of past republics merely by
creating a mixed government. Thus, while the politicians addressed themselves to matters of statecraft, the historians would
use their writings to inculcate that virtue which they saw as the
mainspring of the republic.

The historians' ethical project was simplicity itself. At its heart
was their aim to assert the primacy of people's responsibility for
the future. This was the lesson of the revolutionaries who, it
should be remembered, "procured their own emancipation
from foreign thraldom, by the sacrifice of their heroes and their
friends," and who had "by inconceivable labor and exertion obtained the prize."[62] The historians sought no guarantees save
virtue itself for the people's future conduct—not in nature (the

logic of which pointed to decline in any case), nor in such over-arching principles as Progress, nor even in government itself. There was, as they saw it, no way to institutionalize the future. It would have to be lived, as the revolutionaries had lived it, as strenuous republicans in the face of contingency.

8

The Romance of the Revolution

History is almost always written by the winners, by articulate members of a society's dominant group who seek to legitimate the exalted status of that group, and either to rationalize the status quo or at least to define the parameters within which future change is properly to occur. The revolutionary histories are no exception. In them we hear the voices of history's winners, confidently asserting the validity of their heroes' actions and the legitimacy of their authority. The historians sought to justify the Revolution, to validate a particular constellation of ideological and cultural principles, and to establish, they insisted, the only legitimate set of conceptual and explanatory categories that future generations could use to discover the truth of their revolutionary past. We should expect no less of history's winners.

Yet if we reasonably expect "winners' history" to justify, validate, legitimate, and rationalize, it is rarely obvious how its authors accomplish these aims. The important issue is not *whether* historians encode their works with philosophical, ideological, and cultural values, it is *how* they do so. "[T]he test of every revolutionary movement," writes Northrop Frye, "comes when it must establish continuity with what has preceded it."[1] To pass that test the revolutionary historians employed various strategies, some subtle and inventive, others blatant and transparent. To justify the Revolution, for example, they altered the traditional theory of Natural Law, forcing a difficult philosophical problem to yield to a fertile and imaginative approach. At the same time, however, they also relied on the crudest sort of conspiracy theory, a kind of demonology—the effectiveness of which may be evidenced in the massive neglect of the Loyalists for nearly two centuries—which only history's winners could unblushingly support. Similarly, the historians displayed great ingenuity when, in their efforts to validate the principles of republicanism, they described history in terms of a complex dialectic involving the interaction of ideology, ethics, and language. But at the same time, those efforts to validate republican ideology easily degenerated into a simplistic view of history as a struggle between good guys and bad guys, Us and Them—once again, winners' history.

Of all the strategies the historians employed, none is more important nor more difficult to assess than that of narrative form itself, for narrative is at once the subtlest and most conventional mode of historical presentation. I argued in Chapter 6 that the historians eagerly tied the language and style of historical writing to the ideology of the Revolution in order to create a distinctively American historiography that was capable of rendering republican experience. The historians recognized that history's lessons were subtly tinted by the shades of meaning conveyed through language, images, and modes of description, quite apart from the overt statements they might make about events. Still more than in language and style, however, the historians injected values and principles in the very form in which they told their story. For narrative form is not merely a conduit through which arguments are made and facts related; it is in itself, argues Louis O. Mink, "a primary cognitive instrument" rivalled "only by theory and by metaphor as irreducible ways of making the flux of experience comprehensible." Through narrative, "a story generates its own imaginative space," and while historiographers may properly concern themselves with the truth claims of specific statements in a narrative, the narrative, by virtue of its form, makes claims about a truth that transcends its individual statements, a truth that inheres in the complex form of the narrative itself. In short, "the cognitive function of narrative form . . . is not just to relate a succession of events but to body forth an ensemble of interrelationships of many different kinds as a single whole."[2]

In what form did the revolutionary historians narrate their history? "In every age the ruling social or intellectual class tends to project its ideals in some form of romance," Northrop Frye observes, "where the virtuous heroes and beautiful heroines represent the ideals and the villains the threats to their ascendancy."[3] The revolutionary histories are indeed romances, heroic stories of adventure and overcoming, for only romance could simultaneously capture "the truth" of the Revolution and make it accessible to future generations in an endlessly repeatable story. Before outlining the romance of the Revolution, it is necessary to clear away some theoretical underbrush in which eighteenth-century romance is entangled.

Presentation and Representation:
Romance and Historical Truth

As legend had it, when Sir Walter Raleigh was locked up in the Tower of London he witnessed one day a drama occurring in the yard beneath his window. The next day he related what he saw to a visitor, describing the incident in detail and the instantaneous conclusions he drew as an eyewitness. One man, whom Raleigh judged from his dress to be an officer, was assaulted by another. Before falling, the officer managed to draw his sword and to stab his assailant. Knocked senseless, the officer was carried away "by the servants of justice," while the lifeless body of his assailant was removed by others, "apparently his friends," through the crowd that had gathered.

Raleigh's visitor was shocked at the account, not because it depicted a bloody and violent scene, but because Raleigh was "perfectly mistaken in his whole story." The visitor challenged every detail of the narrative, observing that Raleigh's

> officer was no officer, but a servant of a foreign ambassador; that this apparent officer gave the first blow; that he did not draw his sword, but the other drew it, and it was wrested out of his hands, but not till after he had run its owner through the body with it: that after this, a foreigner in the mob knocked the murderer down, in order that he should not escape: that some foreigners had carried off the servant's body: and that orders had arrived from court for the murderer to be tried instantly, and no favour shown, as the person murdered was one of the principal attendants of the Spanish ambassador.

Upset by his friend's challenges, Raleigh hastened to defend his perceptions. "Sir, I may be mistaken as to the officership of the murderer, yet," he insisted, "I know of a certainty, that all my other circumstances are strictly true; because I was a spectator of the whole transaction, which passed on that very spot opposite, where you see a stone of the pavement a little raised above the rest." Whatever satisfaction he may have derived from his defense was short-lived, however, for his friend replied: "Sir Walter, upon that very stone did I stand during the whole affair, and received this little scratch in my cheek, in wresting the sword out of the fellow's hand: and as I shall answer to God, you are totally mistaken." When his friend had departed, Raleigh, shaken by the discussion, looked at his manuscript *History of the World* and pondered: "How many falsehoods are here? If I cannot judge of the truth of an event that passes under my eyes, how shall I truly narrate those which have passed thousands of years before my birth?" and consigned the manuscript to the fire.[4]

Raleigh acted rashly in destroying his history, and if we believe his friend's version of the story rather than Raleigh's we fall into the same trap that Raleigh did, one carefully laid by John Pinkerton, who related the story in 1785. Three stories are told in the anecdote (if we exclude my version of it): Raleigh's and his

THE CULTIVATION OF VIRTUE

friend's, which operate on the same assumptions, and Pinkerton's, which is a story about storytelling and which denies those assumptions. Both Raleigh and his friend—and we, if we believe the friend's story—tacitly assume that a narrative can be said to square with the reality which it attempts to bespeak, and that among the tests of narrative truth-telling, the proximity of the narrator to the actual events is significant. Since Raleigh's friend was physically closer to the scene than Raleigh was, his version must be more accurate. But Pinkerton's aim in relating (or inventing) the anecdote was to present a far deeper challenge to narrative truth claims, for, as he put it, "there is no such thing as truth of fact, or historical truth, known to man. History is merely a species of romance, founded on events which really happened; but the bare events as stated by chronologists are alone true; their causes, circumstances, and effects, as detailed by historians, depend entirely on the fancy of the relater." Since not even one's participation in an event, much less one's proximity to it, could guarantee that one's narrative of it would be truer than another's, Pinkerton challenged even the notion that there are degrees of historical accuracy or veracity. He exempted from his theory only "a certain species of truth, which consists in the relation and connection of things," in "the propriety and consistence[y] of event of character, of sentiment, of language." This species of truth we commonly associate with poetry and novels, not histories, and Pinkerton hammered home his point with self-consciously mocking perverseness: "the whole truth known to man, and not subject to his senses, must be found only in works of fiction."[5]

One can interpret Pinkerton's brief essay on several levels, two of which are important for my purposes. First, we can view it as a relativist challenge to conventional historical epistemology, for the notion that writing itself alters the strict truth of bare events radically undermines the historian's traditional mimetic assumption that the language and form of a narrative can "re-present" external (or extra-textual) reality. Since, for Pinkerton, the mode of presentation qualifies that which is presented, historical truth and knowledge could no longer be seen as functions of historical facts outside the narrative; instead, truth and knowledge (of a different kind) could be seen only as possibilities of the language, form, and interior structures and relations of the narrative itself. In addition, of course, Pinkerton's anecdote mocked historians' claims to objectivity and impartiality, for it questioned the accounts even of eyewitnesses to historical events.

It is clear that the revolutionary historians rejected the kind of philosophical challenge that Pinkerton's views presented. Had they directly engaged his theory they almost certainly would have dismissed it, pointing to it (as they pointed to Gibbon's "novel") as another clear sign of Britain's cultural degeneration. The historians were very much aware that partisan political bias could impede the quest for truth and fatally mar a narrative. But writing as such was another matter and, as practitioners rather than theorists, they took for granted that the aim of historical writing was "to improve the understanding, and correct the various passions of the human soul," whereas the aim of novels and romances was "only to amuse." Indeed, "the more extravagant, absurd, and ridiculous a novel is, the greater is the probability of its success."[6]

On a second, less volatile level, however, Pinkerton's theory represented more of an invitation than a challenge. To say that history was a species of romance and that the consistency, cogency, and persuasiveness of a narrative's interior structures and relationships were crucial tests of its truth, was merely to say that a narrative's form was as important as its content. If the epistemological issue was debatable, on the literary issue they all agreed: the story one wished to tell had to be told in some narrative form, and the form of the story was crucial to its effectiveness. The historians associated language and style with ideological principles; they clothed the truth in a fashion that would improve its beauties. David Ramsay went a step further, drawing a formal analogy between what novelists and historians do: "Novel writers take fiction & make it a vehicle of their opinions on a variety of subjects. I take truth & the facts of history for the same purpose."[7] Although Ramsay was too little aware of the implications of his statement, he was clearly committed to using art in historical writing, not *despite* his devotion to truth and objectivity but *because* of it, for the purpose of art was to serve truth.

The two levels on which I have interpreted Pinkerton's theory involve competing (though potentially complementary) notions of truth and a working definition of "romance" corresponding to each.[8] On the first (or epistemological) level, Pinkerton explicitly rejected the idea that historical narratives could be truthful because they could never establish a direct relationship between the world-of-the-narrative and the world-of-real-events. On this level truth means the traditionally accepted notion of "objective truth," that which is truthful independent of anyone's speaking or writing it. Thus, when he refers to history as "*merely* a species of romance," he clearly means to contrast romance with the truth of facts, the same contrast William Gordon held up from the other side when he wrote to George Washington that he was after "genuine truth and not a fairy tale." Romance on this level means fabrication, distortion, the attempt to make fabulous what one usually assumes to be concrete and real. Nothing could be further from the then-prevailing understanding of historical writing.[9]

On the second (call it the literary) level, truth means something like the believability or persuasiveness of a narrative; unconcerned with any possible relationship between narrative and world, it involves what happens "inside" the narrative to constitute its consistency and cogency. On this level Pinkerton offers no definition of romance. Yet he implies one because his whole point in telling the Raleigh anecdote is to chide historians for believing that their histories could get any closer than a romance could to truth of fact, or historical truth, and because he insists that a literary theory of truth, associated with romance, remains possible. Romance on this level may be regarded as a particular form or genre of narrative, and, even though Pinkerton does not tell us precisely what the genre looks like, he clearly implies that specific examples of it can achieve their own truth by fulfilling his criteria: by being concerned with "the relation and connection of things," with "the propriety and consistence[y] of event, of character, of sentiment, of language." In short, Pinkerton's theory of romance involves the credibility of a certain kind of story and therefore its potential effectiveness. If one narrates one's story persuasively, one can let its relationship to "reality" take care of itself (meaning, presumably, that one can let one's readers supply it).

The revolutionary historians were unwilling to go quite that far. They were committed to using their histories to serve the Revolution and they would never (at least explicitly) give up the assumption that narratives could reflect external reality. Yet they did write a species of romance and they did so for exactly the same ideological and cultural reasons that prompted them to write history in the first place. For only a romance, understood as a particular kind of story, *could* serve the Revolution as the historians meant to serve it. Precisely as they associated the language and style of historical writing with republican ideology and the constellation of values that suffused it, they believed that the ideology and values of the Revolution were bound to the form in which its history was narrated. Indeed, if art were to serve life at all, the historians had to emplot their histories as romances, for only a romance could narrate a heroic story of overcoming which ended successfully and therefore support the historians' aim to establish interpretive hegemony over the future.

Ideology, Romance, and Myth

"What a tale will the page of history unfold when it shall faithfully transmit to the ear of posterity the rapine and devastation of the present aera," exclaimed Mercy Warren, making clear that histories aim to tell a story.[10] If one follows Northrop Frye and others in beginning with the notion that narratives purpose to tell a story, one must acknowledge that a story—any story—must be told according to certain conventions of storytelling.[11] Since there are many stories to tell, the particular set of conventions that governs any given narrative depends, in the first place, on the *kind* of story being told. Except on those rare (and often momentous) occasions when we confront a narrative that seeks to undermine a set of conventions or to blur traditional lines between genres, we expect that stories will be "conventional"—that tragedies will be identifiably tragic (and not comic) and that satires will be satiric (and not romantic).[12] In the second place, Hayden White has argued brilliantly that there are in historical narratives "elective affinities" between "modes of emplotment," "modes of argumentation," and "modes of ideological implication." By this he means that the kind of story being narrated (Romantic, Tragic, Comic, Satiric) tends to affiliate most naturally with certain assumptions and categories of historical explanation (Formist, Mechanistic, Organicist, Contextualist) and with the author's (or narrating persona's) ideological position (Anarchist, Radical, Conservative, Liberal).[13]

As White has argued, "Precisely because the historian is not (or claims not to be) telling the story 'for its own sake,' he is inclined to emplot his stories in the most conventional forms—as fairy tale or detective story on the one hand, as Romance, Comedy, Tragedy, or Satire on the other."[14] Without in the least denying that historians are often highly self-conscious, one may still contend that they typically "fall into"conventions of storytelling, relatively unaware that they are telling a conventional story at all. Their stories may thus be said to be *preformulated*: precisely as they see history through lenses already ground to refract their ideological judgments and explanatory assumptions, they see history in terms of a pre-established story or mode of emplotment. To say that the revolutionary historians wrote a kind of romance, then, is to say that the history of the Revolution was already emplotted romantically for them even before they began writing. Romance was the perfect vehicle for the Revolution's history because it was the mode of emplotment that squared with the historians' apprehension of the period's truth.

As a heroic story of struggle and overcoming, the romance of the Revolution is, to use White's working definition of the term, "fundamentally a drama of self-identification," a drama of "the triumph of good over evil, of virtue over vice, of light over darkness." In most of the histories the story of the Revolution is a "quest-romance," an adventure story centering in a fundamental conflict which represents the pivotal phase in a larger romance.[15] The larger romance of America can be simplified into three main stages:[16] a beginning period (usually 1620–1763) in which we see the birth of the colonies in struggle and adventure, and their developing sense of political and cultural identity, self-reliance, and autonomy amid general peace and security; a second period (usually 1763–1783) centering in the *agon* or conflict between the protagonist (or hero) and the antagonist, which arises because the antagonist threatens the situation and identity of the hero, and which issues in a struggle for independence; and a third period (usually 1783–1787) in which the hero's victory is assured, his identity re-established, and he is exalted. This simple sketch does not yet describe a romance necessarily, for it still involves elements that are potentially tragic or comic (as, indeed, the completed romance will). Crucial to the story's success as a romance is the historians' treatment of the conflict itself. But the story is already decisively not a satire, for if we continue to agree that the historians were committed to the principles of the successful Revolution they depicted, then satire could only betray that commitment.[17]

At the heart of the larger story is the quest-romance, the essential feature of which is the conflict ending in the hero's success. Frye has suggested that the quest proceeds through three major phases: "the stage of the perilous journey and the preliminary minor adventures; the crucial struggle, usually some kind of battle[;] and the exaltation of the hero."[18] The histories generally follow this basic design with respect to the crucial years of conflict between 1763 and 1787. In the twelve years between 1763 and the outbreak of war in 1775, Britain, clearly bent on world domination, threatens the constitutional and political identity of the colonists, throwing into doubt the tradition of self-rule they had taken for granted for more than a century. The constitutional debates over the Stamp Act, Townshend Duties, and Intolerable Acts reveal the colonists' growing apprehension of threat and disorder, a kind of spiritual disorientation born of their innocent faith in Britain's commitment to the ancient constitution. Perceiving that their assertion of traditional rights is scorned and that Britain's threat means slavery and destruction, the colonists are thrown back into the state of nature where force must be met with force or abject submission. In resistance the seeds of national unity and identity are sown.

Threat and resistance give way to the period of the battle, from Lexington and Concord in April 1775, to Yorktown in October 1781 (or, variously, the Treaty of Paris in 1783). During this stage the protagonist fights a life-and-death struggle against overwhelming odds, his discipline and will tested against the evil giant determined to destroy him. In struggle all concealments and disguises are cast off: the British are unmasked as barbarians (shading at times into demons), the Americans as virtuous warriors (shading at times, particularly in the case of George Washington, into demigods). And in struggle occurs transformation: plunged into the dark world of death and destruction, the once-innocent hero learns that he must fight without hesitation, trusting to nothing but his own valor, both to preserve his existence and to re-establish his identity.[19]

Finally, the hero tested and successful in battle, the dragon mutilated and dying if not yet dead, the years between 1783 and 1787 mark the victorious return of peace, the birth of a vision of future glory, and the solidification of the hero's identity. While this critical period is clearly characterized as one of conflict,[20] the conflict resembles that of a comedy rather than a tragedy, because it issues in one of two major symbols of national unity and identity: the Constitution of 1787, or the apotheosis of George Washington who, flowers strewn in his charger's path, rides triumphantly to Philadelphia to lead the new nation.[21]

The great virtue of this story is its simplicity; it is recognizable as a romance among romances, from fable and folklore, from St. George and the Dragon to Scott's Waverley Novels. Its intent is less to inform than to persuade—or, in persuading to inform. For the historians' aim was not to instruct the people in the facts of the Revolution, since they clearly presupposed that everyone then living already knew the facts and that future generations would learn them in due course.[22] The issue was from *whose* story people would learn: *whose* version of the past would emerge dominant? *which* story would hold sway over the future? By writing romance the historians meant to create the "accepted" version of the Revolution. In their romance they would attempt to gather their version of the past with their vision of the future, fusing both in an accessible and comprehensive story that would convey the ideological and cultural values of the revolutionaries and thus provide a source of sustenance for the future.[23]

Romance was the best vehicle for such an aim in part because a romance, like a revolution itself, generally polarizes actions and characters into ethical opposites. Romance thus avoids ethical ambiguity; its characters are rarely subtle, tending to be either for or against the quest. "If they assist it they are idealized as simply gallant or pure; if they obstruct it they are caricatured as simply villainous or cowardly. Hence every typical character in romance tends to have his moral opposite confronting him, like black and white pieces in a chess game."[24] The historians rarely depicted such stark figures, preferring a more credible "realistic" romance.[25] But, as I suggested in Chapter 7, the image of a morality play in which virtuous Americans are pitted against avaricious Britons supports the idea of polarization. Such simple moral dichotomizing could only enhance the story's accessibility, for whatever complexity and ambiguity the historians built upon it are insufficient to obscure its "simplifying of moral facts."[26]

The point of outlining some of the key structural and moral elements of the story of the Revolution is not to reduce the histories to "mere stories." If anything the reverse is true, for to demonstrate that historical stories serve philosophical, ideological, and cultural ends is to show that the historians could not hope to tie together the revolutionaries' aspirations with their actions without elevating their story to the level of a comprehensive historical statement. That the story of the Revolution—or of any revolution, for that matter—should have been structured as a romance is by no means a foregone conclusion. It is a romance only because it was written by historians who supported the principles and values of the Revolution and who depicted a heroic struggle which ended successfully. It is possible to write stories of revolutions in any of the four "mythoi," or generic narrative forms, and it is worth speculating that such Tories as Jonathan Boucher, Peter Oliver, and others wrote of the "rebellion" in tragic or satiric form, certainly not romantically. The same would hold true, of course, for the proponents of a revolution that ended unsuccessfully. In short, the mode of emplotment historians choose (or fall into) will depend upon where they stand with respect to their stories ideologically and upon their mode of historical explanation.

I have described the historians' story as a romance because it is drawn along that genre's pivotal lines and because it reveals the storytellers' commitment to the protagonist's principles and values. One more element characteristic of romance is useful to understanding the histories as romantic stories, an element that refocuses the central theme of Part I: that providence was no longer for the historians a viable mode of historical explanation because it squared neither with their philosophical assumptions nor with the story they wished to tell. To push the point a step further, I would suggest that instead of reducing the romance of the Revolution to the Christian Myth (or Divine Comedy) which ostensibly accommodates it, we see providence as adding a fabulous dimension to the historians' romance.

The historians' references to providence suggest that they saw the story of the Revolution in terms of the cosmic biblical myth. And, in fact, romance not only echoes myth but frequently parallels it closely. Since most myths are stories about the gods, argues Frye, "the distinction between the mythical and the fabulous overlaps a good deal with the distinction between the sacred and the secular." It is thus reasonable and often fruitful to see the hand of God operating in the histories because viewing the histories as chapters in the Divine Comedy establishes a coherent tradition of myth behind them. But, Frye cautions, the distinction between the mythical and the fabulous is not identical to that between the sacred and the secular, and we err if we see romance deriving directly from Christian myth, for "many stories may be mythical . . . without being sacred."[27] Significantly, among such stories "the largest and most important group . . . are the *national stories,* which as a rule shade insensibly *from the legendary to the historical.*"[28] In short, if we overemphasize the hand of providence—and we do so by viewing it causally— we identify the revolutionaries' national story with that of the Hebrews, which required a partisan God who was superior in *kind* to all local deities, instead of seeing that the Americans' national story depicted citizens who were superior in *degree* to other citizens. While the Hebrews' story (like some other national stories) was properly formulated in myth, the revolutionaries' story was appropriately romantic.

What distinguishes romance from myth as literary forms are two central and related issues: first, whereas romances involve identifiably human characters who inhabit a human world, myths (following the archetypal Biblical Comedy) involve divine beings, and, like epics, range broadly through higher and lower (divine and nether) worlds as well as the human world; and second, they are distinguished "by the hero's power of action." Thus, whereas in myth the hero is "superior in *kind* both to other men and to the environment of other men," in romance he is typically "superior in *degree* to other men and to his environment."[29] Since the revolutionary histories were avowedly democratic, the *people* are properly the heroes of the story. And it is arguable that the virtuous Americans as a whole are depicted in the histories as superior in degree to their enemy and even to their environment. We rarely see the Americans impeded by nature (usually the "impediment" turns out to be an unforeseen boon), and we frequently see them using nature to their own advantage, suggesting their mastery over their environment. Similarly, we rarely see the Americans losing a battle because of a superiority of British virtue or courage (though we are often reminded that the Americans are woefully deficient in men and the materials of war, enhancing the romantic view that they won despite the overwhelming odds against them).

Democratic as they may be, however, it is more fruitful to touch briefly on the historians' treatment of the only manifestly dominant figure in the story, George Washington, who is both a metaphor of the people as a whole and something more. Among the historians' most successful strategies was to invest Washington simultaneously with the best qualities of the virtuous Americans and with a touch of the fabulous. Washington thus embodies both the characteristics of the "leader" and of the "typical hero of romance," to use Frye's terms. As a leader he is "superior in degree to other men but not to his natural environment. . . . He has authority, passions, and powers of expression far greater than ours, but what he does is subject both to social criticism and to the order of nature." As romantic hero, Washington is superior in degree to other men and to his environment, one "whose actions are marvelous but who is himself identified as a human being."[30]

As Jeremy Belknap wrote in 1789, comparing Washington with biblical leaders, "George Washington is the greatest and best man that ever appeared at the head of any nation since the days of Moses and Joshua. His speech, his answers to the various addresses, shew such a spirit of devotion, modesty, patriotism, firmness, and integrity, that his country may well expect honour and safety under his administration." These are the characteristics of a great leader, a man doing his best and succeeding in a precarious and risky world. Washington was subject to "the complicated sources of anxiety" that affected all leaders, for his honor, his life, his whole country "hung suspended, not on a single point only, but on many events that quivered in the winds of fortune, chance, or the more uncertain determinations of men." He was, like the heroes of classical antiquity to whom he was frequently compared, a man of "invincible fortitude," of "perfect self possession," a man "looking beyond the present moment, and taking the future into view."[31] He was that virtuous man whom he himself described to John Jay, someone who always tried to anticipate and prevent disastrous contingencies. The man of extraordinary courage, virtue, and prudence, the tireless and self-effacing leader, Washington found himself in the midst of contingent situations from which he always managed to extricate himself and his troops. Such a leader befitted a republican people.

But there is also something more to Washington. He was "the man, in whom, next to God, America confided her fate," a man not only of "consummate prudence" but of a "good destiny" which protected him through the most perilous events.[32] There was indeed something marvelous in his exploits throughout the Revolutionary era, for whenever America's fate depended on his actions he was always there, "as if the chosen instrument of Heaven, selected for the purpose of effecting the great designs of Providence." At times Washington approached the status of a god. "If the people of America should ever relapse into Idolatry," wrote David Ramsay, "our illustrious commander-in-chief would be Jupiter, so universally is he beloved, I had almost said adored."[33]

In John Lendrum's account of the evacuation of Long Island, Washington even pre-empts providence, leaving the divine will to follow in the wake of his heroic actions. In other accounts, soldiers falling around him, bullets piercing his cape, Washington rallies his troops with exemplary courage, riding in front of them into battle and exhorting them to stand their ground.[34] The clear message is that Washington not only epitomizes Roman virtue but is mysteriously associated with the divine. This is the stuff of biblical myth and of Vergilian and Homeric epic. More important, these descriptions hint at the fabulous, and it is precisely the fabulous that often links romance to myth or the secular to the sacred. Thus Washington the sober leader of prudence, discipline, and virtue, merges with Washington the heroic warrior. And the combined image of leader-hero suggests a spectrum of possible descriptions that apply to him, ranging from "the hero of the high mimetic" (who is, significantly, subject to tragedy) to the most exalted heights of the romantic hero (who approaches divinity). Providence in such accounts—particularly when it is manifestly a metaphor of chance—adds a wondrous dimension to the story of the Revolution, enhancing its romantic nature and elevating it to the point where it associates itself with myth.

The histories of the Revolution are thus stories of momentous triumph against the greatest odds. Citizens are transformed into soldiers, merchants into statesmen, common artisans and mechanics into freedom-fighters, almost as beasts are transformed into princes and princesses in fables and legends. Marvelous coincidences occur, defying all calculation and expectation, just in the nick of time to save the Americans or to foil the British. In some of the histories there is even a dark night of the soul, commonly accompanying romantic descent themes, a time when the odds appear to be absolutely insurmountable and when war-weary Americans, morale ebbing, wring their hands in near despair and wonder why they ever began such an impossible enterprise.

At the same time, the antagonist—Great Britain—although viewed sympathetically as a misguided and blundering fool (and therefore potentially the subject of comedy) prior to the war, is later depicted in terms approaching myth: a malignant and evil collossus committing atrocities on the colonists, attempting to enslave the people and their progeny, and betraying the signs of its political and cultural descent into barbarism in its quest for control of the world. One might almost suggest that the historians depicted the war as the fulfillment of a curse, for some argued that independence was a self-fulfilling prophecy resulting from Britain's blind pursuit of corrupt principles. Such a view would tend toward tragedy, and there is in the histories a strong suggestion of Britain's tragic decline as a subplot in America's romantic quest.

This sketch of the romance of the Revolution can (and should) be expanded in places and qualified in others, but the essential point should be clear. As the historians saw it, for the history of the Revolution to be accessible and usable in a republican culture it had to pass into the vernacular; its fundamental principles had to be repeatable endlessly and synoptically, its essential features fused in a story that conveyed in a stroke the full range of experience, fact, and idea. Despite their condemnation of English historians for becoming more concerned with the manner than the matter of historical writing, they recognized that the matter could do no more than edify if the manner were inappropriate. If the story of the Revolution was to succeed in binding the future to the past, if it was to reveal the revolutionaries' and the historians' commitment to a heroic struggle for freedom, republicanism, and virtue, it would have to be simultaneously a part of the Revolution and the articulation of its mythos.

ABBREVIATIONS

For an extensive list of the revolutionary histories, see the bibliography in Arthur H. Shaffer's *The Politics of History: Writing the History of the American Revolution, 1783–1815* (Chicago: Precedent Publishing, 1975). Following are abbreviations of the titles that I have frequently cited.

Adams-Warren Letters: Charles Francis Adams, ed. *Correspondence Between John Adams and Mercy Warren Relating to her "History of the American Revolution."* MHS, *Collections*, 5th ser., 4; rpt. New York: Arno Press, 1972.

Belknap, *New Hampshire:* Jeremy Belknap, *The History of New Hampshire.* 3 vols., Boston, 1792.

Brunhouse, *Writings of Ramsay:* Robert L. Brunhouse, ed., *David Ramsay, 1749–1815: Selections from His Writings.* American Philosophical Society, *Transactions*, N.S., vol. 55, pt. 4 (1965).

Gordon, *History:* William Gordon, *The History of the Rise, Progress, and Establishment of the Independence of the United States of America. . . .* 4 vols. London, 1788.

Gordon Letters: The Letters of William Gordon. MHS, *Proceedings*, 62 (October 1929–June 1930), pp. 303–613.

Holmes, *Annals:* Abiel Holmes, *American Annals; Or, a Chronological History of America from its Discovery in MCCCCXCII to MDCCCVI.* 2 vols. Cambridge, Mass., 1805.

Lendrum, *American Revolution:* John Lendrum, *A Concise and Impartial History of the American Revolution. . . .* 2 vols. Boston, 1795; rpt. Trenton, 1811.

McCulloch, *Concise History*: John McCulloch, *A Concise History of the*

United States, from the Discovery of America, til 1813.... 4th ed. Philadelphia, 1813.

Marshall, *Life of Washington:* John Marshall, *The Life of George Washington, Commander in Chief of the American Forces, During the war which Established the Independence of his Country, and First President of the United States....* 5 vols. Philadelphia, 1804–1807.

MHS: Massachusetts Historical Society.

Morse, *Annals:* Jedidiah Morse, *Annals of the American Revolution* .... Hartford, 1824.

Morse, *History:* Jedidiah Morse, *The History of America in Two Books* .... Philadelphia, 1780.

Pitkin, *Political and Civil History:* Timothy Pitkin, *A Political and Civil History of the United States of America, from the Year 1763 To the Close of the Administration of President Washington....* 2 vols. New Haven, 1828.

Ramsay, *American Revolution:* David Ramsay, *The History of the American Revolution.* 2 vols. Philadelphia, 1789; rpt. London, 1793.

Ramsay, *Revolution of South-Carolina:* David Ramsay, *The History of the Revolution of South-Carolina, From a British Province to an Independent State....* 2 vols. Trenton, 1785.

Ramsay, *South-Carolina*: David Ramsay, *The History of South-Carolina, from its First Settlement in 1607, to the Year 1808.* 2 vols. Charleston, 1809.

Warren, *American Revolution:* Mercy Otis Warren, *History of the Rise, Progress and Termination of the American Revolution. Interspersed with Biographical, Political and Moral Observations.* 3 vols. Boston, 1805.

Warren, "Letter-Book": "The Letter-Book of Mercy Otis Warren." Manuscript in MHS.

WMQ: William and Mary Quarterly.

NOTES

Introduction

1. *The Dictionary of American Biography* (and, in the case of William Gordon, *The Dictionary of National Biography*) is a good starting point for biographical information on some of the historians. This study is preceded by two others, both of which discuss the lives of the historians at greater length than I do here: Arthur H. Shaffer, *The Politics of History: Writing the History of the American Revolution, 1783–1815* (Chicago: Precedent Publishing, 1975), which contains an excellent primary source bibliography, and William Raymond Smith, *History as Argument: Three Patriot Historians of the American Revolution* (The Hague: Mouton, 1966), which discusses David Ramsay, John Marshall, and Mercy Otis Warren. Although little has been written about the historians individually, one's attention to traditional sources of article literature can be rewarding. The *William and Mary Quarterly*, *New England Quarterly*, *Journal of the History of Ideas*, *Early American Literature*, *Church History*, and the *Collections* and *Transactions* of the Massachusetts Historical Society contain relevant information. Unparalleled is Robert L. Brunhouse, ed., *David Ramsay, 1749–1815: Selections from His Writings* in American Philosophical Society, *Transactions*, n.s., 55, pt. 4 (1965). Ministers who wrote history are easier to track down. See Alan Heimert, *Religion and the American Mind, From the Great Awakening to the Revolution* (Cambridge: Harvard University Press, 1966); Nathan O. Hatch, *The Sacred Cause of Liberty: Republican Thought and the Millennium in Revolutionary New England* (New Haven: Yale University Press, 1977); James West Davidson, *The Logic of Millennial Thought: Eighteenth Century New England* (New Haven: Yale University Press, 1977); John F. Berens, *Providence and*

Patriotism in Early America, 1640–1815 (Charlottesville: University of Virginia Press, 1978).

2. White, *Metahistory: The Historical Imagination in Nineteenth-Century Europe* (Baltimore: Johns Hopkins University Press, 1973), p. ix.

3. Adams to Jefferson, July 3, 1813, in Lester J. Cappon, ed., *The Adams-Jefferson Correspondence* (Chapel Hill: University of North Carolina Press, 1959; rpt. Clarion Books, 1971), p. 349. All the following Loyalist works were written prior to 1783, closing, of course, even before the end of military hostilities: Peter Oliver, *Origins and Progress of the American Rebellion* (1781); Joseph Galloway, *Historical and Political Reflections* (1780); George Chalmers, *Political Annals* (1780); Alexander Hewatt, *Historical Account of . . . South Carolina and Georgia* (1779); Israel Mauduit, *Short History of the New England Colonies* (1769); Thomas Hutchinson, *History of Massachusetts Bay* (1764–67); William Smith, Jr., *History of New York* (1757). Oliver's work is more accurately seen as a memoir. Galloway's work was a self-consciously political book, hastily written, he himself said, so that it might be of contemporary value in conciliating the Anglo-American conflict. Book I of Chalmers's work covers the period from colonial settlement to 1688; three subsequent chapters brought it up to 1696—hardly revolutionary history. It, like Galloway's work, was essentially a political book, the work of "a lawyer chiefly interested in constitutional questions," according to Lawrence Henry Gipson ("George Chalmers and the *Political Annals*," in Lawrence H. Leder, ed., *The Colonial Legacy: Loyalist Historians* [New York: Harper Torchbooks, 1971], p. 13). Mauduit's, Hutchinson's (indisputably the best), and Smith's share the same problem of coverage. In addition, though they were all histories and were all written by people who were later known as Tories, it is questionable whether the term "Loyalist" is even applicable to works written prior to 1774, since the labels "Loyalist" and "Tory" had no real meaning before that date because the issues of the Revolution had not yet been fully articulated.

The following Loyalist works were written after the Revolution: George Chalmers, *An Introduction to the Revolt of the Colonies* (first published in 1782, but added to later; the most frequently used edition is that of 1845); William Smith, Jr., *History of Canada* (1805–17); Robert Proud, *History of Pennsylvania* (1790); Jonathan Boucher, *Causes and Consequences of the American Revolution* (1797). Although written after the Revolution, Chalmers's and Smith's works include events only up to 1763. Proud's deals with events of the Revolutionary era, 1763–1783, in only four pages. Boucher's is a collection of his sermons, the latest of which he delivered in 1775, preceded by a marvelous historical account of about a hundred pages.

CHAPTER 1: *Providential History*

1. William Bradford, *Of Plymouth Plantation*, ed. Samuel Eliot Morison (New York: Modern Library, 1952), pp. 61–63; Deut. 3:25–28, 34:1–12. My interpretation of Puritan philosophy of history relies in part on the following sources: Perry Miller, *The New England Mind: The Seventeenth Century* (Boston: Beacon Press, 1965; hereafter cited as *New England Mind*, I), and *Jonathan Edwards* (Cleveland: Meridian Books, 1965), pp. 307–330; Kenneth B. Murdock, *Literature & Theology in Colonial New England* (New York: Harper & Row, 1963), esp. pp. 67–97, "William Hubbard and the Providential Interpretation of History" (American Antiquarian Society, *Proceedings*, 52 (1942):15–37, and "Clio in the Wilderness: History and Biography in Puritan New England," *Church History* 24 (September 1955):221–238; Peter Gay, *A Loss of Mastery: Puritan Historians in Colonial America* (New York: Vintage, 1968); Sacvan Bercovitch, *The Puritan Origins of the American Self* (New Haven: Yale University Press, 1975), and "The Historiography of Johnson's 'Wonderworking Providence,'" *Essex Institute Historical Collections* 54 (April 1968):138–161; John G. Buchanan, "Puritan Philosophy of History from Restoration to Revolution," *Essex Institute Historical Collections*, 54 (July 1968):329–348; J. F. Maclear, "New England and the Fifth Monarchy: The Quest for the Millennium in Early American Puritanism," *WMQ*, 3d ser., 32 (April 1975):223–260; Cecelia Tichi, "Spiritual Biography and the 'Lords Remembrancers,'" and Jesper Rosenmeier, "'With My Own Eyes': William Bradford's *Of Plymouth Plantation*," both in Sacvan Bercovitch, ed., *The American Puritan Imagination: Essays in Revaluation* (London: Cambridge University Press, 1974), pp. 56–73, 77–106. For contemporary non-American historical theory I have relied on: F. Smith Fussner, *The Historical Revolution: English Historical Writing and Theory, 1580–1640* (New York: Columbia University Press, 1962); F. J. Levy, *Tudor Historical Thought* (San Marino, Calif.: Huntington Library, 1964); Paul Hazard, *The European Mind, 1680–1715* (Cleveland: Meridian Books, 1968), esp. pts. I and II. Other obligations are expressed in footnotes below.

2. Ibid., p. 63; Josh. 24:22–23.

3. Soon after his famous description of the wilderness Bradford wrote: "I shall a little return back, and begin with a combination made by them before they came ashore; being the first foundation of their government in this place" (ibid., p. 75).

4. Thomas Hobbes, *Leviathan* (1651; rpt. London: Oxford University Press, 1962), pt. I, chap. 13, pp. 96–97. K. R. Minogue properly

points out that Hobbes was not merely speaking of "a semi-historical myth lodged in the distant past; it is an ever-present abyss which we skirt daily, and thankfully but unwisely forget" ("Thomas Hobbes and the Philosophy of Absolutism," in David Thomson, ed., *Political Ideas* [London: Everyman, 1966], p. 55).

5. John Locke, *Two Treatises of Government*, ed. Peter Laslett, rev. ed. (New York: Mentor, 1965), "Second Treatise," chap. 5, art. 49, p. 343.

6. Michael Walzer, *The Revolution of the Saints: A Study in the Origins of Radical Politics* (New York: Atheneum, 1968), p. 34; see pp. 22–37; David Little, *Religion, Order and Law: A Study in Pre-Revolutionary England* (New York: Harper & Row, 1969).

7. William Hubbard, "The Happiness of a People . . .," in Perry Miller and Thomas H. Johnson, eds., *The Puritans: A Sourcebook of Their Writings*, 2 vols. (New York: Harper & Row, 1963), I, 247.

8. See Maclear, "New England and the Fifth Monarchy"; Buchanan, "Puritan Philosophy of History"; Sacvan Bercovitch, *The American Jeremiad* (Madison: University of Wisconsin Press, 1978); James West Davidson, *The Logic of Millennial Thought: Eighteenth-Century, New England* (New Haven: Yale University Press, 1977); John F. Berens, *Providence and Patriotism in Early America, 1640–1815* (Charlottesville: University of Virginia Press, 1978).

9. Increase Mather, *The Doctrine of Divine Providence Opened and Applyed* (Boston, 1684), pp. 30, 22, 8, 22–23 (hereafter cited as *DDP*).

10. William Ames, *The Marrow of Theology*, trans. with Introduction by John Dykstra Eusden (Boston: Pilgrim Press, 1968), p. 100; Mather, *DDP*, p. 42, "To the Reader."

11. Mather, *DDP*, pp. 11, 30. As William Ames also wrote: God's "Providence extends to all things, not only general but particular" (*Marrow*, p. 107; see pp. 110ff).

12. Ibid., pp. 6, 8. Mather, like Jonathan Edwards nearly a century later, equated God's foreordination of events with His foreknowledge, arguing that "the Foreknowledge of God proveth his decree, For if he knows what shall be, he must needs either *will* or *nill* the Being of it" (*DDP*, p. 7). See Jonathan Edwards, *A Careful and Strict Enquiry into . . . [the] Freedom of the Will* (1754), ed. Paul Ramsey (New Haven: Yale University Press, 1966), sec. 12, pp. 257–269.

13. Thomas Hooker, "A True Sight of Sin," in Miller and Johnson, eds., *The Puritans*, pp. 293–295. See Ames, *Marrow*, "The Consequences of Sin," pp. 116–120. To account simultaneously for God's absolute foreordination and human responsibility, the Puritans distinguished between the command of the will over the mind's (or soul's) internal faculties and its command over external, worldly events. Chief among

the mental faculties, the will was responsible for the mind's leanings and inclinations, but it was ultimately inefficacious and, therefore, not responsible for its complicity in worldly affairs (see Norman S. Fiering, "Will and Intellect in the New England Mind," *WMQ*, 3d ser., 29 [October 1972]:542). Jonathan Edwards both radicalized and simplified the earlier notion of responsibility by arguing that it was an ontological dimension of man's constitution. Paul Ramsey has noted, however, that even Edwards implicitly assumed a distinction between the will's internal and external efficacy: "In describing the soul's being conversant about its own inner action, he must continue to make the same separation between volition and action as when speaking of the soul's being conversant about an external action" (editor's Introduction to Edwards's *Freedom of the Will*, p. 25). See Little, *Religion, Order and Law*, p. 49, n. 81.

14. Oakes, "New England Pleaded with . . . , " quoted in Miller and Johnson, eds., *The Puritans*, p. 81.

15. Mather, *DDP*, pp. 3, 7, 4–5. See Ames, *Marrow*, pp. 97–98.

16. Ibid., pp. 12–14, 15, 17. See Miller, *New England Mind*, I, 228–235.

17. Miller and Johnson, eds., *The Puritans*, p. 83; Mather, *DDP*, p. 26.

18. Levy, *Tudor Historical Thought*, pp. 237, 287; Fussner, *Historical Revolution*, pp. 307, 301. See Leslie Stephen, *History of English Thought in the Eighteenth Century*, 2 vols. (New York: Harcourt, 1962), I, chap. 4, 192–230.

19. Miller, *New England Mind*, I, 229; Murdock, "Hubbard and the Providential Interpretation," p. 22. Regarding the jeremiad, see Miller, *The New England Mind: From Colony to Province* (Boston: Beacon Press, 1966) pp. 27–39 (hereafter cited as *New England Mind*, II); Sacvan Bercovitch, *Horologicals to Chronometricals: The Rhetoric of the Jeremiad* (Wisconsin Literary Monographs, vol. III [Madison, 1973]), pp. 3–124, and *The American Jeremiad* (Madison: University of Wisconsin Press, 1978); David Minter, "The Puritan Jeremiad as a Literary Form," in Bercovitch, ed., *American Puritan Imagination*, pp. 45–55.

20. All quoted in Miller and Johnson, eds., *The Puritans*, pp. 247–248, 250–251, 259, 271. See Edmund S. Morgan, ed., *Puritan Political Ideas*, (Indianapolis: Bobbs-Merrill, 1965); T. H. Breen, *The Character of the Good Ruler: Puritan Political Ideas in New England, 1630–1730* (New York: Norton, 1970).

21. Oakes, "The Soveraign Efficacy of Divine Providence," in Miller and Johnson, eds., *The Puritans*, pp. 351–352.

22. Murdock, "Hubbard and the Providential Interpretation," p. 25.

23. Oakes, "Soveraign Efficacy," pp. 353, 351.

24. Miller, *New England Mind*, I, 229–230; Ames, *Marrow*, p. 107 (emphasis added).

25. Mather, *DDP*, pp. 46–47. See Ames, *Marrow*, p. 108. Murdock and Miller insist that miracles had no place in Puritan orthodoxy, arguing that "a Providence for the Puritan was 'not contrary to nature,' but an instance of 'nature . . . turned off its course'" (Murdock, "Hubbard and the Providential Interpretation," p. 22; Miller, *New England Mind*, I, 228). The distinction between a providence and a miracle, subtle enough even for a Puritan, was that God used means to effect a providence whereas He would, presumably, intervene directly and without means in effecting a miracle. For the twentieth-century observer this sounds like a distinction without a difference. Miller, at any rate, quoted but seems to have neglected the full import of William Perkins's statement: "Sometimes [God] governes according to the usual course & order of nature . . . yet so, as he can and doth most freely order all things by meanes either *above* nature or *against* nature" in *New England Mind*, I, 228 (emphasis added).

26. Mather, *DDP*, p. 42 (emphasis added). Instances of natural wonders were another major concern of historical narratives. Although "enlightened" Americans a century later would scoff at the Puritans' scientific naivete and accuse them of superstition, the notion that natural occurrences—comets, earthquakes, floods, droughts, and the like—were the works of God persisted in Puritan narratives at least to the 1740s. See, e.g., Increase Mather, *Essay for Recording Illustrious Providences* (Boston, 1684); William Hubbard, *A General History of New England* (1682; first published Boston, 1815); Cotton Mather, *Remarkables of the Divine Providence Among the People of New-England* (bk. VI of *Magnalia Christi Americana* [London, 1702]; Thomas Prince, *A Chronological History of New-England*, 2 vols. (Boston, 1736), and *Extraordinary Events the Doing of God* (Boston, 1745).

27. Increase Mather, *A Brief History of the War with the Indians in New-England* (London, 1676), "To the Reader."

28. Ibid; William Hubbard's aim was "to bind up together the most memorable passages of divine providence, during our late, or former troubles with the *Indians*," and, echoing William Bradford, to make his narrative "of use to posterity, as well as to those of the present Generation, to help them both to call to mind, and carry along the memory of such eminent deliverances, and special preservations granted by divine favour to the people here" in *A Narrative of the Troubles with the Indians in New-England* (Boston, 1677), "Dedicatory Epistle." See Anne K. Nelson, "King Philip's War and the Hubbard-Mather Rivalry," *WMQ* 3d ser., 28 (January 1971):615–629.

29. As Puritan theologians never tired of insisting, it would be an error to say that the people caused the war by making God punish them for their neglects and omissions, for to say that would be to make God's will dependent on man's. Instead, God punishes because He "does wonderfully suit his Judgments according to what the sins of men have been" (*DDP*, p. 60). On another occasion Mather wrote: "At the first God did lightly Afflict the Land, but afterward more grievously. And behold his Anger is not turned away but his hand is stretched out still. This very year God has diminished our ordinary [read "ordained"] food in some places of the Countrey[.] He has called for a Drought . . . and the Earth is stayed from her Fruit. In other places Immoderate Raines have fallen, and the flood has carried all away before it. . . . Why has all this been? O there have been great Ommissions; great and General Neglects of duty found among us" (*DDP*, p. 97). The passage records God's action; He is the active subject. To construe man's actions as the cause is to confuse the cause of an event with its occasion. Thus William Ames argued that "although he wills many things which will not take place except upon some antecedent act of the creature, God's act of willing does not itself properly depend upon the act of the creature" (*Marrow*, p. 98).

30. Mather, *Brief History*, pp. 1–2.

31. Miller and Johnson, eds., *The Puritans*, p. 82; Hubbard, *Narrative*, pp. 10–11. Hannah Arendt uses the term "transmundane" in *On Revolution* (New York: Viking, 1963; rpt. Compass Books, 1965), p. 20, See pp. 13–21.

32. Mather, *Brief History*, p. 23.

33. Ibid., pp. 4–6, 21ff.

34. Ibid., p. 22.

35. Ibid., p. 50 (emphasis added).

36. Mather, *An Essay for Recording Illustrious Providences*, p. 130.

37. Mather, *DDP*, p. 21; Ames, *Marrow*, pp. 108–109.

38. It is never completely clear whether the Puritans understood contingency ontologically—as a fundamental feature of objective reality—or epistemologically—as no more than an appearance to finite and unregenerate man. It is not clear, I believe, because such theologians as Increase Mather found it strategically useful to create a different impression on different occasions: sometimes to threaten complacent man with the ultimate contingency of things in order to bring him to faith (and thereby implying its ontological facticity), and sometimes to reassure the overly anxious that all was meaningful in God's universe (thereby implying that contingency was merely apparent, not real). My own view, it should be clear, is that the Puritans felt the world

to *be* contingent, even chaotic, and that they attempted to create order in it, but that they spoke as if they did not create but actually discovered the divine order that suffused it. Since I have tried to represent *their* thought as nearly as possible, I have emphasized the epistemological interpretation throughout.

39. Perry Miller, "The Marrow of Puritan Theology," in *Errand into the Wilderness* (New York: Harper & Row, 1964), p. 65.

40. Cotton Mather, *The Christian Philosopher*, in Kenneth B. Murdock, ed., *Cotton Mather: Selections* (New York: Hafner, 1965), p. 286, 286 n2.

41. Ibid., pp. 291, 296 (emphasis added).

42. Ibid., p. 287.

43. Ibid., pp. 302–307; quoted at pp. 309–311.

44. See George L. Kittredge, "Cotton Mather's Election into the Royal Society," *Publications of the Colonial Society of Massachusetts*, 14 (1913): 81–114, and "Cotton Mather's Scientific Communications to the Royal Society" in American Antiquarian Society, *Proceedings*, 26 (1916):18–57.

45. See Daniel B. Shea, *Spiritual Autobiography in Early America* (Princeton: Princeton University Press, 1968).

46. Cotton Mather, *Magnalia Christi Americana; Or, The Ecclesiastical History of New-England* (London, 1702), "General Introduction," art. 6.

47. The very conventions of authorship also undergo change as Michel Foucault has pointed out. See "What Is an Author?" in *Partisan Review*, 42, no. 4 (1975):603–614.

48. Mather, *Magnalia*, bk. VI, p. 1. Book VI, moreover, specifically concerns special providences. It includes the "Thaumatographia Pneumatica. Relating the Wonders of the Invisible World in Preternatural Occurrences" (pp. 66–83), about which Jeremy Belknap (a historian of revolutionary New Hampshire and Congregational minister) and Ebenezer Hazard (a compiler of revolutionary documents) laughed in ridicule. (See Chapter 2, pp. 67–68.)

49. Although the work was not published until 1774, Edwards had begun writing about the idea in 1739. For Edwards's historical theory it is fruitful to begin with the opposing interpretations by Perry Miller, *Jonathan Edwards*, pp. 307–330, and Peter Gay, *A Loss of Mastery*, pp. 88–117. Davidson's *The Logic of Millennial Thought* is filled with insight into Edwards's philosophy of history, as is Alan Heimert's *Religion and the American Mind: From the Great Awakening to the Revolution* (Cambridge: Harvard University Press, 1966), esp. pp. 59–94. For transformations in Puritan thought more generally, see Bercovitch, *Puritan Origins*, esp. pp. 35–72 concerning Edwards; Miller, *New England Mind*, II; Joseph J. Ellis, *The New England Mind in Transition: Samuel Johnson of Connecticut, 1696–1772* (New Haven: Yale University Press, 1973);

James W. Jones, *The Shattered Synthesis: New England Puritanism Before the Great Awakening* (New Haven: Yale University Press, 1973); Conrad Wright, *The Beginnings of Unitarianism in America* (Boston: Beacon Press, 1966); Robert Middlekauf, *The Mathers: Three Generations of Puritan Intellectuals, 1596–1728* (New York: Oxford University Press, 1971).

50. Heimert, *Religion and the American Mind*, p. 74.

51. Edwards, *Freedom of the Will*, p. 432. See Davidson, *Logic of Millennial Thought*, pp. 29–34; C. C. Goen, "Jonathan Edwards: A New Departure in Eschatology," *Church History*, 28 (1959):25–40.

52. Heimert, *Religion and the American Mind*, p. 77; Miller, *Jonathan Edwards*, p. 313.

53. Ibid., p. 74.

54. *Freedom of the Will*, p. 432. This is reminiscent of William Ames's early notion that God's "conserving" providence was "nothing else than a continued creation, so to speak" (*Marrow*, p. 109).

55. Ibid., pp. 431–432 (emphasis added). See Davidson, *Logic of Millennial Thought*, pp. 81–121.

56. Ibid., p. 185.

57. See ibid., pp. 270ff.

58. Editor's Introduction to *The Freedom of the Will*, pp. 9, 10. See Edwards's letters to Reverend John Erskine, July 25 and August 3, 1757 (ibid., pp. 443–470).

59. Miller, "Religion and Society in the Early Literature of Virginia," in *Errand into the Wilderness*, pp. 99–140. In *The American Jeremiad*, Bercovitch shows how distinctively Puritan forms became more universally American.

60. Between 1747 and 1767, several writers—including William Stith (*History of the Discovery and First Settlement of Virginia* [1747]), William Smith (*History of the Province of New York* [1757; rev. ed. 1762]), Samuel Smith (*History of the Colony of Nova Caesarea, Or New Jersey* [1765]), and especially Thomas Hutchinson (*History of the Colony of Massachusetts-Bay* [1764–67])—wrote colony histories which have been largely ignored, and in which the language of providence is conspicuously absent. To perpetuate the neglect of those narratives here is not to depreciate their intrinsic importance. It is, however, to suggest that not until the revolutionary histories do we see a cohesive group of works that is internally united by concern, theme, and scope, as well as by philosophical, ideological, and aesthetic principles, and that evidences the dramatic change from an earlier mode for which I am arguing.

61. Nathan O. Hatch, *The Sacred Cause of Liberty: Republican Thought and the Millennium in Revolutionary New England* (New Haven: Yale University Press, 1977), p. 40. Hatch's work and Davidson's *Logic of Millen-*

nial Thought are the best studies of millennialism in Revolutionary America. Also very useful are Berens, *Providence and Patriotism*; Ernest Lee Tuveson, *Redeemer Nation: The Idea of America's Millennial Role* (Chicago: University of Chicago Press, 1968), which deals mostly with a later period; J. F. Maclear, "The Republic and the Millennium," in Elwyn A. Smith, ed., *The Religion of the Republic* (Philadelphia: Fortress Press, 1971), pp. 183–216; Bercovitch, *American Jeremiad*; Hatch, "The Origins of Civil Millennialism in America: New England Clergy, War with France, and the Revolution," *WMQ*, 3d ser., 31 (July 1974):407–430; Stephen J. Stein, "An Apocalyptic Rationale for the American Revolution," *Early American Literature*, 9 (Winter 1975):211–225.

62. Shaffer, *The Politics of History: Writing the History of the American Revolution, 1783–1815* (Chicago: Precedent Publishing, 1975), p. 50.

63. Hatch is the only recent commentator who refuses to presuppose the immutability of Puritan ideas in the Revolutionary era (see *Sacred Cause*, pp. 1–20). For another view of religion in the period, see Bernard Bailyn, "Religion and Revolution: Three Biographical Studies," *Perspectives in American History*, 4 (1970):85–169.

64. Scholars who have recently discussed the sermons of minister-historians have neglected their histories—an understandable, if serious, omission since these historians are specifically concerned with religious thought. As I will suggest at greater length in Chapter 2, the neglect is glaring, particularly in light of these scholars' attempts to draw close connections between religious and historical consciousness. The failure to discuss the minister-historians' historical writings may point to the assumption that a single body of principles consistently unites the corpus of a person's writings, an assumption which in this case leads to error. Thus, for example, Alan Heimert (the only one who *does* mention a minister's historical work) refers to William Gordon as "the Calvinist historian of the Revolution," and to Gordon's history as "the most extensive Calvinist history of the Revolution" (*Religion and the American Mind*, pp. 351, 570). Perry Miller discussed Gordon's sermons, but not his history ("From the Covenant to the Revival," in James Ward Smith and A. Leland Jamison, eds., *Religion in American Life*, vol. I, *The Shaping of American Religion* [Princeton: Princeton University Press, 1961], pp. 336–337). Hatch, Bercovitch, and Heimert cite Jeremy Belknap's sermons, but not his historical works (*Sacred Cause*, pp. 123–124, 132, 151–152; *American Jeremiad*, p. 135; *Religion and the American Mind*, pp. 325–326). Berens mentions Abiel Holmes's 1795 sermon on the "Freedom and Happiness of America," but fails to discuss his *American Annals* or other historical writing (*Providence and Patriotism*, p. 133). And Hatch, Heimert, and Davidson discuss Jedidiah Morse's religious views

without mentioning his histories (*Sacred Cause*, pp. 130-132; *Religion and the American Mind*, p. 535; *Logic of Millennial Thought*, pp. 289-290, 292, 296).

65. Warren, *American Revolution*, III, 345.

CHAPTER 2: *The Invisible Hand*

1. Gordon, *History*, II, 568-569.

2. Jonathan Edwards, "Remarks on the Essays on the Principles of Morality and Natural Religion ... " in Edwards, *Freedom of the Will*, ed. Paul Ramsey, (New Haven: Yale University Press, 1957; rpt. 1966), pp. 459, 462.

3. Ibid., p. 449 (emphasis added). Hume wrote: "What the vulgar call chance is nothing but a secret and conceal'd cause" in *A Treatise of Human Nature* (1739), ed. L. A. Selby-Bigge; rev. ed. P. H. Nidditch (Oxford: Oxford University Press, 1978), pp. 130, 404. See Hume, *An Inquiry Concerning Human Understanding* (1748), ed. Charles W. Hendel (Indianapolis: Bobbs Merrill, 1955), pp. 69-111.

4. William Gordon to Mrs. Elizabeth Smith, July 30, 1775 (*Gordon Letters*, p. 315); Benjamin Trumbull, *A General History of the United States of America ... Or, Sketches of the Divine Agency ...* especially in the late Memorable Revolution (Boston, 1810), p. 1.

5. As John Marshall called them in *Life of Washington*, II, 361.

6. Ramsay, *Revolution of South-Carolina*, II, 206. In his *History of the American Revolution*, Ramsay varied the third sentence as follows: "The Americans, confident of the justice of their cause, considered this event as an interposition of Providence in their favour" (*American Revolution*, II, 237).

7. Ibid., II, 208. See *American Revolution*, II, 236-239.

8. Lendrum, *American Revolution*, II, 177-178.

9. Holmes, *Annals*, II, 443.

10. Warren, *American Revolution*, II, 313-314.

11. William Raymond Smith suggests that Warren did in fact mean to imply that a miracle had been wrought, and that "the support of Providence is the conspicuous theme running throughout Mrs. Warren's history" in *History as Argument: Three Patriot Historians of the American Revolution* (The Hague: Mouton, 1966), pp. 91 n35, 100.

12. Warren, *American Revolution*, II, 239 (emphasis added).

13. Holmes, *Annals*, II, 188 n2. See ibid., II, 238 n3, 444-445; II, 171, 286-287; Lendrum, *American Revolution*, I, 275-276, 332-334.

14. David Hume, *Inquiry*, p. 123. See David Fate Norton and Richard

H. Popkin, eds., *David Hume: Philosophical Historian* (Indianapolis: Bobbs-Merrill, 1965).

15. Bloch, *The Historian's Craft* (New York: Vintage, 1953), p. 125. See Leo Braudy, *Narrative Form in History & Fiction: Hume, Fielding, & Gibbon* (Princeton: Princeton University Press, 1970), pp. 250–253. Also see W. B. Gallie, *Philosophy and the Historical Understanding*, 2d ed. (New York: Schocken, 1968), esp. pp. 40ff., 87ff.

16. See Nathan O. Hatch, *The Sacred Cause of Liberty: Republican Thought and the Millennium in Revolutionary New England* (New Haven: Yale University Press, 1977); John F. Berens, *Providence and Patriotism in Early America, 1640–1815* (Charlottesville: University of Virginia Press, 1978); James West Davidson, *The Logic of Millennial Thought: Eighteenth-Century New England* (New Haven: Yale University Press, 1977); Alan Heimert, *Religion and the American Mind, From the Great Awakening to the Revolution* (Cambridge: Harvard University Press, 1966); Perry Miller, "From the Covenant to the Revival," in James Ward Smith and A. Leland Jamison, eds., *Religion in American Life*, vol. I: *The Shaping of American Religion* (Princeton: Princeton University Press, 1961), pp. 322–368; J. F. Maclear, "The Republic and the Millennium," in Elwyn A. Smith, ed., *The Religion of the Republic* (Philadelphia: Fortress Press, 1971), pp. 183–216; Stephen J. Stein, "An Apocalyptic Rationale for the American Revolution," *Early American Literature*, 9 (Winter 1975):211–225.

17. Jeremy Belknap to Ebenezer Hazard, October 22, 1789 and Hazard to Belknap, October 29, 1789 (MHS, *Collections*, 5th ser., 3:198, 202). Also see Belknap to Hazard, November 11, 1789 (ibid., pp. 204–205). A year earlier Hazard suggested that Belknap's projected biographical study might benefit by including "valuable shreds" from Daniel Neal's *History of the Puritans* and Mather's *Magnalia*, though he recognized that those shreds would need to be "wove into a new web." (Hazard to Belknap, January 11 and 16, 1788 [ibid., p. 2]). See Davidson, *Logic of Millennial Thought*, p. 268.

18. Gordon to Gates, August 5–12, 1776 (*Gordon Letters*, p. 324).

19. Gordon to George Washington, March 5, 1777, and to Horatio Gates, February 25, 1778 (*Gordon Letters*, pp. 333, 378). See Gordon's "A Discourse Preached December 15, 1774 . . ." in John Wingate Thornton, ed., *The Pulpit of the American Revolution*, 2d ed. (Boston, 1876), pp. 197–226, and "The Separation of the Jewish Tribes, after the death of Solomon . . . July 4, 1777," in Frank Moore, ed., *The Patriot Preachers of the American Revolution* (n.p., 1860), pp. 159–185; Miller, "From the Covenant to the Revival," pp. 322–368.

20. Barthes, *Writing Degree Zero*, trans. Annette Lavers and Colin

Smith (Boston: Beacon Press, 1970), p. 16; Culler, *Structuralist Poetics: Structuralism, Linguistics, and the Study of Literature* (Ithaca: Cornell University Press, 1975), p. 134; see chaps. 6 and 7. The most important and insightful study of the conventions of historical writing is Hayden White's *Metahistory: The Historical Imagination in Nineteenth Century Europe* (Baltimore: John Hopkins University Press, 1973), pp. 1–42; also see White's "The Historical Text as Literary Artifact," in Robert H. Canary and Henry Kozicki, eds., *The Writing of History: Literary Form and Historical Understanding* (Madison: University of Wisconsin Press, 1978), pp. 41–62. Bernard Bailyn also provides fruitful insight into the ways in which conventions make thought "arrange itself" in his study of Stephen Johnson, Congregational minister of Lyme, Connecticut ("Religion and Revolution: Three Biographical Studies," *Perspectives in American History*, 4 [1970]:125–139.

21. An alternative to my argument here is that we *not* rely on the recent interpretations of Revolutionary era sermons (cited above, n16). Since none of the historians, except Hatch, seriously questions the meaning of providential language in the sermons, it is possible that they have failed to see the politicization of theology even beyond the point that Hatch suggests, and that not even ministers were using providence to describe the active, intrusive, causal deity on which Puritan philosophy of history rested.

22. Holmes, *Annals*, I, 57n. Holmes's work presents a particularly interesting opportunity to compare the narratives of the Revolution with those of the seventeenth century. As cofounder of the Massachusetts Historical Society, Holmes had access to many of the early histories in both manuscript and published form. His footnotes indicate that he frequently relied upon seventeenth-century narratives in constructing the first volume of his *Annals*. He was, moreover, responsible for the publication of William Hubbard's *General History of New-England* (1684) in 1815. An example or two proves illuminating.

According to Holmes, relying upon Thomas Prince's work, "A severe drought prevailing at this time [1621] in Plymouth, the government set apart a solemn day of humiliation and prayer; and soon after, in grateful and pious acknowledgement of the blessing of copious showers, and supplies of provisions, a day of public thanksgiving" (*Annals*, I, 227). This straightforward report of the Puritans' activities appears in Prince's history as follows: "July Notwithstanding our great Pains and Hopes of a large Crop, God seems to blast them and threaten sorer Famine by a Great Drought and Heat . . . so as the Corn withers both the Blade and the Stalk, as if 'twere utterly Dead: Now are our Hopes overthrown and we discouraged, our Joy being turned into Mourning. . . . Upon this the Publick Authority sets apart a solemn day of Humiliation and Prayer to seek the Lord in this Distress who was pleased to give speedy Answer, to our and the Indians Admiration" (*A Chronological History of New-England. . .* , 2 vols. [Boston, 1736], I, 137–138). The difference in narrative voice could hardly be more obvious. Where Prince reveals through his language his commitment to an active, interceding deity, Holmes maintains a distance and lack of engagement.

Or, Holmes again: "At the close of this year [1633], and in the following winter, the small pox broke out again among the natives of Massachusetts, and made great devastations among this unhappy race, destined, by various means, to ultimate extermination" (*Annals*, I, 273). This time Holmes cited William Hubbard's *General History*, written at the relevant point: "In the year 1633, it pleased God to visit the Colony of Plymouth with a pestilential fever, whereof many died, upwards of twenty, men, women, and children, which was a great number out of a small company of inhabitants. . . . [I]n the end of that year and winter following a great mortality happened among the Massachusetts Indians, whereby thousands of them were swept away, which came by the small pox." Underscoring the principle of his narrative, Hubbard concluded about the deaths of only twenty settlers but thousands of Indians: "Thus, in a sense as it was of old, God cast out the heathen to make room for his people" (*General History*, pp. 194–195).

23. Warren, *American Revolution*, I, 353–354.

24. Ibid., III, 345.

25. See, for example, ibid., I, 354–359.

26. Ibid., I, 92–93. Abiel Holmes added: "Incidents, apparently small, are often productive of important consequences" (*Annals*, II, 26).

27. Lendrum, *American Revolution*, II, 195–197, quoting at 197. Mercy Warren's account is by far the most interesting and detailed. See *American Revolution*, II, chap. 20, through III, chap. 21.

28. Lendrum, *American Revolution*, II, 9; Ramsay, *Revolution of South-Carolina*, II, 215; Warren, *American Revolution*, I, 189, 92. To enumerate examples of the various constructions of chance would be to pull the histories apart page by page. John Lendrum spoke of "good luck" and even hinted at "magic" (*American Revolution*, II, 31, 119); William Gordon wrote of "random shots" and events being "unlucky" (*History*, II, 565, 475); John Marshall referred to "untoward events" and "unknown causes" (*Life of Washington*, II, 361; III, 252). All the historians played upon the concepts of chance, accident, fortune, luck, happenstance, and so forth throughout their histories.

29. Pitkin, *Political and Civil History*, I, 260. The petition was that of

the Massachusetts Assembly calling for the removal of governor Hutchinson. Benjamin Franklin was widely thought to have stolen the letters or, at least, to have transmitted them to the Sons of Liberty. See Carl Van Doren, *Benjamin Franklin* (New York: Viking, 1938; rpt. Compass Books, 1964), pp. 440ff. Whatever the source, Franklin pointed out how important he thought the letters were: "I have reason to believe [that they] laid the foundation for most if not all our present grievances" (Van Doren, *Franklin*, p. 443). See Bernard Bailyn, *The Ordeal of Thomas Hutchinson* (Cambridge: Harvard University Press, 1974), pp. 224ff. John Lendrum referred to the finding of the letters as "an accidental discovery" (*American Revolution*, I, 252).

30. Ibid., I, 262. In another of those inconsistent usages that tend to undermine the traditional meaning of providence, William Gordon referred to the discovery of Hutchinson's letters as "providential" in a newspaper essay of June 5, 1775, but in his *History* described it as "an accident" (*Gordon Letters*, pp. 313-14; *History*, II, 28-29). Although dealing with the *absence* of providential language is treacherous, it is perhaps worth noting that neither Ramsay (*American Revolution*, I, 92), nor Marshall, (*Life of Washington*, II, 151), nor the minister Jedidiah Morse (*Annals of the American Revolution*, p. 167) discussed the discovery of the letters in providential terms.

31. Marshall, *Life of Washington*, IV, 342-358, quoting at pp. 349, 356. Marshall also appears to be more interested in "virtue" (or "virtu") and "fortuna" than in providence. J. G. A. Pocock discusses these concepts and their history in western political theory in *The Machiavellian Moment: Florentine Political Thought and the Atlantic Republican Tradition* (Princeton: Princeton University Press, 1975), pp. 31-48 and elsewhere.

32. Ibid., III, 530-531.

33. Lendrum, *American Revolution*, I, 382-384.

34. Ibid., p. 383. Also see ibid., I, 219, 330, 398-399; Pitkin, *Political and Civil History*, I, 3, 31-32, 117, 382-383; II, 43; Holmes, *Annals*, II, 370-371; Gordon, *History, II,* 514-515; McCulloch, *Concise History*, p. 86.

35. Warren, *American Revolution*, I, 176.

36. Ibid., III, 423; I, 127, 16.

37. Quoted in Ramsay, *Revolution of South-Carolina*, I, 109; Pitkin, *Political and Civil History*, I, 359ff.

38. Ibid., I, 126-127; Pitkin, *Political and Civil History*, I, 359-360. Pitkin included a lengthy extract of Drayton's charge in Appendix, 21.

39. Gordon to Adams, November 30, 1782 (*Gordon Letters*, p. 476). I do not wish to imply that ministers dealt with political themes covertly. As Nathan O. Hatch points out, "Few New England clergymen

throughout the eighteenth century avoided the charge that they made politics, rather than divinity, their study. Fewer still answered this accusation by retreating from the political implications of religion" (*Sacred Cause*, p. 97).

40. Lendrum, *American Revolution*, I, 310. See Ibid., II, 204; McCulloch, *Concise History*, pp. 44ff; Ramsay, *American Revolution*, II, 324. Gordon, *History, I*, 418. Also see Warren, *American Revolution*, II, 221–222 for another view.

41. Galloway, *Historical and Political Reflections on the Rise and Progress of the American Rebellion* . . . (London, 1780), esp. pp. 23–32. See J. F. MacClear, "New England and the Fifth Monarchy: The Quest for the Millennium in Early American Puritanism," *WMQ*, 3d ser., 32 (April 1975), 223–260. See Chapter 5.

42. Lendrum, *American Revolution*, II, 142, 147. John McCulloch and Jedidiah Morse referred to André as the "unfortunate major" (*Concise History*, p. 135; *Annals of the American Revolution*, p. 337). Also see Warren, *American Revolution*, II, 259–265. Charles Stedman, a member of the Welsh Fusileers attached to Cornwallis's army, wrote of André's capture as "the intervention of unfortunate circumstances," and as an "unfortunate train of incidents, which unexpectedly, and almost unavoidably, led him into that situation." He too saw the young major as "the unfortunate André," and viewed the whole affair as "tragic" (*The History of the Origin, Progress, and Termination of the American War*, 2 vols. [Dublin, 1794], II, 249–253). One would not, of course, expect to see a British officer or a Tory contrue events in the same way that the patriot historians did. But to say this is to acknowledge that providence had become an ideological construct.

43. Gordon, *History*, II, 574. It is also noteworthy that Gordon's question appears at the end of a paragraph. He opens the next paragraph as follows: "Gates after a victory acknowledged in general orders a Providence, but did not presume upon it, so as to neglect the dictates of human prudence" (ibid., p. 569). Gordon's juxtaposition of his question against a mundane statement of fact is open to various interpretations, but it seems to have the effect of deflating the momentousness of the question by implying that providence somehow benefitted from being acknowledged in general orders.

44. Braudy, *Narrative Form*, pp. 230, 158–171, quoted at p. 160.

45. Ibid., p. 86.

46. Ibid., p. 230, pp. 216–217.

47. Ibid., p. 229.

48. Marshall, *Life of Washington*, IV, 291.

49. Georges Sorel, *Reflections on Violence*, trans. T. E. Hulme and J. Roth (New York: Macmillan, 1950; rpt. Collier Books, 1974), p. 50.

50. Miller, "Covenant to Revival," p. 343. See Chapter 8.

CHAPTER 3: *Contingency, Complexity, and the Shape of History*

1. Marshall, *Life of Washington*, II, 365, 368–369 (emphasis added).

2. Ibid., pp. 323–324. Marshall heightened the sense of contingency by noting that Montgomery had been killed by an "accidental" shot fired by an unknown Canadian (II, 331). He also observed about a later American scheme to capture Canada: "A plan . . . consisting of so many parts, to be prosecuted both from Europe and America, by land and by water, which, to be successful, required such a harmonious co-operation of the whole, such a perfect coincidence of events, appeared to [Washington] to be exposed to too many accidents, to risk upon it interests of such high value (III, 574).

3. Condie, "Biographical Memoir," in Lendrum, *American Revolution*, II, 246.

4. See W. B. Gallie, *Philosophy and the Historical Understanding*, 2d ed. (New York: Schocken, 1968), pp. 110ff.

5. Marshall, *Life of Washington*, IV, 252; Ramsay, *Revolution of South-Carolina*, II, 266; Marshall, *Life of Washington*, III, 574; Ramsay, *Revolution of South-Carolina*, II, 267; Holmes, *Annals*, I, 113.

6. R. G. Collingwood, *The Idea of History* (New York: Oxford University Press, 1956), pp. 80–81. See Arthur H. Shaffer, *The Politics of History: Writing the History of the American Revolution, 1783–1815*, (Chicago: Precedent Publishing, 1975), p. 111.

7. Peter Gay, *The Enlightenment, An Interpretation*, vol. II: *The Science of Freedom* (New York: Knopf, 1969), pp. 380–390.

8. Edward Gibbon, *The Decline and Fall of the Roman Empire*, 3 vols. (New York: Modern Library, n.d.), I, 207.

9. John Bigland, *Letters on the Study and Use of Ancient and Modern History* . . . (London, 1805; rpt. Philadelphia, 1814), pp. 84, 342.

10. Ibid., p. 341.

11. Jonathan Boucher, *A View of the Causes and Consequences of the American Revolution* . . . (London, 1797), pp. i–vi, xix–xx.

12. Ramsay, *Revolution of South-Carolina*, II, 43; Gibbon, *Decline and Fall*, I, 207. See Leo Braudy, *Narrative Form in History & Fiction: Hume, Fielding, & Gibbon* (Princeton: Princeton University Press, 1970), pp. 213–268. See Chapters 7 and 8.

13. See Ernst Cassirer, *The Philosophy of the Enlightenment*, trans. Fritz C. A. Koelln and James T. Pettegrove (Boston: Beacon Press, 1955), chap. 5, esp. pp. 209–216; Gay, *The Enlightenment*, II, 390.

14. Holmes, *Annals*, I, 197; Gordon, *History*, I, 179–180.

15. See Gallie, *Philosophy and the Historical Understanding*, pp. 105–110. Apparently reduced to frustration, John Marshall sometimes relied on the construction: "*Whatever*" the causes may have been (*Life of Washington*, II, 428, 453).

16. See Chapter 5.

17. See Lester H. Cohen, "Explaining the Revolution: Ideology and Ethics in Mercy Otis Warren's Historical Theory," *WMQ* 3d ser., 37 (April 1980); Shaffer, *Politics of History*, chap. 3; Also see Chapter 7.

18. Pitkin, *Political and Civil History*, I, 4 (emphasis added). John Marshall also wrote of "those powerful causes which had lately been brought into operation" (*Life of Washington*, V, 456; III, 272).

19. Marshall, *Life of Washington*, III, 83, 330.

20. Lendrum, *American Revolution*, I, 232–233. See Warren, *American Revolution*, I, 54. Shaffer, *Politics of History*, chaps. 3 and 4.

21. Pitkin, *Political and Civil History*, I, 4; Noah Webster, *Letters to a Young Gentleman Commencing His Education: To Which is Subjoined a Brief History of the United States* (New Haven, 1823), p. 276 (emphasis added).

22. Herbert Butterfield, *The Whig Interpretation of History* (New York: Norton, 1965).

23. Ramsay, *American Revolution*, II, 43, 234; *Revolution of South-Carolina*, II, 200.

24. Ibid., I, 74.

25. Warren, *American Revolution*, I, 189; Marshall, *Life of Washington*, II, 199–200; Gordon, *History*, II, 569.

26. Lendrum, *American Revolution*, I, 403; II, 2 (emphasis added).

27. Hume, *A Treatise of Human Nature*, ed. L. A. Selby-Bigge; rev. ed. P. H. Nidditch (Oxford: Oxford University Press, 1978), p. 173.

28. Hume, *An Inquiry Concerning Human Understanding* (1748), ed. Charles W. Hendel, (Indianapolis: Bobbs-Merrill, 1955), pp. 95, 118. See pp. 34, 50, 69–71, 92, 154–155. See *Treatise*, pp. 124–155.

29. Bolingbroke quoted in Dorothy A. Koch, "English Theories Concerning the Nature and Uses of History, 1735–1791," (Ph.D. diss., Yale University, 1946), p. 29. Joseph Galloway similarly observed that "it is not uncommon for contrary extremes to produce the same effects" in *Historical and Political Reflections* (London, 1780), p. 113. Also see Marshall, *Life of Washington*, V, 519–520.

30. Warren, *American Revolution*, I, 62 (emphasis added).

31. Ramsay, *Revolution of South-Carolina*, I, 175. See Chapter 5.

32. Ramsay, *American Revolution*, II, 305.

33. Pitkin, *Political and Civil History*, I, 400; Warren, *American Revolution*, II, 307.

34. Hayden White, *Metahistory: The Historical Imagination in Nineteenth Century Europe* (Baltimore: Johns Hopkins University Press, 1973), p. 18.

35. Ibid., pp. 17–19.

36. Gordon, *History*, I, Preface. See Lionel Gossman, "History and Literature: Reproduction or Signification," in Robert H. Canary and Henry Kozicki, eds., *The Writing of History: Literary Form and Historical Understanding*, (Madison: University of Wisconsin Press, 1978), pp. 3–39; Braudy, *Narrative Form, passim*; White, *Metahistory*, esp. pp. 1–42.

37. Reynolds, *Discourses on Art*, ed. Robert R. Wark (London: Collier-Macmillan, 1969), pp. 202 (Discourse 13: December 11, 1786), 80 (Discourse 5: December 10, 1772).

38. Gordon, *History*, II, 39–46. See Gordon to Samuel Wilcon [Wilton?], April 6–May 6, 1776 in MHS, *Proceedings*, 60 (October 1926–June 1927): 363.

39. Richardson quoted in Ian Watt, *The Rise of the Novel: Studies in Defoe, Richardson and Fielding* (Berkeley: University of California Press, 1957; rpt. 1971), pp. 192, 193. Instead of using chapters to divide his *History*, Gordon used dated letters to a European correspondent (the real existence of whom was irrelevant to Gordon's purposes). By dating the letters, Gordon could refer to events that occurred only before the date on which he ostensibly wrote. He also had these fictitious letters cross his correspondent's in the mails. Both devices seem to have been intended to enhance the feeling of immediacy in much the way Richardson suggested.

40. See Braudy's excellent discussions of Fielding's *Tom Jones* and Gibbon's *Decline and Fall, Narrative Form*, pp. 144–180, 240–268. Also see Chapter 8.

CHAPTER 4: *The Hinge of the Revolution*

1. Quoted in Pitkin, *Political and Civil History*, II, 476 (emphasis added).

2. Marshall, *Life of Washington*, III, 451.

3. Lendrum, *American Revolution*, I, 382–383. Abiel Holmes wrote of the same event that "there appears to have been a deficiency either of skill or of vigilance" (*Annals*, II, 356).

4. Ibid., I, 399. The "enterprise" was Washington's subsequent capture of Princeton and his victorious march back across New Jersey.

5. Warren, *American Revolution*, I, 353–354.

6. Cooper, *North America*, p. 69; Holmes, *Annals*, II, 331; Gordon, *History*, II, 39.

7. Lendrum, *American Revolution*, II, 184; Gordon, *History*, II, 583–584; Warren, *American Revolution*, III, 109.

8. Ramsay, *Revolution of South-Carolina*, II, 34, 43–44; Gordon, *History*, II, 504–505. A formal inquiry was held to investigate Sullivan's actions at Staten Island, and while Sullivan was acquitted of any legal culpability Gordon had no misgivings about holding him historically responsible nevertheless.

The most illuminating account of historical responsibility was written by Charles Stedman, a member of a Welsh troop attached to Cornwallis's army. After losing the battle of Saratoga, General John Burgoyne was called before parliament to defend his actions. Stedman analyzed Burgoyne's testimony as follows: "In the whole of general Burgoyne's vindication . . . his method was to state a necessity for every one of his measures taken singly, and not as links of one chain or system of action." Burgoyne, that is, was a poor historian. Worse yet, however, in his defense Burgoyne took "care to pass over one material circumstance, that *that necessity* invariably originated, on his own part, from some previous omission or blunder" (*American War*, I, 356, emphasis added). Neither Stedman nor the American historians would argue that circumstances never created a virtual necessity, sufficient to overpower human efforts. But such a qualification merely heightens the sense of efficacy and responsibility in history, for in this and many other cases necessity was seen to arise from specific actions.

9. Warren, *American Revolution*, III, 309, 322, 201.

10. Condie, "Biographical Memoir," in Lendrum, *American Revolution*, II, 247; Lendrum, *American Revolution*, I, 381.

11. Peter Gay, *The Enlightenment, An Interpretation*, vol. II, *The Science of Freedom* (New York: Knopf, 1969), p. 387.

12. Quoted in Pitkin, *Political and Civil History*, II, 216–217.

13. Warren, *American Revolution*, I, 134; Ramsay, *Revolution of South-Carolina*, I, 22. See Warren, ibid., I, 109–111; Lendrum, *American Revolution*, I, 234–235; Hubley, *American Revolution*, p. 28.

14. Lendrum, *American Revolution*, I, 381. Quincy quoted in Pitkin, *Political and Civil History*, I, 264.

15. Lendrum, *American Revolution*, I. 275 (emphasis added); Miller, "From the Covenant to the Revival," in James Ward Smith and A. Leland Jamison, eds., *Religion in American Life*, vol. I, *The Shaping of*

American Religion (Princeton: Princeton University Press, 1961), p. 337. Historians of the "civil millennialism" of the Revolutionary era have for the most part ignored the problem of human efficacy, although raising it would provide a means for testing the role of providence in patriot sermons. Only John F. Berens has addressed himself to the issue explicitly, though his notion that Americans continued to believe in "the subordination of human to providential causation in God's moral government of the world," seems to be the leading assumption made by other scholars as well. Berens, *Providence and Patriotism in Early America, 1640–1815* (Charlottesville: University of Virginia Press, 1978), p. 88. I, obviously, disagree with his view. For others, see Chapter 1, n 61.

16. Ramsay, *Revolution of South-Carolina*, II, 18. See Chapter 7.

17. Lendrum, *American Revolution*, I, 223.

18. Quoted in Edmund S. Morgan and Helen M. Morgan, *The Stamp Act Crisis: Prologue to Revolution* (New York: Collier, 1967), p. 87. The Morgans argue essentially the same thing, pointing out that one of Grenville's principal strategies in devising the Stamp Act was intentionally to fail to state the sum he wanted the colonies to raise. By forcing the colonists to agree to a tax without knowing the amount was to "set a precedent for being consulted about any future taxes" (ibid, p. 82).

19. Quoted in Pitkin, *Political and Civil History*, I, 164. See Warren, *American Revolution*, III, 179.

20. Ibid., I, 173. See Ramsay, *Revolution of South-Carolina*, I, 8. These statements resound with echoes of the conspiracy theories used both by patriot and Tory historians. See Chapter 5.

21. Warren, *American Revolution*, I, 45; Lendrum, *American Revolution*, I, 251; Pitkin, *Political and Civil History*, I, 221.

22. Pitkin, *Political and Civil History*, II, 225.

23. Ramsay, *American Revolution*, II, 353–354 (emphasis added). See McCulloch, *Concise History*, p. 158; Warren, *American Revolution*, I, 229–230; Pitkin, *Political and Civil History*, I, 155.

24. Williams, *Natural and Civil History of Vermont* (1794), quoted in *Massachusetts Magazine*, 6, no. 12 (December 1794): 752–753.

25. Warren, *American Revolution*, III, 389, 434, 297; I, 155. See Warren to Abigail Adams, March 15, 1779 ("Letter-Book," p. 175).

26. Ibid., pp. 327–328. Both Hannah Arendt and the theologian of history Karl Lowith have questioned whether Christian historical theory could support the notion that *any* human historical event could be construed as being "new." See Arendt, *On Revolution* (New York: Viking, 1963; rpt. 1965), p. 20; Lowith, *Meaning in History* (Chicago: University of Chicago Press, 1964), pp. 166ff.

27. Ramsay, *American Revolution*, II, 356.

28. Hume, *An Inquiry Concerning Human Understanding* (1748), ed. Charles W. Hendel (Indianapolis: Bobbs-Merrill, 1955), p. 93. See Leo Braudy, *Narrative Form in History & Fiction: Hume, Fielding & Gibbon* (Princeton: Princeton University Press, 1970), pp. 39–65 for a discussion of Hume's movement away from a concern with the sameness of human nature.

29. Gay, *The Enlightenment, II*, 380. See ibid., pp. 167–174 for Gay's discussion of Enlightenment theories of human nature.

30. Hume, *Inquiry*, p. 95 (emphasis added); Gay, *The Enlightenment*, II, 380; Dorothy A. Koch, "English Theories Concerning the Nature and Use of History, 1735–1791" (Ph.D. diss., Yale University, 1946), pp. 318ff.

31. Quoted in Arthur H. Shaffer, *The Politics of History: Writing the History of the American Revolution, 1783–1815* (Chicago: Precedent Publishing, 1975), p. 67.

32. Warren, *American Revolution*, III, 330; to John Adams, October 1775 ("Letter-Book," p. 157); Gordon to Horatio Gates, January 24, 1783 (*Gordon Letters*, p. 483). See Gordon to Gates, June 17, 1779 (*Gordon Letters*, p. 415). Also see Chapter 7.

33. Arthur H. Shaffer provides the best discussion of the historians' environmentalism, *The Politics of History*, chaps. 4 and 5. Bernard Sheehan's excellent analysis treats the metaphysics of environmentalism, *Seeds of Extinction: Jeffersonian Philanthropy and the American Indian* (New York: Norton, 1973), esp. pp. 15–44. In my "Eden's Constitution: The Paradisiacal Dream and Enlightenment Values in Late Eighteenth Century Literature of the American Frontier," *Prospects*, 3 (1977): 83–109, I mention some of the more important works that deal with naturalistic environmentalism.

34. See Shaffer, *Politics of History*, chap. 4. John Lendrum, for example, wrote that "the inhabitants of the north are hardy, industrious, frugal, and in general intelligent; those of the south are more luxurious, indolent, and uninformed," though he hastened to add that, "like all general views," this one "admits of great limitation, and many exceptions" (*American Revolution*, I, 209).

35. See, for example, Warren, *American Revolution*, I, 154–155; II, 327; Warren to Hannah Winthrop, 1774 ("Letter-Book," p. 71). Also see Leo Marx, *The Machine in the Garden: Technology and the Pastoral Ideal in America* (New York: Oxford, 1964), esp. pp. 73–144; Daniel J. Boorstin, *The Lost World of Thomas Jefferson* (Boston: Beacon Press, 1948; rpt. 1968); Arthur O. Lovejoy, *The Great Chain of Being: The Study of the History of an Idea* (Cambridge: Harvard University Press, 1936; rpt. New York: Harper & Row, 1965), chap. 6.

36. Warren, *American Revolution*, III, 83 (emphasis added).

37. Ramsay to Thomas Jefferson, May 3, 1786 (Brunhouse, ed., *Writings of Ramsay*, p. 101). In this letter Ramsay acknowledged receipt of a copy of Jefferson's recently printed *Notes on Virginia*, the discussion of blacks in which prompted Ramsay's observations on nature and society. Blacks and native Americans were crucial in the development of this nascent American anthropology. See Sheehan, *Seeds of Extinction*; Winthrop D. Jordan, *White Over Black: American Attitudes Toward the Negro, 1550–1812* (Chapel Hill: University of North Carolina Press, 1968), esp. pp. 287–294, 429–569.

38. Ramsay, *American Revolution*, II, 315ff.

39. Warren to John Adams, July 16, 1807 (*Adams-Warren Letters*, p. 330).

40. Ramsay, "Oration of 1778" (Brunhouse, ed., *Writings of Ramsay*, pp. 188–189).

41. See Chapter 7.

CHAPTER 5: *Justifying the Revolution*

1. See in general Carl Lotus Becker, *The Declaration of Independence: A Study in the History of Political Ideas* (1922; rpt. Vintage Books, n.d.); Leo Strauss, *Natural Right and History* (1950; rpt. Phoenix Books, 1974); Otto Gierke, *Natural Law and the Theory of Society, 1500–1800*, trans. Ernest Barker (Cambridge, 1950), esp. chap. 2; Garry Wills, *Inventing America: Jefferson's Declaration of Independence* (Garden City, N.Y.: Doubleday, 1978); Caroline Robbins, *The Eighteenth Century Commonwealthmen* (Cambridge: Cambridge University Press, 1968), esp. pp. 67–72. Part of this chapter appeared in "The American Revolution and Natural Law Theory," *Journal of the History of Ideas*, 39 (July–September 1978): 491–502.

2. Warren, *American Revolution*, I, viii (emphasis added), Lendrum, *American Revolution*, I, 107. See Gordon, *History*, II, 295; Pitkin, *Political and Civil History*, I, 3; Ramsay, *Revolution of South-Carolina*, I, Preface; *American Revolution*, I, Preface.

3. Morse, *Annals*, p. 109.

4. Warren, *American Revolution*, I, 280–281; see III, 414.

5. Pitkin, *Political and Civil History*, I, 363, 364.

6. Ramsay, *American Revolution*, I, 335, 338.

7. Gordon, *History*, II, 296–297. See Morse, *Annals*, p. 246.

8. Morse, *Annals*, p. 255.

9. Warren, *American Revolution*, I, 145; see John Locke, *Two Treatises*

of Government, ed. with Introduction by Peter Laslett (Cambridge, 1960; rpt. Mentor Books, 1963), *Second Treatise,* chaps. 2 and 16; Strauss, *Natural Right and History,* pp. 202-251.

10. Ramsay, *American Revolution,* I, 347.

11. Marshall, *Life of Washington,* II, 413.

12. Gordon, *History,* II, 297. See Belknap, *New Hampshire,* II, 405.

13. Morse, *Annals,* p. 246 (emphasis added).

14. Ramsay, *American Revolution,* I, 337; Gordon, *History,* II, 289. See Marshall, *Life of Washington,* II, 412-413.

15. John Locke, *An Essay Concerning Human Understanding* (1690), collated and annotated by Alexander Campbell Fraser, 2 vols. (New York, 1959), II, 176-178.

16. Peter Gay, *The Enlightenment: An Interpretation: The Rise of Modern Paganism* (New York: Knopf, 1967), p. 18; Strauss, *Natural Right and History,* chaps. 5 and 6.

17. Warren, *American Revolution,* III, 423.

18. Daniel Walker Howe, *The Unitarian Conscience: Harvard Moral Philosophy, 1805-1861* (Cambridge: Harvard University Press, 1970), p. 29.

19. Robert Green McCloskey, ed., *The Works of James Wilson,* 2 vols. (Cambridge: Harvard University Press, 1967), I, 145-146.

20. Ibid., p. 147. See Wilson's "Of the General Principles of Law and Obligation," ibid., pp. 97-125.

21. Ibid.

22. Jefferson's "Summary View of the Rights of British America..." (1774) can be read as a harbinger of the processive theory of Natural Law. Like his Declaration of Independence, however, it is still more an uneasy mixture of the historical and the transcendent than a synthesis of them.

23. Warren, *American Revolution,* III, 327. See Ramsay, *History of South Carolina,* II, 75.

24. Quoted in Pitkin, *Political and Civil History,* I, 191 (emphasis added).

25. See Edmund Burke, "Speech on Conciliation with the Colonies" (March 22, 1775), Introduction and Notes by Jeffrey Hart (Chicago: Gateway Editions, 1964), *passim;* Strauss, *Natural Right and History,* pp. 294-323; Sheldon S. Wolin, *Politics and Vision: Continuity and Innovation in Western Political Thought* (Boston, 1960), pp. 409-410; Leslie Stephen, *History of English Thought in the Eighteenth Century,* 2 vols. (1876; rpt. Harbinger Books, 1962), II, 197ff.

26. Morse, *Annals,* p. 99. See Ramsay, *Revolution of South-Carolina,* II, 213; Warren, *American Revolution,* I, 274.

27. Ibid., p. 92.
28. Quoted in Lendrum, *American Revolution*, I, 244.
29. Pitkin, *Political and Civil History*, I, 85. Jedidiah Morse observed that taxation and representation were one right which amounted to "a privilege of ancient date" (*Annals*, p. 98).
30. Ramsay, *American Revolution*, I, 16.
31. Warren, *American Revolution*, III, 370.
32. Ibid., pp. 306–307.
33. Lendrum, *American Revolution*, I, 204; McCulloch, *Concise History*, p. 32; Ramsay, *American Revolution*, I, 27.
34. See Ramsay, *American Revolution*, I, 28ff.
35. Compare Burke's "Speech on Conciliation" with his *Reflections on the Revolution in France*, ed. Thomas H. D. Mahoney (Indianapolis: Bobbs-Merrill, 1955), esp. pp. 39–102. Mahoney summarizes the point as follows: "One of the main reasons why Burke opposed the French Revolution was precisely because the French were breaking violently with their past instead of using it . . . as the foundation for the future" (Ibid., p. xxii).
36. Jonathan Boucher, *A View of the Causes and Consequences of the American Revolution* . . . (Repro. of 1797 edition; Russell and Russell, 1967), p. xx.
37. Gordon, *History*, II, 295.
38. Bailyn, *The Ideological Origins of the American Revolution* (Cambridge: Harvard University Press, 1967), p. 95; see pp. 94–133. Also see Bailyn, *The Origins of American Politics* (New York: Vintage, 1970); Pauline Maier, *From Resistance to Revolution: Colonial Radicals and the Development of American Opposition to Britain, 1765–1776* (New York: Vintage, 1972), pp. 183–197.
39. Warren to Macaulay, June 9, 1773 ("Letter-Book," p. 2).
40. Warren to Macaulay, December 29, 1774 (ibid., pp. 3–5). Warren used the same language in her history, *American Revolution*, I, 41.
41. Warren to Macaulay, December 29, 1774 (ibid., p. 3). See Warren to Abigail Adams, March 15, 1779 (ibid., p. 175); to Martha Washington, 1776 (ibid., p. 119); to Catharine Macaulay, February 18, 1777 (ibid., pp. 17–19). See Chapter 7.
42. Lendrum, *American Revolution*, I, 295.
43. Ibid., I, 223, 232.
44. Ramsay, *Revolution of South-Carolina*, I, 8; Pitkin, *Political and Civil History*, I, 157, 161. See Ramsay, *Revolution of South-Carolina*, I, 9.
45. Morse, *Annals*, p. 97; Warren, *American Revolution* I, 37, 50.
46. Warren, *American Revolution*, I, 65; Gordon, *History*, I, 330–331.
47. Ramsay, *South-Carolina*, I, 134; *Revolution of South-Carolina*, I, 28.

48. Pitkin, *Political and Civil History*, I, 107; Lendrum, *American Revolution*, I, 113.

49. Noah Webster, *Letters to a Young Gentleman Commencing his Education: To Which is Subjoined a Brief History of the United States* (New Haven, 1823), pp. 271, 273. Timothy Pitkin added: "Though apparently mild at first, [Andros] soon discovered the rapacity of the ancient governors of a Roman province." He was, in short, "the true representative of his master" (*Political and Civil History*, I, 116).

50. Pitkin, *Political and Civil History*, I, 118–119; Warren, *American Revolution*, I, 41.

51. Morse, *Annals*, p. 60; McCulloch, *Concise History*, p. 40. See Holmes, *Annals*, I, 265. Several historians presented Bacon's Rebellion as a glorious precursor of the American Revolution, sometimes dwelling on the numerological significance of its occurring in 1676. See Wilcomb E. Washburn, *The Governor and the Rebel: A History of Bacon's Rebellion in Virginia* (Chapel Hill: University of North Carolina Press, 1957), esp. pp. 1–17. The historians saw a number of revolutionary images prefigured in seventeenth-century conflicts. See, e.g., Marshall, *Life of Washington*, I, 68ff; Pitkin, *Political and Civil History*, I, 72ff., 101ff. Also see Wesley Frank Craven, *The Dissolution of the Virginia Company: The Failure of a Colonial Experiment* (New York: Oxford, 1932).

52. Ramsay, *American Revolution*, I, 345. See Jeremy Belknap to Ebenezer Hazard, April 16, 1782 (MHS, *Collections*, 5th ser., 2: 123–126). In light of my discussion in Chapter 4, it should be noted that the use of a conspiracy theory and the notion of a self-fulfilling prophecy presupposes the historical efficacy of man. As Gordon Wood has observed: "American Whigs, like men of the eighteenth century generally, were fascinated with what seemed to the age to be the newly appreciated problem of human motivation and causation in the affairs of the world. In the decade before independence the Americans sought endlessly to discover the supposed calculations and purposes of individuals or groups that lay behind the otherwise incomprehensible rush of events. . . . The belief in conspiracy grew naturally out of the enlightened need to find the human purposes behind the multitude of phenomena, to find the causes for what happened in the social world just as the natural scientist was discovering the causes for what happened in the physical world" ("Rhetoric and Reality in the American Revolution," *WMQ* 3d, 23 [January 1966]: 17). It is no accident, then, that Ramsay refers to British actions as the "efficient cause" of the separation from Britain. Equally important, the conspiracy theory presupposes a theory of intention that locates people's motives not in what

they say but in what they do, which also presupposes that people's actions are efficacious in history.

53. Joseph Galloway, *Historical and Political Reflections on the Rise and Progress of the American Rebellion* ... (London, 1780), pp. 3-5.

54. Ibid., pp. 101-102, 111.

55. Ibid., pp. 24-29.

56. Ibid., pp. 31, 54-55. Galloway almost certainly intended his work to be *politically* effective. Writing in 1780, a particularly difficult time for the colonies, Galloway used a strategy of divisiveness, distinguishing between the people at large and that "dangerous combination of men" in order, presumably, to reach a potentially moderate audience and woo them back to loyalty. Thus the following: "In short, the colonists at this moment are in that very despotism in which Charles II found the people of Britain at the time of his restoration. They have seen the arts and frauds of their leaders, and are daily suffering under their treachery and tyranny; their country has been drained of its labourers, and remains uncultivated; their commerce is ruined, and every necessary of life is extravagantly dear, and but few to be obtained; and to increase this part of their distress, the little property remaining is daily seized, and nothing returned for it but money of no value, insomuch that they have wasted upwards of £40,000,000 sterling in forging their own chains. Laws the most unjust, oppressive, and sanguinary, have been made for their government. Children have been driven from their parents, and husbands from their wives, into the field, to support the tyranny of their rulers; and more than one fifth part of their white inhabitants who were capable of bearing arms, have already perished in a war, unjust and unnatural. . . . Disarmed, ruined, and incapable of assisting themselves, they are looking up to Great Britain with impatience for deliverance from yet more grievous misfortunes" (ibid., p. 116.

Jonathan Boucher's strategy was similar to Galloway's though, written after the war, it was less strident: "[T]he bulk of the people of America were as innocent of any premeditated purpose of revolting, as the people of England, properly so called, were of abetting them in their revolt. But whilst this statement lessens their guilt, it probably aggravates their folly. Owing to an unhappy concurrence of various causes, they suffered themselves to be made the dupes of a few desperate democrats in both countries, who thus misled them (as it is the hard fate of the people always to be misled) merely that they might be made their stepping-stones into power" (*Causes and Consequences*, p. xv n).

57. Ramsay, *American Revolution*, I, 332-333.

58. Ibid., p. 335. See Morse, *Annals,* p. 246.

59. Ibid., pp. 27-28.

60. Ibid., pp. 28-29.

61. Ibid., p. 29. See ibid., pp. 31ff, for Ramsay's summary.

62. The argument for prior independence, like the conspiracy theory, had been prefigured in the pamphlet literature of the 1760s. The authors of the pamphlets tended to emphasize English rights—rights guaranteed by the English constitution regardless of where Englishmen lived—and colonial rights as guaranteed by the charters. But there was already apparent in the pamphlets a shift toward a Natural Rights argument with an emphasis on traditional American legal practices, foreshadowing the historians' historicizing of Natural Law and their argument for prior independence. In "The Colonel Dismounted" (1764), for example, Richard Bland showed how Virginia was settled at the colonists' own expense and argued that they retained their rights as Englishmen because those rights were guaranteed by the original charter. Significantly, Bland also tied constitutional rights to traditional practices, arguing that the power of the General Assembly, "by a constant and uninterrupted usage and custom," has been exercised "for more than 140 years" (in Bernard Bailyn, ed., *Pamphlets of the American Revolution, 1750-1776,* vol. I, *1750-1765* [Cambridge: Harvard University Press, 1965], p. 323, see pp. 319ff). Similarly, James Otis associated Natural Rights with the origins of the colonies and with the practices of the colonists from the beginning ("The Rights of the British Colonies Asserted and Proved" [1764], ibid., pp. 436-470). By the 1770s the argument for prior independence was even more explicit. See, for example, Thomas Jefferson, "Summary View of the Rights of British America" (1774). The English philosopher and proponent of the American cause Richard Price made perhaps the strongest case for prior independence and for the notion that Britain was attempting to enslave a foreign nation by conquest, in "Observations on the Nature of Civil Liberty, The Principles of Government, and the Justice and Policy of the War with America . . ." (6th ed., London, 1776).

The historians, writing a decade and more later, cultivated the argument by joining the principle of prior independence with the conspiracy theory in an effort to demonstrate that Britain had caused the Revolution by violating Americans' Natural Rights. Like Ramsay, John McCulloch argued that "the emigrants were at the whole charge of transporting themselves, and purchasing their lands from the natives. And it was owing to their perseverance and industry, that the country was changed from a desolate wilderness, to a land abounding with every thing fit for the habitation of civilized man" (*Concise History*, p. 36; see pp. 47, 230–231). Timothy Pitkin argued that the Mayflower Compact "contained the elements of those forms of government peculiar to the new world" (*Political and Civil History*, I, 33; see pp. 54, 109, 153–154). John Lendrum saw seventeenth-century New England approaching "very near to an independent commonwealth" (*American Revolution*, I, 143; see pp. 108, 120, 214). And John Marshall believed that "the colony of Massachusetts . . . had been conducted, from its commencement, very much on the plan of an independent society" (*Life of Washington*, I, 105–106; see pp. 24, 25). Also see Warren, *American Revolution*, I, 52, 155; III, 413.

CHAPTER 6: *An American History*

1. Ramsay, *Revolution of South-Carolina*, I, viii–ix.

2. Ramsay, *American Revolution*, I, x; Gordon, *History*, I, i–ii; Warren, *American Revolution*, I, vi.

3. Adams to Belknap, July 24, 1789 (MHS, *Collections*, 6th ser., 4: 438); Adams to Jefferson, July 3, 1813 in Lester J. Cappon, ed., *The Adams-Jefferson Correspondence* (Chapel Hill: University of North Carolina Press, 1959; rpt. New York: Clarion Books, 1971), p. 349.

4. Adams to Warren, August 15, 1807 (*Adams-Warren Letters*, p. 463).

5. Warren to Adams, May 8, 1780 ("Letter-Book," pp. 179–180); December 28, 1780 (ibid., p. 183 [emphasis added]). For Warren's illuminating letters to Adams, 1775–1786, see ibid., pp. 152–195. See Warren to Samuel Otis, December 22, 1772 (ibid., p. 450).

6. Warren to Charles Warren, August 29, 1780 ("Letter-Book," pp. 351–352).

7. Some of the canons that governed eighteenth-century English historiography emerged a century earlier. See F. Smith Fussner, *The Historical Revolution: English Historical Writing and Thought, 1580–1640* (New York: Columbia University Press, 1962). For the eighteenth century see Dorothy A. Koch. "English Theories Concerning the Nature and Uses of History, 1735–1791" (Ph.D. diss, Yale University, 1946); Leo Braudy, *Narrative Form in History & Fiction: Hume, Fielding & Gibbon* (Princeton: Princeton University Press, 1970); Hayden White, *Metahistory: The Historical Imagination in Nineteenth Century Europe* (Baltimore: Johns-Hopkins University Press, 1973), pp. 45–80.

8. Ramsay to Morse, August 12, 1807 (Brunhouse, ed., *Writings of Ramsay*, p. 160); Warren to Adams, August 7, 1807 (*Adams-Warren Letters*, p. 424); Belknap, *New Hampshire*, I, v; Holmes, *Annals*, I, iv; Pitkin, *Political and Civil History*, I, 7.

9. To Benjamin Rush, April 13, 1786; to Elias Boudinot, April 13, 1786; to John Adams, September 20, 1787; to Charles Thomson, September 20, 1809 (in Brunhouse, ed., *Writings of Ramsay*, pp. 99–100, 114, 164).

10. May 3, 1786 (ibid., pp. 101–102). Regarding Ramsay's political activities, see Brunhouse, Introduction. Ramsay was "chairman" of the Continental Congress from November 23, 1785, to May 15, 1786, in the absence of an ailing President John Hancock (ibid., p. 94 n 1).

11. October 25, 1782 ("Letter-Book," p. 184). Adams was incensed at Warren's work, particularly insofar as it discussed himself personally and his role in the Revolution. His letters to Warren (in *Adams-Warren Letters*) are a study in vitriol.

12. August 30, 1781 (*Gordon Letters*, pp. 457–458). See Gordon to Washington, July 23, 1778 (ibid., p. 405).

13. June 18, 1783 (ibid., p. 493).

14. March 16, 1778 (ibid., p. 393). Gordon also wrote to Gates telling him of his visit to Mount Vernon to use Washington's papers. On June 2, "I sat into work and followed it closely, rising by day light and being at his books as soon as I could read, and continued until evening, breaking off only for meals, and never went once to visit tho' invited. By the 19th about two o'clock I had finished, having searched and extracted thirty and three folio volumes of copied letters of the General's, besides three volumes of private, seven volumes of general orders, and bundles upon bundles of letters to the General. Don't you think I labored hard?" (August 31, 1784 [ibid., p. 506]).

15. Lionel Gossman, "History and Literature: Reproduction or Signification," in Robert H. Canary and Henry Kozicki, eds., *The Writing of History: Literary Form and Historical Understanding* (Madison: University of Wisconsin Press, 1978), pp. 3–39. See Koch, "English Theories"; Braudy, *Narrative Form*. This chapter will make clear that the revolutionary historians were familiar (in some cases intimately so) with the writings of contemporary English historians. This point squares with Henry May's treatment of the general penetration and spread of European Enlightenment ideas in late-eighteenth-century America in *The Enlightenment in America* (Oxford: Oxford University Press, 1976). David Lundberg and May also provide an enormously useful guide to the availability of certain European books in America with "The Enlightened Reader in America" in *American Quarterly*, 28 (Summer 1976):

262–271, and including twenty additional pages of graphs tracing the fates of various European books in American libraries.

16. Gossman, "History and Literature," p. 12.

17. March 16, 1778 (*Gordon Letters,* p. 393).

18. Gordon to Gates, October 16, 1782 (ibid., p. 475). Gordon's work did in fact suffer in the American press and even among his friends. See, e.g., the Jeremy Belknap–Ebenezer Hazard correspondence between June 21 and August 27, 1789 (MHS, *Collections,* 5th ser., 3: 145–163). *The Independent Chronicle,* June 18, 1789, ran a piece on Gordon's *History* in which Gordon was called a "mercenary scribbler, who makes books with no other view than to gain a few pence." The reviewer, "Americanus," added: "In every part of his history, there is a very remarkable want of truth, and integrity, but the arrows of his envy and malevolence, are so blunted by his indiscretion in his attacks, and the want of decency in his stile and manner, that they do no injury, either to the characters they are pointed at, or to the country which he wishes to wound and injure" (*Gordon Letters,* pp. 557–558).

19. *American Magazine,* June 1788, p. 467; July 1788, pp. 536–537.

20. Ibid., p. 537.

21. *Massachusetts Magazine,* 1 (July 1789): 441.

22. Ibid., July 1789, pp. 441–442. Mercy Warren also criticized Gibbon both for his style and for his heterodox religious attitudes: to Winslow Warren, March 1785 ("Letter-Book," pp. 309–310); to George Warren, July 1795 ("Letter-Book," pp. 419–420).

23. "On the Literature, Wit and Taste of the European Nations," *Columbian Magazine,* 2 (August 1788): 424–426 (continued from July 1788, ibid., pp. 384–388). For a historical interpretation of the relationship between fiction and history, see Gossman, "History and Literature." Also see Chapter 8.

24. *Massachusetts Magazine,* 1 (August 1789): 476. It might be noted that these views echo those of Gibbon himself. In the opening paragraph of his *Memoir* Gibbon wrote: "Truth, naked, unblushing truth, the first virtue of more serious history, must be the sole recommendation of this personal narrative" (M. M. Reese, ed., *Gibbon's Autobiography* [London: Routledge and Kegan Paul, 1971], p. 1). Much of Gibbon's *Essay on the Study of Literature* (London, 1764) was devoted to style and taste and their relationship to truth. For Gibbon's historical writing and theory, see Braudy, *Narrative Form;* the Summer 1976 issue of *Daedalus,* devoted to Gibbon, contains several excellent articles and provides a fruitful introduction to his writings.

25. Ibid., p. 476; Webster, *Dissertations on the English Language . . .* (Boston, 1789), Appendix, pp. 393–394. The Appendix was printed in *Mas-*

sachusetts Magazine, 1 (October, November, and December 1789): 605–608, 658–661, 743–746.

26. In his "Memorial to the Legislature of New Yorrk" (January 18, 1783), Webster wrote of the need "to reform the abuses and corruptions" of American speech, arguing that America must be "rendered as independent and illustrious in letters as she is already in arms and civil policy" (Harry R. Warfel, ed., *Letters of Noah Webster* [New York: Library Publishers, 1953], pp. 5–6).

27. *Dissertations*, p. 397.

28. Ibid., p. 406.

29. Webster, *A Collection of Essays and Fugitiv Writings on Moral, Historical, Political and Literary Subjects* (Boston, 1790), p. 94. See John Bigland, *Letters on the Study and Use of Ancient and Modern History* (Philadelphia, 1806), pp. 124–125, 158. On Webster's theories of culture and language, see Vincent Paul Bynack, "Language and the Order of the World: Noah Webster and the Idea of an American Culture" (Ph.D. diss., Yale University, 1978).

30. Warren to Winslow Warren, December 24, 1779 ("Letter-Book," pp. 240–243). In this letter Warren also criticized David Hume, who enjoyed a surprisingly good reputation among the historians despite his "Tory" politics and skeptical philosophy, and Lord Bolingbroke, about whom the consensus of opinion was overwhelmingly positive. Warren expressed great admiration for Gibbon's style, though she preferred [Adam?] Ferguson's because it was less "flowery" and because Ferguson refrained from sneering at religion (to Winslow Warren, March 1785 [ibid., pp. 309–310]). Also see Warren to Winslow Warren, March 25, 1780; to Charles Warren, August 29, 1780, and January 1, 1784 (ibid., pp. 245, 351–352, 354–355); Jeremy Belknap to Ebenezer Hazard, regarding the style of Samuel Johnson, September 12, 1783 (MHS, *Collections*, 5th ser., 2: 247).

31. "Critical Reflections on Style," *Massachusetts Magazine*, 4 (April 1792): 237–238.

32. Blair, "Literary Character of Swift," *Massachusetts Magazine*, 3 (December 1791): 757–758; Mercy Warren to Winslow Warren, December 24, 1779 ("Letter-Book," p. 243); Benjamin Rush to David Ramsay, November 5, 1778 (Brunhouse, ed., *Writings of Ramsay*, p. 57). See *Massachusetts Magazine*, 4 (January 1792): 4–5; Ramsay to Rush, February 3, 1779 (Brunhouse, ed., *Writings of Ramsay*, p. 58). Warren to John Adams, April 27, 1785 ("Letter-Book," p. 191); Belknap-Hazard letters concerning Oliver Goldsmith's writings, July 1 and July 26, 1782, and July 18, 1783 (MHS, *Collections*, 5th ser., 2: 135–137, 142, 233); Blair, *Lectures on Rhetoric and Belles Lettres* (London, 1783), II, 274.

33. *Massachusetts Magazine,* 4 (December 1792): 741.

34. Ibid., 3 (September 1791): 568. See 3 (November and December 1791): 698–702, 759–761; 4 (May 1792): 321.

35. Brunhouse, ed., *Writings of Ramsay,* p. 220; *Columbian Magazine,* I (September 1786): 22.

36. *American Magazine,* September 1788, pp. 739–740; *Massachusetts Magazine,* 3 (September 1791): 569. The reviewer of Minot's history also referred to "those elegant and judicious historians, Mr. Belknap and Dr. Ramsay" (*American Magazine,* September 1788, p. 742).

37. Madison to Thomas Jefferson, March 27, 1786 (Brunhouse, ed., *Writings of Ramsay,* p. 226). See Ramsay to Belknap March 11, 1795 (ibid., p. 140); Ramsay to John Eliot, November 26, 1788 (ibid., p. 123), praising Minot's work; Belknap to Hazard, August 2, 1788, and Hazard to Belknap, August 21, 1788, regarding Minot's work (MHS, *Collections,* 5th ser., 3: 55, 59). The review of Ramsay's work appeared in *Columbian Magazine,* 4 (June 1790): 373–377. Similarly, a reviewer of Samuel Williams's history remarked that his style "exhibits a *native* majesty, not deprived of the charms of variety by the refinements of modern civilization" in *Massachusetts Magazine,* 6 (December 1794): 748, emphasis added.

38. Ramsay to John Coakley Lettsom, October 29, 1808 (Brunhouse, ed., *Writings of Ramsay,* p. 163).

39. See Chapter 7.

40. Webster, *Essays,* p. 87. An older Webster was certain about the causal relationship between language and politics: "It is obvious to my mind, that popular errors proceeding from a misunderstanding of words, are among the efficient causes of our political disorders" (*Observations on Language* [1839], quoted in Richard M. Rollins, "Words as Social Control: Noah Webster and the Creation of the American Dictionary" in *American Quarterly,* 28 [Fall 1976]: 424). Also see Rollins, "Noah Webster: Propagandist for the Revolution" in *Connecticut History,* 18 (November 1976): 22–43).

41. Webster, *Dissertations,* pp. 397–398.

42. November 12, 1807, in Charles Burr Todd, *Life and Letters of Joel Barlow: Poet, Statesman, Philosopher* (New York: G. P. Putnam's Sons, 1886; rpt. New York: DaCapo, 1970), p. 247.

43. August 2, 1787 ("Letter-Book," p. 22).

44. Arthur H. Shaffer, *The Politics of History: Writing the History of the American Revolution, 1783–1815* (Chicago: Precedent Publishing, 1975), pp. 3–4.

45. Quoted in Robert E. Spiller, ed., *The American Literary Revolution, 1783–1837* (New York: New York University Press, 1967), p. 8. Regard-

ing cultural nationalism and the fine arts, see Lillian B. Miller, *Patrons and Patriotism: The Encouragement of the Fine Arts in the United States, 1790–1860,* (Chicago: University of Chicago Press, 1966). David Ramsay, who wrote history despite its financial disappointments, thought "the trade of an author is a very poor one in our new world," and longed "to see the day when an author will at least be on an equal footing with a taylor or shoemaker in getting his living" (to William Gordon, January 18, 1786 [Brunhouse, *Writings of Ramsay,* p. 96]; to Benjamin Rush, May 1, 1787 [ibid., p. 112]).

    46. Quoted in Spiller, ed., *American Literary Revolution,* p. 23.

    47. October 15, 1785 (Merrill D. Peterson, ed., *The Viking Portable Jefferson* [New York: Viking, 1975], pp. 393–394). See Mercy Warren to her sons James, Winslow, Charles, and George ("Letter-Book," pp. 213–438).

    48. Rush, *Essays, Literary, Philosophical and Moral,* 2d ed. with additions (Philadelphia, 1806), pp. 14–15; "A Letter by Dr. Benjamin Rush Describing the Consecration of the German College at Lancaster, June 1787 (Lancaster, Pa., 1945), pp. 1 and *passim;* Webster, "On the Education of Youth in America," *Essays,* p. 23. See Webster, *A Compendious Dictionary of the English Language* (Hartford and New Haven, 1806), Preface; Rollins, "Words as Social Control"; Shaffer, *Politics of History,* p. 41.

    49. Ramsay, "Oration of 1778" (Brunhouse, ed., *Writings of Ramsay,* p. 190).

    50. *Universal Asylum and Columbian Magazine,* 6 (April 1791): 237.

    51. *Massachusetts Magazine,* 1, (August 1789): 475.

    52. *American Magazine,* 1 (September 1788): 740, emphasis added; *Columbian Magazine,* 4 (June 1790); 374.

    53. Webster to John Canfield, January 6, 1783 (Warfel, ed., *Letters of Webster,* p. 4); Webster, *Dictionary* (1806), Preface, pp. xviii, xv, xvi.

    54. Koch, "English Theories," pp. 151–227; Isaac Kramnick, ed., *Lord Bolingbroke: Historical Writings* (Chicago: University of Chicago Press, 1972), pp. xi–xii; Braudy, *Narrative Form,* pp. 21–30.

    55. Quoted in Koch, "English Theories," pp. 182, 203–222. See pp. 163–201.

    56. Priestley, *Lectures on History and General Policy,* 2 vols. (Philadelphia, 1803), I, 2–4. See Kramnick, ed., *Bolingbroke,* pp. 70–77.

    57. Koch, English Theories," pp. 224–225, emphasis added. See pp. 226–27.

    58. See Gordon S. Wood, *The Creation of the American Republic, 1776–1787* (Chapel Hill: University of North Carolina Press, 1969), esp. pp. 344–389.

59. Warren, *American Revolution*, III, 324–325. As in a few other cases, Warren lifted her own words from earlier letters, in this instance from a letter to Catharine Macaulay (May 31, 1791, "Letter-Book," p. 30).

60. Ibid., pp. 73–74, 336–337. See Chapter 7.

61. February 2, 1814 (*Adams-Warren Letters*, p. 505).

62. To Benjamin Rush, August 31, 1809 in John A. Schutz and Douglass Adair, eds., *The Spur of Fame: Dialogues of John Adams and Benjamin Rush, 1805–1813* (San Marino, Calif.: The Huntington Library, 1966), p. 152.

63. To Thomas Jefferson, July 3, 1813 (Cappon, ed., *Adams-Jefferson Correspondence*, p. 349). Jefferson ought not to have been surprised by Adams's sentiments, since Jefferson had written some years before to Joel Barlow saying that Marshall's work, then nearing completion, "is intended to come out just in time to influence the next presidential election. It is written, therefore, principally with a view to electioneering purposes." Jefferson, however, did not condemn Marshall's work because it was politically motivated. To the contrary, he pointed out what a useful political strategy it served and recommended it to his own followers (Todd, *Life and Letters of Barlow*, p. 154).

64. November 30, 1782 (*Gordon Letters*, p. 476); August 13, 1785 (ibid., p. 514). Also see Gordon to Adams, October 4, 1785 (ibid., pp. 521–522).

65. Belknap, *New Hampshire*, I, v.

CHAPTER 7: *The Historian of the Revolution as a Revolutionary Historian*

1. Enlightenment historians made "no attempt ... to lift history above the level of propaganda," observed R. G. Collingwood. But, added Peter Gay, it had to be "propaganda in behalf of the truth, and it would be effective propaganda only if it were the truth" (Collingwood, *The Idea of History*, [New York: Oxford University Press, 1956], p. 81; Gay, *The Enlightenment, An Interpretation: The Science of Freedom* [New York: Knopf, 1969], p. 384).

2. Gordon to John Adams, June 5, 1777 (*Gordon Letters*, p. 340); Ramsay to William Henry Drayton, September 1, 1779; to Benjamin Rush, August 6, 1786 (Brunhouse, ed., *Writings of Ramsay*, pp. 64, 105).

3. This chapter is deeply indebted to Bernard Bailyn, *The Ideological Origins of the American Revolution* (Cambridge: Harvard University Press, 1967), and *The Origins of American Politics* (New York: Vintage, 1970); Gordon S. Wood, *The Creation of the American Republic, 1776–1787*

(Chapel Hill: University of North Carolina Press, 1969); and J. G. A. Pocock, *The Machiavellian Moment: Florentine Political Thought and the Atlantic Republican Tradition* (Princeton: Princeton Unversity Press, 1975), esp. pp. 462–552.

4. See Lester H. Cohen, "Explaining the Revolution: Ideology and Ethics in Mercy Otis Warren's Historical Theory," *WMQ,* 3d ser. (April 1980). Much of the material concerning Warren in this chapter derives from the earlier article.

5. Warren to John Adams, August 15, 1807 (*Adams-Warren Letters,* p. 453).

6. Warren to Winslow Warren, September 1785; to Winslow Warren, November 20, 1780; to John Adams, December 28, 1780 ("Letter-Book," pp. 314–315, 256–257, 183); Warren, *American Revolution,* I, viii. Warren identified "the old patriots" with "the pure principles of republicanism" in a letter to Catharine Macaulay, August 2, 1787 (ibid., p. 22).

7. Quoted in Isaac Kramnick, ed., *Lord Bolingbroke: Historical Writings* (Chicago: University of Chicago Press, 1972), p. xvi. The best short discussion of the exemplary theory is by George H. Nadel, "Philosophy of History Before Historicism," *History and Theory,* 3, no. 3. (1964): 291–315. Also see Kramnick, ed., *Bolingbroke,* pp. xv–xxxix; Dorothy A. Koch, "English Theories Concerning the Nature and Use of History, 1735–1791," (Ph.D. diss., Yale University, 1946), esp. pp. 58–72. The following discussion is also indebted to: Paul Hazard, *The European Mind, 1680–1715* (Cleveland: Meridian Books, 1968), pp. 29–52; Leslie Stephen, *History of English Thought in the Eighteenth Century,* 2 vols. (New York: Harcourt, 1962), II, 141–157; Richard H. Popkin, *The History of Scepticism, From Erasmus to Descartes* (New York: Harper & Row, 1968); Carl L. Becker, *The Heavenly City of the Eighteenth Century Philosophers* (New Haven: Yale University Press, 1932, 1967), pp. 71–118; Leo Braudy, *Narrative Form in History & Fiction: Hume, Fielding & Gibbon* (Princeton: Princeton University Press, 1970), pp. 21–30.

8. Ramsay, *Revolution of South-Carolina,* I, vi; Gordon, *History,* I, i (emphasis added).

9. Ramsay to John Eliot, April 7, 1810 (Brunhouse, ed., *Writings of Ramsay,* p. 166); Gordon, *History,* I, i.

10. Nadel, "Philosophy of History." Bolingbroke attributed his famous maxim—"history is philosophy teaching by examples"— to Dionysius of Halicarnassus, who attributed it in turn to Thucydides (Nadel, ibid., p. 301; Koch, "English Theories," p. 58 n 1).

11. Plutarch, *The Lives of the Noble Grecians and Romans,* trans. by John Dryden and revised by Arthur Hugh Clough (New York: Modern Li-

brary, n.d.), p. 293. For the influence of classical writers on Americans in the Colonial Era, see Richard M. Gummere, *The American Colonial Mind and the Classical Tradition: Essays in Comparative Culture* (Cambridge: Harvard University Press, 1963); H. Trevor Colbourn, *The Lamp of Experience: Whig History and the Intellectual Origins of the American Revolution* (Chapel Hill: University of North Carolina Press, 1965), pp. 21–25; Howard Mumford Jones, *O Strange New World: American Culture, The Formative Years* (London: Chatto and Windus, 1965), pp. 227–272.

12. Nadel, "Philosophy of History," pp. 294–295. The revolutionary histories abound with references to "Roman virtue" and related classical images. As Nadel points out, Christian views of virtue tempered the more militaristic and heroic attitudes of the Romans with love and compassion. But the Americans seem to have had no difficulty in assimilating Roman virtue into their christianized version of the exemplary theory.

13. John Bigland, *Letters on the Study and Use of Ancient and Modern History* (Philadelphia, 1806), pp. 27ff. See Koch, "English Theories," pp. 228–243.

14. Fordyce, *Dialogues Concerning Education* (London, 1745–48), and Turnbull, *Observations Upon Liberal Education* (London, 1742), quoted in Koch, "English Theories," pp. 300, 311.

15. Quoted in Koch, "English Theories," p. 150. See Hazard, *European Mind,* pp. 29–52, 99–115; Popkin, *History of Scepticism.*

16. Quoted in Koch, "English Theories," p. 143; see pp. 133–150. Also see David Fate Norton and Richard H. Popkin, eds., *David Hume: Philosophical Historian* (Indianapolis: Bobbs-Merrill, 1965), pp. ix–xxxi; Braudy, *Narrative Form,* pp. 31–91.

17. Koch, "English Theories," p. 58; see pp. 13–18. See Kramnick, ed., *Bolingbroke,* Introduction.

18. Mather, *Magnalia Christi Americana: Or, The Ecclesiastical History of New England* (London, 1702), General Introduction, sec. 5. In light of his protestations about impartiality, see his "Life of John Winthrop" (ibid., bk. 2, chap. 4). Also see Sacvan Bercovitch, *The Puritan Origins of the American Self* (New Haven: Yale University Press, 1975), pp. 1–34.

19. Warren to Catharine Macaulay, February 1, 1777 ("Letter-Book," p. 10).

20. Warren, *American Revolution,* I, 1–2. I have adopted the term "avarice" as the antithesis of virtue both because the historians used the word so frequently in their published and private writings and because it conveys more precisely than the traditional "vice" (which they also used) a *lust* for wealth, power, luxury, and distinction. "Vice" is too passive to capture their sense of a willful (even if blind) pursuit. At the

same time, while the historians believed that avarice led to "corruption," both "corruption" and "commerce" (as J. G. A. Pocock has used the latter term) are systemic concepts that go beyond their more limited and personalized image of avarice. See Pocock, "Virtue and Commerce in the Eighteenth Century," *Journal of Interdisciplinary History,* 3 (Summer 1972): 120–134, and *The Machiavellian Moment,* pp. 462–505.

21. As I pointed out in Chapter 4, the historians, like other enlightened Americans, tended to emphasize the role of environment in shaping human conduct. Although they paid lip service to contemporary theories of "human nature," they were less interested in explaining history in terms of fundamental passions or appetites that determined behavior, than in a notion of "human character," which they saw as the developing product of a multiplicity of social and personal forces. Thus Warren may have discerned a "propensity in human nature" for people to "tyrannize" their fellows, but she argued more emphatically that "the character of man is never finished until the last act of the drama is closed," and that people's conduct owes "*more* to the existing state or stage of society" than to the nature or disposition of mankind (to John Adams, October 1775 ["Letter-Book," p. 157]; to John Adams, July 16, 1807 [*Adams-Warren Letters,* p. 330]; *American Revolution,* III, 83 [emphasis added]).

22. Bolingbroke quoted in Koch, "English Theories," p. 25; Warren to James Warren, Jr., 1773; to George Warren, February 17, 1793 ("Letter-Book," pp. 217, 406). She also wrote to James in 1776 that "all writers on morals, religion, and philosophy agree, that the great business of life is the regulation of the passions and the subjugating those appetites which tend to inflame them and to weaken the powers of the mind until it forgets the law of reason" (ibid., p. 218).

23. Warren, *American Revolution,* I, 2, (emphasis added).

24. Ibid., p. 3; to John Adams, December 1786 ("Letter-Book," p. 197); *American Revolution,* I, 216, 70. "In all ages," she wrote, "mankind are governed less by reason and justice, than by interest and passion" (III, 309).

25. Warren, *American Revolution,* III, 73–74.

26. Ibid., I, 40.

27. Pitkin, *Political and Civil History,* I, 123, 303; Warren, *American Revolution,* I, 25; Lendrum, *American Revolution,* I, 231.

28. Warren to Hannah Lincoln, June 12, 1774; to Mrs. E. Lothrop, 1775 ("Letter-Book," pp. 33, 97); Lendrum, *American Revolution,* I, 255. See Warren to Mrs. Temple, August 1775; to Hannah Winthrop, 1774 ("Letter-Book," pp. 92, 71).

29. Warren, *American Revolution,* III, 399; Warren to Janet Montgomery, November 25, 1777 and September 27, 1778; Warren to

John Adams, August 2, 1775 ("Letter-Book," pp. 41-42, 153); Warren, *American Revolution*, III, 330. The historians repeated many atrocity stories, which are important for present purposes only insofar as they reflect the historians' view that Britain had degenerated into barbarism. See Gordon, *History*, II, 543ff., III, 14ff, 44ff, 88-89; Lendrum, *American Revolution*, I, 400, 255; McCulloch, *Concise History*, pp. 47, 137; Ramsay, *Revolution of South-Carolina*, II, 217. Such Tories as Joseph Galloway, Jonathan Boucher, and Peter Oliver also tended to view history in terms of virtue and avarice and to agree that avarice was the principal cause of a nation's decline. But, of course, they saw the American "rebellion" as the product of the *colonists'* acquisition of wealth and their consequent decline into luxury and licentiousness. The Americans, they argued, had gained enormously during the French and Indian War, but instead of repaying England in gratitude as well as in pounds sterling, they repudiated all responsibility to the mother country. Thus, while Britain floundered in debt after the war, the Americans, wrote Galloway, would "riot in luxury and dissipation without contributing a reasonable proportion of those aids which were necessary to [their] own safety" in Galloway, *Historical and Political Reflections* (London, 1780), p. 10. See Boucher, *A View of the Causes and Consequences of the American Revolution* (London, 1797; rpt. Russell and Russell, 1967), pp. xvii-xviii; Oliver, *Peter Oliver's Origin and Progress of the American Rebellion,* ed. Douglass Adair and John Schutz (Stanford: Stanford University Press, 1967), p. 50.

30. Warren to Hannah Winthrop, 1774 ("Letter-Book," p. 70).

31. Warren to John Adams, October 15, 1778 (ibid., p. 167); Ramsay, *American Revolution*, II, 316; *Revolution of South-Carolina*, II, 144. See McCulloch, *Concise History*, p. 226.

32. Warren, *American Revolution*, I, 68, 226-227, 147. See Marshall, *Life of Washington,* II, 161; IV, 244-245; Lendrum, *American Revolution*, II, 169. It is worth noting in light of the following discussion that the historians tended to write more optimistically in their histories than in their private correspondences. This is true, no doubt, in part because by the time they wrote their narratives the military success of the revolutionaries had eased some of their apprehensions. But it is also true because their histories were exhortations, designed to offer hope to future generations even as the historians harbored personal doubts about the likelihood of ultimate victory. See Cohen, "Explaining the Revolution."

33. *Notes on the State of Virginia,* ed. William Peden (Chapel Hill: University of North Carolina Press, 1954), p. 161.

34. Ibid.

35. *Massachusetts Magazine,* 3 (July 1791): 408; Galloway, *Historical*

and Political Reflections, p. 1. See Stow Persons, "The Cyclical Theory of History in Eighteenth Century America," *American Quarterly*, 6 (Summer 1954); 147–163; Peter Burke, "Tradition and Experience: The Idea of Decline from Bruni to Gibbon," and J. G. A. Pocock, "Between Machiavelli and Hume: Gibbon as Civil Humanist and Philosophical Historian," *Daedalus*, Summer 1976, pp. 137–152, 153–169.

36. Warren to James Otis, 1775; to John Adams, October 15, 1778 ("Letter-Book," pp. 94, 167). See Gordon to John Adams, June 5, 1777 (*Gordon Letters*, p. 340); Warren to Catharine Macaulay, August 2, 1787 and [September?] 17, 1786; to Winslow Warren, July 17, 1782; to John Adams, May 8, 1780 ("Letter-Book," pp. 22, 19–20, 277, 179–180).

37. Warren to John Adams, December 1786; to Catharine Macaulay, August 2, 1787 ("Letter-Book," pp. 195, 23). Hazard to Belknap, July 10, 1784 (MHS, *Collections*, 5th ser., 2: 371).

38. Gordon to "The Independent Chronicle," February 26, 1778 (*Gordon Letters*, p. 381); Ramsay to Benjamin Rush, August 3, 1779 (Brunhouse, ed., *Writings of Ramsay*, p. 64). See Gordon to George Washington, June 12, 1780; to Horatio Gates, May 25, 1781 (*Gordon Letters*, pp. 434, 455); Ramsay to John Eliot, August 6, 1785 (Brunhouse, ed., *Writings of Ramsay*, p. 90); Warren to John Adams, October 25, 1782 ("Letter-Book," p. 185).

39. Ramsay to John Eliot, August 6, 1785 (Brunhouse, ed., *Writings of Ramsay*, pp. 90–91).

40. Warren, *American Revolution*, III, 336–337. David Ramsay echoed Warren's theme in his Oration of 1794: "Had I a voice that could be heard from New Hampshire to Georgia, it should be exerted in urging the necessity of disseminating virtue and knowledge among our citizens" (Brunhouse, ed., *Writings of Ramsay*, p. 195).

41. Warren, *American Revolution*, II, 287; Lendrum, *American Revolution*, II, 170, 90.

42. Ramsay, *Revolution of South-Carolina*, II, 83–85. See Marshall, *Life of Washington*, IV, 191ff.

43. Ibid., p. 93.

44. Warren, *American Revolution*, I, 4–5.

45. Mercy Warren most brilliantly exploited the contrast between the generation of the revolutionaries and the "rising generation," a strategy that grew out of her plays. See Cohen, "Explaining the Revolution."

46. Ibid., III, 279–280.

47. Marshall, *Life of Washington*, V, 591–592; Warren, *American Revolution*, III, 279; II, 236–237.

48. See Sacvan Bercovitch, *The American Jeremiad* (Madison: University of Wisconsin Press, 1978); Nathan O. Hatch, *The Sacred Cause of*

Liberty: Republican Thought and the Millennium in Revolutionary New England (New Haven: Yale University Press, 1977); Richard L. Bushman, *From Puritan to Yankee: Character and the Social Order in Connecticut, 1690–1765* (New York: Norton, 1970), esp. chaps. 12 and 13.

49. The historians' attitude toward American corruption was tied to their political beliefs. Significantly, of all the major historians only Mercy Warren was an ardent Antifederalist. Ramsay, Gordon, Marshall, Morse, Holmes, Lendrum, and Pitkin all supported the Constitution and believed that the new frame of government would itself help to check the corruption they saw rampant in America between 1777 and 1786. Their histories may thus be read in part as "Federalist" documents, although that interpretation tends to minimize the ethical dimension for which I have been arguing. The following discussion should make clear that all the historians, regardless of their opinion of the Constitution, emphasized the priority of ethics to institutions, adopting a position that Gordon S. Wood has identified with Antifederalist political sociology. Federalists, on the other hand—proponents of the Constitution and later members of the Federalist political faction—"hoped to create an entirely new and original sort of republican government—a republic which did not require a virtuous people for its sustenance" (*Creation of the American Republic*, p. 475; see chaps. 11 and 12.

50. J. B. Bury, *The Idea of Progress: An Inquiry into its Growth and Origin* (New York: Macmillan, 1932; rpt. Dover Books, 1955), pp. 4–7.

51. Ramsay, *American Revolution*, II, 353.

52. Ibid., p. 354 (emphasis added). See Warren, *American Revolution*, III, 368–369.

53. Warren, *American Revolution*, I, vi–vii.

54. Ibid., III, 424, 429.

55. Ibid., pp. 324–326.

56. See Gordon Wood's excellent discussion in *Creation of the American Republic*, chaps. 11 and 12.

57. Jefferson to Pendleton, August 26, 1776 in Merrill D. Peterson, ed., *The Viking Portable Jefferson* (New York: Viking, 1975), p. 357. William Gordon also quoted George Washington as saying, "I do not mean to exclude altogether the idea of patriotism. I know it exists, and I know it has done much in the present contest: but I will venture to assert, that a great and lasting war can never be supported on this principle alone. It must be aided by a prospect of interest or some reward" ([to John Bannister, Jr., April 21, 1778] in Gordon, *History*, III, 64).

58. John Adams to Mercy Warren, August 19, 1807 (*Adams-Warren Letters*, pp. 472–473).

59. As Adams wrote in his *Defence of the Constitutions of Government in*

the United States of America: "Happiness, whether in despotism or democracy, whether in slavery or liberty, can never be found without virtue. The best republics will be virtuous, and have been so; but we may hazard a conjecture, that the virtues have been the *effect* of the well ordered constitution rather than the *cause*" in Charles Francis Adams, ed., *The Works of John Adams* 10 vols. (Boston, 1850–56), VI, 219 (emphasis added).

60. Warren to Adams, March 1776 ("Letter-Book," pp. 163–164).

61. *The Spirit of the Laws*, trans. Thomas Nugent (New York: Hafner, 1962), p. 20, (bk. 3, art. 3).

62. Warren, *American Revolution*, III, 309, 322. See Chapter 4.

CHAPTER 8: *The Romance of the Revolution*

1. Frye, *The Secular Scripture: A Study of the Structure of Romance* (Cambridge: Harvard University Press, 1976), pp. 144–145.

2. Mink, "Narrative Form as a Cognitive Instrument," in Robert H. Canary and Henry Kozicki, eds., *The Writing of History: Literary Form and Historical Understanding* (Madison: University of Wisconsin Press, 1978), pp. 131, 143–144.

3. Frye, *The Anatomy of Criticism: Four Essays* (Princeton: Princeton University Press, 1957; rpt. 1973), p. 186.

4. The anecdote appears in "On the Truth of Fact and Truth of Nature," *New York Magazine*, 2, no. 5 (May 1791): 258–260. The title of the extract states: "From Heron's Letters," suggesting that the author was Robert Heron (1764–1807), an essayist who was an assistant of Hugh Blair, the Scottish rhetorician and divine. Actually, the author was John Pinkerton (1758–1826), a Scottish historian, geographer, poet, and essayist who wrote *Letters of Literature* (London, 1785) under the pseudonym Robert Heron (his mother's surname). The anecdote appears in *Letters of Literature*, pp. 213–219. For Pinkerton see DNB.

5. Ibid., p. 259. Pinkerton clearly went beyond the notion that one *could* alter the truth by one's use of language, style, or form. As John Bigland wrote in a comment typical of Enlightenment England: "Truth may be disguised in various manners. It is not always [necessary] for that purpose to substitute downright falsehood: a little diversity of colouring in the picture, will sometimes alter the representation. A little exaggeration, or misrepresentation, will, in some cases, have a powerful effect in creating false appearances and inculcating erroneous ideas" in *Letters on the Study and Use of Ancient and Modern History* (London, 1805; Philadelphia, 1806, 1814), p. 117.

6. "On the Study of History," *Universal Asylum and Columbian Magazine*, 9 (October 1792): 227. See "Truth and Fiction," *Massachusetts Magazine*, 5, no. 9 (September 1793): 552–553; a review of *The Hapless Orphan* (a novel), ibid., 5, no. 7 (July 1793): 432. Thomas Jefferson was a conspicuous exception to those who would distinguish sharply between fictional and historical works. In a letter to Robert Skipwith (August 3, 1771) he argued that "the entertainments of fiction are *useful* as well as pleasant." As long as fiction aimed to instruct people in public and private virtue, it was as useful as history. "I appeal to every reader of feeling and sentiment whether the fictitious murther [sic] of Duncan by Macbeth in Shakespeare does not excite in him as great [a] horror of villainy, as the real one of Henry IV by Ravaillac as related by Davila?" One took one's moral lessons where one could find them, from history when it was sufficiently lively and exemplary, from fiction when history was deficient. Thus, "considering history as a moral exercise, her lessons would be too unfrequent if confined to real life. Of those recorded by historians few incidents have been attended with such circumstances as to excite in any high degree this sympathetic emotion of virtue. We are therefore wisely framed to be as warmly interested for a fictitious as for a real personage. The spacious field of imagination is thus laid open to our use, and lessons may be formed to illustrate and carry home to the mind every moral rule of life" in Merrill D. Peterson, ed., *The Portable Thomas Jefferson* (New York: Viking, 1975), pp. 349–351 (emphasis added). Benjamin Rush also wrote that "I am disposed to believe with Sir Robert Walpole that all history (that which is contained in the Bible excepted) is a romance, and romance the only true history," though he wrote the comment in frustration over what he saw as historians' distortions (to John Adams, August 14, 1805 in John A. Schutz and Douglass Adair, eds., *The Spur of Fame: Dialogues of John Adams and Benjamin Rush, 1805–1813* [San Marino, Calif.: Huntington Library, 1966], p. 32).

7. Gordon to Horatio Gates, March 16, 1778 (*Gordon Letters*, p. 393); Ramsay to John Coakley Lettsom, October 29, 1808 (Brunhouse, ed., *Writings of Ramsay*, p. 163).

8. The concept of "Romance" is much hazier in literary theory than one might expect. Few attempts have been made to deal with it generically. Instead, literary scholars seem for the most part to treat it historically, wittingly or unwittingly following Clara Reeves's 1785 distinction between "Romance" and "Novel," the key to which is that "Romance" tends to be "fabulous" and more properly the product of "imagination," whereas "Novel" tends to be more "realistic," associating itself with the "probable." As recently as 1966 Robert Scholes and Robert Kellogg cited Reeves's distinction with evident approbation. It is worth quoting

at some length: "The Romance is an heroic fable, which treats of fabulous persons and things.—The Novel is a picture of real life and manners, and of the times in which it is written. The Romance in lofty and elevated language, describes what never happened nor is likely to happen.—The Novel gives a familiar relation of such things, as pass every day before our eyes, such as may happen to our friend, or to ourselves; and the perfection of it, is to represent every scene, in so easy and natural a manner, and to make them appear so probable, as to deceive us into a persuasion (at least while we are reading) that all is real." (Quoted in *The Nature of Narrative* [New York: Oxford University Press, 1966], pp. 6–7.) Among the principal difficulties with this distinction is that, with little if any modification of the descriptions, we could change the word "Romance" to the word "fiction" and "Novel" to "history," arguing that fictions are fanciful, fabulous, and imaginative, whereas histories are realistic and probable. But this still begs the question that Pinkerton raised and it suggests more problems than it answers, for one still faces the questions what fanciful and realistic mean.

The larger problem is simply this: to understand style, form, genre, and related issues one must turn to literary theory, since historians are embarrassingly unconcerned with such problems; but at the same time, literary scholars are almost entirely concerned with the conventions of fiction and too little interested in the conventions of historical writing. I have tried in this chapter to work on the assumption that "narrative" is logically prior to both "historical narrative" and "fictional narrative" and that the distinction between them is fundamentally conventional rather than intrinsic.

My discussion in this chapter is indebted principally to the following: Frye, *Anatomy* and *The Secular Scripture;* Hayden White, *Metahistory: The Historical Imagination in Nineteenth-Century Europe* (Baltimore: Johns Hopkins University Press, 1973); White, "The Historical Text as Literary Artifact," Lionel Gossman, "History and Literature: Reproduction or Signification," and Mink, "Narrative Form as a Cognitive Instrument," all in Canary and Kozicki, eds., *The Writing of History,* pp. 41–62, 3–39, 129–149; Leo Braudy, *Narrative Form in History & Fiction: Hume, Fielding & Gibbon* (Princeton: Princeton University Press, 1970); W. B. Gallie, *Philosophy and the Historical Understanding,* 2nd ed. (New York: Schocken, 1968); Jonathan Culler, *Structuralist Poetics: Structuralism, Linguistics, and the Study of Literature* (Ithaca: Cornell University Press, 1975); Robert Scholes, *Structuralism in Literature: An Introduction* (New Haven: Yale University Press, 1974); Ian Watt, *The Rise of the Novel: Studies in Defoe, Richardson and Fielding* (Berkeley: University of California Press, 1957; rpt. 1971); Karl Kroeber, *Romantic Narrative Art* (Madison: University of Wisconsin Press, 1966); John G. Cawelti, *Adventure,*

Mystery and Romance: Formula Stories as Art and Popular Culture (Chicago: University of Chicago Press, 1976); Roland Barthes, "Historical Discourse," in Michael Lane, ed., *Introduction to Structuralism* (New York: Harper Torchbooks, 1970); Scholes and Kellogg, *The Nature of Narrative;* David Levin, *History as Romantic Art: Bancroft, Prescott, Motley, and Parkman* (Stanford: Stanford University Press, 1959; rpt. New York: AMS Press, 1967).

9. Gordon to George Washington, June 18, 1783 (*Gordon Letters,* p. 493). Noah Webster's 1806 *Compendious Dictionary* is illuminating here: Romance, *n*: "a fiction, fable, fabulous story;" *v:* "to tell or write fables." Romantic, *adj:* "wild, irregular, improbable, false." Romanticness, *n*: "a romantic state, wild." History, *n:* "a narration of facts, actions, wars &c." Historically, *adv:* "by way of history, regularly."

10. Warren to Martha Washington, 1776 ("Letter-Book," p. 118). The story Warren outlined in the letter is itself a romance.

11. Scholes and Kellogg write that "by narrative we mean all those literary works which are distinguished by two characteristics: the presence of a story and a story-teller. . . . For writing to be narrative no more and no less than a teller and a tale are required" (*Nature of Narrative,* p. 4). While I accept their fundamental elements of narrative (assuming that it is possible to define "story"), a third element seems to me as necessary as the first two, namely, an audience. Whether or not we can ever know anything about the nature and composition of a narrative's audience, an audience is always implied in the narrative itself and thus figures in the narrative's structure (see Walter J. Ong, S.J., "The Writer's Audience is Always a Fiction," *PMLA,* 90, no. 1 [January 1975]: 9–21).

12. Northrop Frye argues that generic narratives share conventions with one another. Thus, for example, "as comedy blends into irony and satire at one end and into romance at the other, if there are different phases or types of comic structure, some of them will be closely parallel to some of the types of irony and of romance" (*Anatomy,* p. 177; see ibid., pp. 158–239). Even in the most formulaic narratives where conventions seem to be rigidly established—as in detective stories—a certain sharing of conventions occurs so that the stories are not completely predictable (see Cawelti, *Adventure, Mystery and Romance*).

13. White, *Metahistory,* pp. 5–29. The term "emplotment" in its various forms is White's. It signifies "the way by which a sequence of events fashioned into a story is gradually revealed to be a story of a particular kind" (ibid., p. 7; see pp. 5–11). White argues that his "elective affinities" are not absolutes: "On the contrary, the dialectical tension which characterizes the work of every master historian usually arises from an effort to wed a mode of emplotment with a mode of argument

or of ideological implication which is inconsonant with it" (ibid., p. 29). Nevertheless, insofar as the idea of elective affinities implies a kind of predictability, White runs the risk of reductionism, as do I by adopting his principles. White, in my judgment, avoids reductionism splendidly. It might also be noted that, while White argues that one can begin with any of the three categories and read the other two with a fair degree of accuracy, I am much more concerned with emplotment as a *function* of ideology and mode of argumentation.

14. Ibid., p. 8, n6.

15. Ibid., pp. 8–9; Frye, *Anatomy*, pp. 186ff.

16. These three phases parallel in a condensed form Frye's six phases of each of the four mythoi. See *Anatomy*, pp. 177–186 (Comedy), 198–203 (Romance), 219–223 (Tragedy), 226–229 (Satire).

17. Frye and White view romance and satire as polar forms. While a Satiric Romance is plausible, if one means by it a form "intended to expose, from an Ironic standpoint, the fatuity of a Romantic conception of the world," a Romantic Satire is "a contradiction in terms." The "archetypal theme" of Satire, writes White, "is the precise opposite" of the Romantic drama. Satire is "a drama of diremption, a drama dominated by the apprehension that man is ultimately a captive of the world rather than its master, and by the recognition that, in the final analysis, human consciousness and will are always inadequate to the task of overcoming definitively the dark force of death, which is man's unremitting enemy" (*Metahistory*, pp. 9–10; Frye, *Anatomy*, pp. 163–239). It is worth noting that Jeremy Belknap wrote a historical satire (in political allegory), *The Foresters* (1792), which may be viewed as a crude precursor of Washington Irving's *Knickerbocker History of New York* (1809), which, through parody, systematically undermined the dominant conventions of enlightened narrative. While Belknap was perfectly capable of adopting an ironic stance toward history, the story he told in *The Foresters* was different in kind from the romance he told in his *History of New Hampshire*.

18. Frye, *Anatomy*, p. 187.

19. See Frye, *Secular Scripture*, chaps. 4 and 5.

20. As I argued in Chapter 7, the conflict the historians described in the "critical period" was a genuine one which could end tragically. But romance is an open-ended mode, and we may view the historians' portrayal of events between 1777 and 1786 as a strategy for indicating that a new story—potentially either tragic or romantic—was beginning. The new story would be told by future historians (see Frye, *Secular Scripture*, pp. 174, 186; Mink, "Narrative Form as a Cognitive Instrument," p. 143).

21. See Ramsay, *American Revolution*, II, 344–349; Marshall, *Life of Washington*, V, 153–159. Even an Antifederalist and critic of Washington like Mercy Otis Warren on the whole wrote glowingly of Washington and the Constitution. Although she sometimes referred to human history as a "tragedy," she apparently found the romantic mode so compelling as a unifying social and ideological force that she was unwilling to risk its effectiveness by deflating such important symbols as the Constitution and the hero of the Revolution.

22. John Marshall made explicit what the others took for granted: "The American War was a subject of too much importance to have remained thus long unnoticed by the literary world. Almost every event worthy of attention, which occurred during its progress, has been gleaned up and detailed" (*Life of Washington*, I, ix).

23. See Frye, *Secular Scripture*, chap. 6.

24. Frye, *Anatomy*, p. 195.

25. Karl Kroeber discusses realistic romance in *Romantic Narrative Art*, pp. 189–190.

26. Frye, *Secular Scripture*, pp. 139, 50. Conspiracy theories and the references to British degeneration evidence this kind of polarizing.

27. Frye, *Secular Scripture*, pp. 8, 88. See pp. 92, 107, 132–133; *Anatomy*, pp. 315ff. Frye's whole work, as the title suggests, treats romance as the secular scripture. His superb discussion deals with the divergences and convergences of sacred and secular narratives.

28. Ibid., p. 8 (emphasis added).

29. Frye, *Anatomy*, pp. 33–34, 188. Regarding "epic" see pp. 315–326.

30. Ibid.

31. Jeremy Belknap to Ebenezer Hazard, May 8, 1789 (MHS, *Collections*, 5th ser., 3: 123–124); Warren, *American Revolution*, II, 228–229; Marshall, *Life of Washington*, I, iv; II, 527; V, 9.

32. Lendrum, *American Revolution*, I, 330; Condie, "Biographical Memoir," in Lendrum, *American Revolution*, II, 247.

33. Marshall, *Life of Washington*, I, iv; Ramsay to Nathanael Greene, June 9, 1782 (Brunhouse, ed., *Writings of Ramsay*, p. 70). See Ramsay to Benjamin Rush, June 20, 1779 (ibid., p. 61). On January 6, 1777, William Gordon wrote to Washington himself after the great victories at Trenton and Princeton: "Having made my acknowledgments to the God of hosts, I now thank and congratulate your Excellency" (*Gordon Letters*, pp. 331–332).

34. See, e.g., Gordon, *History*, II, 401–402; Marshall, *Life of Washington*, II, 551–553, 555–556; Ramsay, *American Revolution*, I, 323; Lendrum, *American Revolution*, I, 400.

INDEX

Accident, 28–29, 59, 66, 68, 71–75, 80, 87, 108. *See also* Chance; Contingency.
Adams, John, 19, 80, 122, 141, 162–164, 166, 169, 183, 187, 200, 209–210
Adams, Sam, 117
Addison, Joseph, 168
America: colonial history of, 97, 150–151, 153–154, 159, 221; corruption in, 185–187, 204; historiography of, 47–53
Ames, Fisher, 107–109, 113, 118
Ames, William, 28, 79
Andros, Edmund, 151–152
Arnold, Benedict, 81, 84, 86
Articles of Confederation, 187
Avarice, 179, 192–194, 205–206; in America, 199, 204, 207; in Britain, 198. *See also* Corruption; Virtue.

Bacon's Rebellion, 152
Bailyn, Bernard, 147
Baldwin, Ebenezer, 67
Barlow, Joel, 176
Barnard, John 34
Belknap, Jeremy, 16, 162; on impartiality, 164, 183; and providential interpretation, 67–68; on truth and style, 162, 173–174; on virtue, 201; on George Washington, 226

Bigland, John, 90–91
Blair, Hugh, 172–173
Bolingbroke, Henry St. John, 52, 100, 165, 168, 173, 188, 191, 193
Boston Massacre, 72–73
Boston Tea Party, 115
Boucher, Jonathan, 92, 145–146, 161, 224
Bradford, William, 23–26, 47
Braudy, Leo, 82–83
Bunker Hill, Battle of, 104–106, 110
Burgh, James, 181
Burgoyne, John 57–58, 105
Burke, Edmund, 142–144

Calvin, John, 25
Calvinism, 45
Causes in history: chain of, 97–101; and consequences, 72–73, 84, 93, 95–96, 101, 113, 115; moral, 71, 91, 99; natural, 69–71, 88, 91, 98–99; "powerful and efficient," 95, 98, 108; primary and secondary, 35–36, 96–97. *See also* Historical causation.
Chance, 15–16, 25, 28–29, 59, 66, 71, 74, 80, 82, 86, 88–89, 94, 108–109, 111, 126; and providence, 28–30, 53, 58–60, 71–77, 83, 101, 111, 119. *See also* Contingency.
Chesterfield, Philip Dormer Stanhope, Earl of, 171–174

281

Pitkin, Timothy, 16, 113; on causes, 95–96; on chance, 75; on civil liberty, 119; on colonial history, 195; on conspiracy, 149, 151–152; on the Constitution, 118, 120; on independence, 135; and providential interpretation, 79; on scholarship, 165; on taxation and representation, 117, 142

Plutarch, 189

Polybius, 43, 52, 191

Popular consent, 131–132. *See also* Republicanism.

Priestley, Joseph, 181

Prince, Thomas, 47

Princeton, Battle of, 72

Progress, Idea of, 205–206

Providence, historical theory of, 23–53, 69, 88, 91, 108–110, 189, 206; and chance, 39, 57–77, 85; and Divine Comedy, 224–225; and drama, 67, 76–78; and foreordination, 31–32, 61, 82; and immanence, 125–127; and politics, 66, 77–82; in Revolutionary era, 48–53; in revolutionary histories, 60–85; and romance, 228; and special providence, 31–32, 34, 36, 42, 60–61, 66, 68. *See also* History: necessity and inevitability in; History: sacred.

Puritans, 66, 79–80, 83, 97, 127, 154, 191: historians, 24, 27–31, 34, 113, 204; political theory of, 26, 34, 40. *See also* Providence, historical theory of.

Quebec, 86

Quincy, Josiah, 115

Raleigh, Sir Walter, 214–216

Ramsay, David: 16, 19, 179, 187; on causes and consequences, 97–98, 101, 111; on colonial rights, 143; on conspiracy, 149–150, 153; on the Constitution, 118, 120, 206–207; on corruption and virtue, 185–186, 197, 201–203; on environmen-

talism, 123–124; on exemplary theory, 175, 188–189; on facts and conjecture, 92; on the future, 116; on history and fiction, 217–218; on human nature, 123–124; on independence, 135, 138, 155–159; and nationalism, 174; on objectivity, 161, 163–165; and providential interpretation, 62–64, 67, 79; on style and truth, 173, 180; on taxation and representation, 142–143; on George Washington, 227

Reason, 34, 41–42, 85. *See also* Human character; Human efficacy.

Republicanism: 16, 20, 22, 50, 52, 127, 154, 175, 185, 187, 200–201, 204, 208, 210 213, 229; and government, 123–124, 186, 208, 210; and history, 179, 196, 205–206. *See also* Ideology.

Revolutionary historians, self-awareness of, 15–16, 18, 22, 87–91, 94, 163, 186, 201–203

Reynolds, Sir Joshua, 104

Richardson, Samuel, 104–105

Right of Revolution, 131–134, 157

Robertson, William 52, 165

Romance, 15, 20, 22, 212–229; and ideology, 220–221, 223, 229; and myth, 20, 224–226; and truth, 214, 218

Rome, history of, 89–90

Rush, Benjamin, 164, 173, 177–179, 183

Salem (Mass.), 115

Saratoga, Battle of, 57, 73, 97, 111

Savannah, Siege of, 111

Separatists, 24–25, 93

Sermonic literature, 49–51, 67, 82

Shaffer, Arthur H., 49, 122, 177, 231

Shaw, Peter, 181

Shays's Rebellion, 187

Sherwood, Samuel, 67

Stamp Act, 75, 93, 95–97, 116–117, 147, 149, 155, 222. *See also* Great Britain: policies of.

The Revolutionary Histories

Designed by Richard E. Rosenbaum.
Composed by The Composing Room of Michigan, Inc.
in 10 point Baskerville V.I.P., 3 points leaded,
with display lines in Baskerville.
Printed offset by Thomson/Shore, Inc. on
Warren's Number 66 Antique Offset, 50 pound basis.
Bound by John H. Dekker & Sons, Inc.
in Holliston book cloth
and stamped in All Purpose foil.

Library of Congress Cataloging in Publication Data

Cohen, Lester H.   1944–
    The Revolutionary histories.

    Bibliography: p.
    Includes index.
    1.   United States—History—Revolution, 1775–1783—Historiography.   I.   Title.
E209.C63   1980   973.3'07'2   80-11243
ISBN 0-8014-1277-3